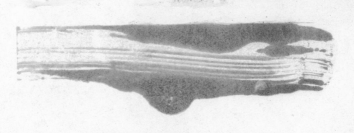

Planning in the Curriculum

Planning in the Curriculum

A Reader edited by Victor Lee and
David Zeldin for the *Purpose and
Planning in the Curriculum* Course
at the Open University

HODDER AND STOUGHTON

in association with
The Open University

British Library Cataloguing in Publication Data

Planning in the curriculum.
  1. Curriculum planning
  I. Lee, Victor   II. Zeldin, David
  375'.001   LB1570

ISBN 0 340 28775 6

Photo Typeset by Macmillan India Ltd., Bangalore.

Printed and bound in Great Britain
for Hodder and Stoughton Educational,
a division of Hodder and Stoughton Ltd,
Mill Road, Dunton Green, Sevenoaks, Kent,
by Richard Clay (The Chaucer Press) Ltd, Bungay, Suffolk

Contents

Preface   vii
General Introduction   1

Part One   School, college and the curriculum   3

1.1   The idea of school   5
    Michael Oakeshott

1.2   The school as a hierarchical community   8
    Gary Easthope

1.3   Alternative schools: a conceptual map   11
    Terrence E. Deal and Robert R. Nolan

1.4   School-based curriculum development   18
    Malcolm Skilbeck

1.5   Authority and participation   35
    Terry Moore and Denis Lawton

1.6   The notion of the ethos of a school   41
    John Dancy

1.7   Leadership in middle management   47
    Denys John

1.8   Ideology and management in a garbage
    can situation   51
    Kristian Kreiner

1.9   Aspects of accountability   64
    East Sussex Accountability Project

1.10   Keeping the primary school under review   69
    Inner London Education Authority Inspectorate

1.11   The methods of evaluating   79
    Robert E. Stake

Part Two   Teachers, learners and the curriculum   89

2.1   A model for classroom teaching   92
    Michael J. Dunkin and Bruce J. Biddle

2.2   Classroom research: a cautionary tale   104
    David Hamilton and Sara Delamont

2.3   A typology of teaching styles   118
    Neville Bennett

2.4   The types of behavioural objectives   142
    Hilda Taba

2.5   The form of objectives   160
    Ralph W. Tyler

2.6   The teaching of literary appreciation   175
    F. R. Leavis

Contents

2.7 The importance of structure 178
Jerome S. Bruner

2.8 A process model 182
Lawrence Stenhouse

2.9 Implications of classroom research for professional development 189
John Elliott

2.10 Against dogmatism: alternative models of teaching 199
Bruce Joyce and Marsha Weil

2.11 Technology: the analytic style 213
I. K. Davies

2.12 Conventional classrooms, 'open' classrooms and the technology of teaching 220
Ian Westbury

2.13 Meaning making 230
Neil Postman and Charles Weingartner

2.14 Power or persons: two trends in education 233
Carl R. Rogers

2.15 A critique of Logo as a learning environment for mathematics 242
Tim O'Shea

Index 251
Acknowledgments 257

Preface

This Reader is the second of two volumes compiled to accompany Open University course E204, 'Purpose and Planning in the Curriculum'. Whereas the first Reader, *Challenge and Change in the Curriculum*, is concerned with planning at the national level and the themes of innovation and change, *Planning in the Curriculum* deals with curriculum planning at the institutional and classroom levels. Although *Planning in the Curriculum* is designed for students of the course, it will also stand in its own right as a source book of ideas for anyone interested in the curriculum in classroom, school or college.

It is not necessary to become an undergraduate of the Open University in order to take E204. Further information about this course may be obtained by writing to: The Admissions Office, The Open University, PO Box 48, Walton Hall, Milton Keynes, MK7 6AB.

General Introduction

Planning in the Curriculum is divided into two sections – Part One: 'School, College and the Curriculum', and Part Two: 'Teachers, Learners and the Curriculum'. The main thrust of the extracts and papers in Part One concerns curriculum at the level of school and college, while in Part Two the perspective is at classroom level. What must be stressed, however, is that this is not a case of simple dichotomies. So, while it is perfectly true that Part Two will emphasize, for example, such issues as curriculum decision-making within educational institutions, it is equally true that it will treat such issues as the role of the classroom teacher in the preparation and implementation of curriculum proposals. In other words, both parts attempt to deal with curriculum studies as a whole, but give emphasis to different areas.

This arrangement complements the articles in the companion Reader *Challenge and Change in the Curriculum* which deal with a critical analysis of the contribution of national and local bodies to curriculum policy-making and with the problems involved in attempting to promote curriculum.

The extracts and articles selected reflect some of the critical issues of our time and recent developments in curriculum studies. So, for example, they cover such issues as the debate about a common curriculum, how curriculum tasks may be planned and organized, the influence of pressure groups and alternative forms of schooling, and the relationship between school organization, curriculum and school ethos. Important ideas which affect curriculum are given particular prominence such as accountability, authority and evaluation. Questions are posed which are designed to help teachers assess their own work and that of the school. What are the different modes of accountability? All in all, this Reader tries to show curriculum studies as a field of applied research where theories must be judged both by their intellectual worth and by their practical relevance.

This selection should be of particular interest as it is offered at a time when the teacher's responsibilities are being widened to include participation in whole school curriculum planning, evaluation and accountability. Thus, in addition to classroom expertise, teachers are also being required to be versed in policy-making, organization and management of the curriculum. Teachers must do more than teach. These readings should therefore be of interest and assistance to primary and secondary teachers, college lecturers, and also to education administrators involved in curriculum planning and implementation.

Part One

School, college and the curriculum

Part One contains articles and extracts which examine curriculum issues within educational institutions. In Part Two specific classroom concerns are examined. In schools and colleges teachers are given wide discretion to plan the curriculum, but they are also expected to work within broad prescriptive limits. Schools and colleges have, therefore, some freedom to determine their practices so long as these are not inconsistent with the publicly accepted functions of education.

Part One examines alternative forms of schooling and curriculum, including the hidden or paracurriculum, that is, what is also taught and learned parallel to the formal or explicit curriculum. It explores the educational ideologies, the structures, organizational forms and arrangements which sustain the curriculum. It discusses the issues which involvement in the planning of the school or college curriculum, evaluation and accountability, raise for teachers, administrators and others. The papers have been chosen for the issues they raise rather than the prescriptions which they may contain, and are presented as illustrative rather than definitive statements of current debate.

In the first paper Michael Oakeshott examines the traditional views which define the idea of 'school'. He suggests that these should include an initiation into an inheritance, a commitment to learning, a personal relationship between teacher and pupil, a certain detachment from immediate concerns, and a recognition of continuity and community in the institution. Gary Easthope uses the notion of a 'hierarchical community' to explore the development of the English public schools. He discusses ways in which these schools have provided a regime and a curriculum which continues to attract clients. Terrence Deal and Robert Nolan outline the relationships between educational ideology, school organization and curriculum. They indicate ways in which the purposes and the organization of schools may be distinguished, and alternative courses of action identified and developed.

In a seminal paper, Malcolm Skilbeck explains and argues for the idea of an institution-based approach. Skilbeck discusses the range of curriculum decisions and identifies the decision-makers who may be involved. He outlines the elements of a strategy for heads and teachers to analyse their situation, to identify acceptable aims and pedagogical methods, and to organize themselves, and others, in their pursuit. Terry Moore and Denis Lawton summarize the Weberian notions of authority and power and link them with the possibilities of pupil and teacher participation in curriculum decisions in schools. John Dancy analyses the ethos of schools in terms of values, aims, attitudes and procedures. His analysis suggests a way in which curriculum decisions about individuals, the school community and school work may be pursued. Denys John uses a systems analysis to examine the tasks of middle managers in schools. He identifies the diversity of responsibilities and suggests ways in which curriculum tasks may be planned and organized. Kristian Kreiner provides an account of curriculum decision-making in which parents and teachers were involved in a non-authoritarian Danish free school. He describes the process in which goals were ambiguous, pedagogical methods were unclear and participation was fluid.

Accountability and evaluation are increasingly important issues in schools and colleges. An extract from the East Sussex Accountability Project describes six different modes of accountability and discusses ways in which schools may effect their accountability responsibilities. An Inner London Education Authority seminal paper provides a list of questions which are designed to help primary teachers assess their own work and that of their schools. In the final paper in this section, Robert Stake discusses some common dimensions in educational evaluation and distinguishes between approaches which are adopted by different interest groups.

1.1   The idea of school

Michael Oakeshott

At home in the nursery, or in the *kindergarten*, in the early years of childhood, attention and activity, when they begin to be self-moved, are, for the most part, ruled by inclination; the self is inclination. Things and occurrences (even when they have been expressly designed or arranged by adults) are gifts of fortune known only in terms of what can be made from them. Everything is an opportunity, recognised and explored for the immediate satisfaction it may be made to yield. Learning, here, is a by-product of play; what is learned is what may happen to be learned.

But education, properly speaking, begins when, upon these casual encounters provoked by the contingencies of moods, upon these fleeting wants and sudden enthusiasms tied to circumstances, there supervenes the deliberate initiation of a new-comer into a human inheritance of sentiments, beliefs, imaginings, understandings and activities. It begins when the transaction becomes 'schooling' and when learning becomes learning by study, and not by chance, in conditions of direction and restraint. It begins with the appearance of a teacher with something to impart which is *not* immediately connected with the current wants or 'interests' of the learner.

The idea 'School' is, in the first place, that of a serious and orderly initiation into an intellectual, imaginative, moral and emotional inheritance; an initiation designed for children who are ready to embark upon it. Superimposed upon these chance encounters with fragments of understanding, these moments of unlooked-for enlightenment and those answers imperfectly understood because they are answers to unasked questions, there is a considered *curriculum* of learning to direct and contain the thoughts of the learner, to focus his attention and to provoke him to distinguish and to discriminate. 'School' is the recognition that the first and most important step in education is to become aware that 'learning' is not a 'seamless robe', that possibilities are not limitless.

Secondly, it is an engagement to learn by study. This is a difficult undertaking; it calls for effort. Whereas playful occupations are broken off whenever they cease to provide immediate satisfactions, learning, here, is a task to be persevered with and what is learned has to be both understood and remembered. And it is in this perseverance, this discipline in inclination, that the indispensable habits of attention, concentration, patience, exactness, courage and intellectual honesty are acquired, and the learner comes to recognize that difficulties are to be surmounted, not evaded. For example, in a profuse and complicated civilization such as our own, the inheritance of human understandings, modes of thinking, feeling and imagination, is to be

Source: OAKESHOTT, M . (1971) 'Education: The engagement and its frustration', in *Proceedings of the Philosophy of Education Society*, Vol. 5, No. 1, January 1971.

encountered, for the most part, in books or in human utterances. But learning to read or to listen is a slow and exacting engagement, little or nothing to do with acquiring information. It is learning to follow, to understand and to re-think deliberate expressions of rational consciousness; it is learning to recognize fine shades of meaning without overbalancing into the lunacy of 'decoding'; it is allowing another's thoughts to re-enact themselves in one's own mind; it is learning in acts of constantly surprised attention to submit to, to understand and to respond to what (in this response) becomes a part of our understanding of ourselves. And one may learn to read only by reading with care, and only from writings which stand well off from our immediate concerns: it is almost impossible to *learn* to read from contemporary writing.

The third component of the idea 'School' is that of detachment from the immediate, local world of the learner, its current concerns and the directions it gives to his attention, for this (and not 'leisure' or 'play') is the proper meaning of the word *schole*. 'School' is a place apart in which the heir may encounter his moral and intellectual inheritance, not in the terms in which it is being used in the current engagements and occupations of the world outside (where much of it is forgotten, neglected, obscured, vulgarized or abridged and where it appears only in scraps and as investments in immediate enterprises) but as an estate, entire, unqualified and unencumbered. 'School' is an emancipation achieved in a continuous re-direction of attention. Here, the learner is animated, not by the inclinations he brings with him, but by intimations of excellences and aspirations he has never yet dreamed of; here, he may encounter, not answers to the 'loaded' questions of 'life', but questions which have never before occurred to him; here, he may acquire new 'interests' and pursue them uncorrupted by the need for immediate results; here, he may learn to seek satisfactions he had never yet imagined or wished for.

For example, an important part of this inheritance is composed of languages, and in particular of what is to be the native language of the new-comer. This he has already learned to speak in its contemporary idioms and as a means of communicating with others of his kind. But at 'School' he learns something more which is also something different. There, studying a language is recognizing words as investments in thought and is learning to think more exactly; it is exploring its resources as themselves articulations of understandings. For, to know a language merely as a means of contemporary communication is to be like a man who has inherited a palace overflowing with expressions, intimations and echoes of human emotions, perceptions, aspirations and understandings, and furnished with images and emanations of human reflection, but in whose barbaric recognition his inheritance is merely that of 'a roof over his head'. In short, 'School' is 'monastic' in respect of being a place apart where excellences may be heard because the din of worldly laxities and partialities is silenced or abated.

Further, the idea 'School' is that of a personal transaction between a 'teacher' and a 'learner'. The only indispensable equipment of 'School' is teachers: the current emphasis on apparatus of all sorts (not merely 'teaching' apparatus) is almost wholly destructive of 'School'. A teacher is one in whom some part or politic to which they could give allegiance. Just as team games provided a microcosm of the total school community so too did the house. In this way the school was formed of competing social groups all owing allegiance to the total community. The house system was a means of monitoring and developing the spiritual side of the 'whole man'. [. . .]

[. . .] Team games were seen as particularly appropriate for developing the 'character' of pupils and the role of team captain, as it was expected to be exercised in public schools, was precisely the type of leader that was desired. In short the leaders the schools developed were not individualists but leaders in the stable 'hierarchical community' of the school who were expected to become leaders in the stable 'hierarchic community' of a locality upon leaving school.

The public school today remains a 'hierarchical community' with the head as the sovereign. Lambert (1968) in his study of public schools found that when compared with state schools the social order took primacy over the individual in that the pupils preferred social qualities rather than individual qualities, the school was seen to promote a herd instinct and the heads preferred leavers oriented towards the collective rather than the individual. Similarly traditional values were more highly regarded, the structure of the community was more hierarchical and the individual was expected to be loyal and committed to the school.

Although the public school remains more of a 'hierarchical community' than the state school, state schools also strove to be hierarchical communities because the public schools became the ideal to which all English schools subscribed. They became the model for all schools because when state education was expanded the schools with the highest status, the grammar schools created by the 1907 Act, received as heads men who had been teachers, and often house-masters, in the public schools and they appointed as teachers men who if they had not taught in a public school had themselves been taught in such a school before going to Oxford or Cambridge. In turn the training colleges for teachers were staffed by ex-grammar school teachers. These men made the training colleges 'hierarchical communities' (Shipman, 1967) and both in this way and by precept they passed on the ideal to their students to carry into the new secondary modern schools and later still the comprehensive schools.

So pervasive is the concept in English education that it is unthinkable to conceive of a school that is not committed to the development of its pupils' personalities, does not have a headteacher and does not espouse and value the concept of the school as a 'hierarchical community'. The ideal school is spoken of, by headteachers at speech days, as a ship – isolated, hierarchical, total in its control of all aspects of life and one in which the officers are concerned for the welfare of the men. Of course state schools are not isolated and nor do they have the total control over all aspects of life so characteristic of a boarding school or a military unit. Their 'hierarchical community' remains therefore a pale copy of the public school: lacking control over all their pupils' lives they extend their control as far as they can by the use of homework and the insistence upon the wearing of uniform outside the school; lacking a full house system they set up copies which often exist solely as a means of dividing up the school into teams for the sports day; lacking the full hierarchical paraphernalia of a public school they none the less create prefects, and monitors with powers, often much more limited than those given to pupils in public schools, to discipline other pupils. One thing they do not lack – the conception of the headteacher as the unchallengeable sovereign. Underlying all these devices is the model of the public school and the valuation of the school as a 'hierarchical community'. [. . .] Inextricably bound up with the concept of the school as a 'hierarchical community' is the idea of the head as its sovereign. [. . .]

A school is what its headmaster makes of it; no matter how much decentralisation, how much diffusion of authority and influence there may be, it is the influence of the headmaster that is for better or worse, the principal formative agent (a public school headmaster cited by Weinberg, 1969).

The power exercised by the head in an English school is formidable, and [. . .] [is] limited only by the willingness of his subjects to obey his commands but whose right to give commands is not disputed by his subjects. Such a powerful figure was an historical creation of the nineteenth century. The growth in size of educational establishments in the nineteenth century necessitated some form of co-ordination. The autocratic head was the form adopted because it was congruent with the most successful organisations in nineteenth-century England, the industrial factories which were run by autocratic entrepreneurs and within education the example of the 'hierarchical community' of Rugby presupposed a sovereign ruler. Problems of size also face large comprehensive schools today and it has been suggested that such schools would lead to a diminution of the power of the head. This has not occurred because the school is still conceived of as a 'hierarchical community' and such a conception requires a sovereign head. One of the paradoxes of the great power that is given to heads is that although it was originally given to encourage them to fulfil societal goals it gives them sufficient resources to resist societal pressures and even to act against societal goals.

References

BARON, GEORGE (1955) 'The English notion of the school.' Unpublished paper, University of London Institute of Education.

LAMBERT, R. *et al.* (1968) *New Wine in Old Bottles*. London: Bell.

SHIPMAN, M. (1967) 'Education and college culture.' *British Journal of Sociology*, 18, pp. 425–34.

WEINBERG, I. (1969) *The English Public Schools. the sociology of elite education*. New York: Atherton.

1.3 Alternative schools: a conceptual map

Terrence E. Deal and Robert R. Nolan

Educational ideologies

Ideologies reflect the intellectual patterns of any culture or movement. An ideology conditions what individuals believe and value and how they view the world. Ideologies influence how people behave, how they relate, and what they expect. Ideologies are transmitted by music, literature, the media, and word of mouth. Ideologies are reflected in institutions, affect institutional goals or norms, and define important structural or technical patterns within organizations. [. . .]

Schools, like other complex organizations, are influenced, buffeted, and defined by ideologies. Following, and expanding somewhat the work of Kohlberg and Mayer (1972), we have identified four existing educational ideologies which educational organizations presently face. These four ideologies provide patterns of thinking that influence instructional approaches, student-teacher interaction, curriculum content, organizational structure, and all other facets of life in schools. Each has different sources, metaphors, conceptions of students and learning, and emphases (Kohlberg and Mayer, 1972). They are summarized in Table 1.

The first ideology represents the traditional pattern of educational thinking. In the 'school as filling station' students are empty vessels to be filled by the wisdom of the ages. The next three ideologies represent patterns of thought which have more commonly influenced alternative schools.

The 'school as a greenhouse' ideology reflects many of the ideas and values of the countercultural revolution of the 1960s. From this vantage point students are viewed as flowers who, if left alone, will blossom forth. As a variation of this theme, the 'school as a tool' emphasizes the potential of schools as an instrument for bringing about social change. Schools are seen as a means to a more just social order; students are seen as change agents.

The 'school as a marketplace' ideology finds roots in the Progressive movement of the 1930s and, although itself an alternative ideology, represents in many respects a synthesis of the 'school as a filling station' and 'school as a greenhouse' perspectives. Schools are seen as a marketplace in which students engage in a continual transaction with social beliefs, values, and information.

In practice, of course, those ideologies are rarely found in pure form. Some schools, run by 'true believers', probably come close. Generally, however, the ideologies are combined in diverse ways, yielding eclectic approaches. Inconsistencies, conflict, and indecision may characterize individuals or organizations who strongly espouse more than one.

Source: *School Review*, November 1978, pp. 36–44.

Table 1 Four educational ideologies

	'School as a Filling Station'	'School as a Greenhouse'	'School as a Tool'	'School as a Marketplace'
Sources	The 'classicists'	The 'romanticists', Rousseau, Neill	The 'revolutionists'	The 'progressives', Dewey
Metaphor	Kids as empty vessels	Kids as plants	Kids as agents of social change	Kids as philosophers, bargaining agents, and problem solvers
Source of knowledge	Outside	Inside	The new regime	Interaction between inside and outside
Main task of schools	Transmit to present generation bodies of information, rules and values of the past	Create a permissive environment in which innate qualities can unfold	Change the society	Create an environment that will nourish a natural conflict or negotiation between students and society
Emphasis	Traditional, established	Unique, novel, and personal	Create individuals for a new social order Using the schools as a lever for affecting social change	Resolvable but genuine problems or conflicts between the established and the emerging

Note—Based, in part, on the conceptualization of Kohlberg and Mayer, 1972.

Schools as organizations

Educational ideologies become imbedded, intentionally or unintentionally, in educational organizations. Like all organizations (Udy, 1965), schools have five major components or subsystems: goals, technologies, formal structure, informal patterns and norms, and an environment. Goals are general statements of purpose which give a school a direction; technologies are the instructional practices, approaches, and programs which are employed to reach these goals; formal structures define the role of students, administrators, teachers, and parents and help determine how these roles relate to one another; informal patterns and norms interact with the formal structure to help determine what really goes on in a school; and the environment consists of everything external to a school – parents, community people, and other organizations – to which a school must relate in carrying out its principal tasks. Educational ideologies potentially have an impact on each of the organizational components in schools.

Interlacing educational ideologies with the organizational framework yields four basic organizational models. Each model is produced by applying the values, beliefs, and ideas of a particular ideology to the five parts of a school's organization. In reality, of course, one would probably not find these models in their pure form. As organizations, schools are loose collectives (Meyer and Rowan, 1975) and thus may contain individuals who operate from different ideological perspectives. Local communities may exhibit individuals or groups from all persuasions. It is also possible that one aspect of school organization may be influenced by one ideology while a second element is influenced by another. A school, for example, could have a tight formal structure and a loose instructional program. As with individuals, however, schools probably lean toward one ideology or another. But some schools may contain smaller departments, pods, or units, each of which operates from a radically different ideological base. These models are outlined in Table 2.

The first organizational model represents the application of the classical or 'school as a filling station' ideology. This is the traditional school organization which processes age-graded batches of students through a fairly regimented set of activities. Within a classroom the teacher makes instructional decisions and the student follows them. Within a school the principal makes decisions which teachers are expected to carry out. Informal patterns emphasize autonomy and competition. The schools' internal workings, by and large, are buffered from the community.

The 'do your own thing' school organization is typical of many schools which were begun in the early 1960s. Following the 'school as a greenhouse' ideology, such schools exist primarily to provide a protected place for students to grow on their own. What students learn as well as how, when, and where they learn it varies according to individual wants and whims. Within the classroom, students make instructional decisions with little input or interference from teachers. Teachers, in fact, are defined as fellow learners.

Table 2   School organization

Goals	Program	Formal Structure	Environment	Informal Processes and Norms
Traditional				
Transmit knowledge and traditional cultural values and norms	Age-graded 'batches' of students move through discipline-based courses; teacher lectures, students recite and are tested on their 'knowledge'; emphasis on existing knowledge	Schoolwide: decisions are made and conflicts resolved by hierarchical superiors; evaluations occur at end of a program or performance; roles divided by age or subject areas. Classroom: teacher makes instructional decisions (objectives, activities, evaluation); teacher active, student passive	Learning and central decisions of the school 'buffered' from immediate environment	Autonomy of individual teacher; competition
Do Your Own Thing School				
Remove barriers to 'natural' acquisition of knowledge and personal growth	Students individually learn whatever captures their interest at that moment	Schoolwide: little or no formal authority; decisions made by consensus; conflicts resolved in similar manner; no formal evaluation. Classroom: students choose objects and activities; students initiate, teachers respond	Buffered from school: occasionally used as site for learning depending on immediate desires of students	Extremely important because of low degree of formalization; 'if it feels right, do it'; freedom; harmony

Revolutionary School

Use the school to change society; shape students into change agents	Students learn the doctrine and techniques to bring about major social change; emphasis on doctrine and proper social consciousness	School wide: authority wielded by single individual or small group which interprets the revolutionary doctrine Classroom: teachers responsible for developing the students as change agents, imparting to them relevant doctrine and technique	Viewed as target of school's central activities	Influenced heavily by revolutionary doctrine; 'the end justifies the means'

Negotiation School

Provide an environment where students can interact with and solve problems	Students individually participate in a variety of activities worked out jointly between teachers and students; competency-based contracts; learning takes place at diverse times and in a variety of locations; emphasis on a tension between what kids want and what they need	Schoolwide: Some decisions made by consensus, others by hierarchical superiors; various strategies for resolving conflicts; clearcut distinctions between who makes which decisions and how various kinds of conflicts are resolved; emphasis on continuous evaluation to improve programs or performance Classroom: teachers and students make decisions jointly (objectives, activities, and evaluation criteria); students active in making individual decisions; teachers active in developing options; negotiation	Used as a site for learning; formal channels for bringing community and parents into decision making; specific roles and responsibilities for community and parent 'teachers'	Cooperation; interdependence; conflict as natural process; integration of informal and formal

Schoolwide decisions are normally made by consensus within the 'inner community', which shields itself from impact or influence from the external environment. Because of the loose formal structure, informal norms become exceedingly important. Such norms emphasize freedom, harmony, and 'if it feels right, do it'.

The 'revolutionary' school, based on the 'school as a tool' ideology, highlights the role of school in changing society. The program emphasizes the acquisition of the doctrine, tools, and techniques for accomplishing social change. Students are expected to become change agents. The teacher's role is highly autocratic. And the school itself is usually overseen by a single individual or small group which is responsible for interpreting the revolutionary doctrine around which the school is intimately structured. The informal norms, like the formal structure, are infused with the revolutionary doctrine. The community environment is seen as a thing to be acted upon. Having the environment eventually conform to the basic philosophy and structure of the school is the primary aim.

The 'negotiation' school, fostered by the beliefs and values of the 'school as a marketplace' ideology, exists to provide an environment where students can pursue and solve real-life problems. In some ways, the negotiation school resembles the do your own thing school. But in other key areas the two are fundamentally different. In the negotiation school, what is learned is determined by a tension between what a student wants and needs. Structurally, the negotiation school is a mixture of authority, autonomy, and consensus. Some schoolwide decisions are made by those in positions of authority, others are made by group consensus. In the classroom some decisions are made by teachers and students jointly; others are made by students individually. The teacher expands instructional options although students ultimately choose objectives, activities, and evaluation criteria. The tension between the role of student and teacher represents the heart of the negotiation school approach.

In the negotiation school, informal norms are integrated with the formal structure and emphasize cooperation, interdependence, and conflict as a natural process. The community environment is intimately connected with the school. The community provides problems which are a central focus of the curriculum. Parents and individuals from the community participate in the school's instructional activities as 'teachers'. They are also involved in making key policy decisions. In both instructional and policy areas, the roles of outside people as well as the rules for their participation are fairly well defined. The blurring of the internal-external boundaries increases the atmosphere of the marketplace of educational transaction of the negotiation school.

References

KOHLBERG, L. and MAYER, R. (1972) 'Development as the aim of education.' *Harvard Educational Review*, Vol. 42, No. 4, pp. 449–96.

MEYER, J. W. and ROWAN, B. (1975) 'Notes on the structure of educational organizations.' A revised version is reprinted in MEYER, M. W. and Associates (1978) *Environments and Organizations*. San Francisco, Calif.: Jossey-Bass.

UDY, S. H. (1965) 'The comparative analysis of organizations', in MARCH, J. G. (ed.) *The Handbook of Organizations*. Chicago, Ill.: Rand McNally.

1.4 School-based curriculum development

Malcolm Skilbeck

The concept, and the case for school-based curriculum development

What it is

School-based curriculum development is a new name for an old idea. The idea is that the best place for designing the curriculum is where the learner and the teacher meet. For example, unlike the Sophists, who claimed to have plans and schemes to teach anyone useful knowledge and pre-defined techniques like debating, Socrates built up his curriculum in and through relationships with students who displayed an aptitude for philosophical and mathematical reasoning. This was school-based curriculum development with the public places of Athens serving as the school and the joint dialectical experience of the teacher, his peers and his pupils constituting the curriculum. There were at hand scribes like Plato who produced *post hoc* accounts of the substance of these discussions, thus providing texts for two millennia of philosophy instruction, much of it more in the mode of the Sophists than of Socrates.

The point of these opening remarks is to suggest not only that the idea of school-based curriculum is an old one, but also that it *is* an idea, even an educational philosophy, and not simply a method or a technique. As an idea or an educational philosophy, school-based curriculum development makes a number of claims:

(*a*) The curriculum is, for the learner and the teacher, made up of experiences; these should be experiences of value, developed by the teacher and learner together from a close and sympathetic appraisal of the learner's needs and his characteristics as a learner.

(*b*) Freedom for teacher and for pupils is a necessary condition for the full educational potential of these experiences to be realised. This freedom should extend to allow the teacher to define objectives; set targets; select learning content; modulate the range and tempo of learning tasks; determine what is appropriate in the form of both criteria and techniques; and assess the extent to which the potential value of the learning situation has been realized. Conversely, teacher and pupil need to be freed from onerous burdens and constraints which interfere with education. This constellation of freedoms must involve the teacher and the pupil; it also involves, as we shall see, other agencies in a network of freedoms and constraints.

Source: SKILBECK, M. (1975) *School-based Curriculum Development and Teacher Education.* Mimeographed paper.

(*c*) The school is a human social institution, a place in which educational experiences can occur naturally and easily, although not without effort. It engages in complex transactions with the environment which involve exchange of ideas, resources and people through a network of communication systems. The school's responsiveness to this environment, which is not at all the same thing as uncritical adjustments to its demands, depends upon its freedom to build up its own curriculum in part as an exchange system with that environment. The school is, or may be, staffed by professionals who know what they are doing and who are capable of defining not only relevant learning experiences but also the support system required if those experiences are to become a reality in the lives of pupils.

(*d*) Curriculum development is an intellectually demanding and onerous task which calls into play all the teacher's competencies and skills; its success depends upon the development of quite substantial support systems.

(*e*) School-based curriculum development does not preclude curriculum development at other levels than the school, nor does it deny a creative role to others than teachers and pupils. One of the major tasks for policy makers is to help allocate types of curriculum decision to different agencies and interests from local to national level, and to design the necessary structures for sustaining curriculum development at all levels.

(*f*) Teachers, if suitably trained, can act effectively as curriculum developers, but part of the necessary support system for school-based curriculum development is an extensive in-service education programme whose main features are only now beginning to be worked out.

As stated above, school-based curriculum development is a new name for an old idea. Why has the name been introduced, and how can we explain the manifestations in many different educational systems of school and teacher freedom to make and remake the curriculum? The answers to these two questions are, of course, linked: the name itself signifies the growing evidence of greater teacher freedom and autonomy, of dissatisfaction with imposed curricula, however scholarly in inception and elegant in form, of support systems which presuppose and facilitate teacher-curriculum development, and of courses in colleges and universities which encourage teachers to think critically and creatively about the curriculum. For these and other reasons it has become imperative to recognize the emergence of a movement, an ideology, perhaps; hence the term school-based curriculum development, which refers to a phenomenon and to an attempt to rationalize, assess and strengthen that phenomenon.

In the simplest terms, school-based curriculum development claims that of all our educational institutions and agencies, the school and the school-teacher should have the primary responsibility for determining curriculum content, the learning resources needed for this content, and teaching, learning and evaluation procedures. Many objections and qualifications can be and have been made to this claim. As stated, it is too simple, since it does not acknowledge the complexity of curriculum decision-making in any national system. The case for school-based curriculum development is nevertheless a strong one. We shall consider first the arguments for it, and a model for school-based curriculum development which has practical value for schools, then the criticisms of and alternatives to school-based curriculum development, and, finally, some of the major implications for a policy and programme of teacher education.

The case for school-based curriculum development

(*a*) Some of the arguments advanced for school-based curriculum development have been touched upon already. The principal argument favouring school-based curriculum development is the need for the teacher and the learner to enjoy the freedom to form educative relationships. Externally imposed syllabuses, textbooks, examinations all define educational values and set certain standards which are, of course, important from the standpoint of the individual as well as for national and social purposes; however, they make the spontaneity, flexibility and diversity which are an equally important part of education much more difficult to achieve. The learner's first-hand experience is consequently neglected despite its rich educational potential. Such external demands on the school, when organized into a curriculum, can also be ideologically very powerful and hence a source of concern for democratic societies. We need a system for curriculum development that combines the advantages of national policy-making, national centres for the production of materials and for research and development, with the flexibility, adaptability and professionally satisfying features of local initiative and creativity.

(*b*) In the United Kingdom, there is widespread agreement that primary education has benefited in many different ways from the reduction of external constraints on the curriculum. A similar freedom is enjoyed by university teachers who would never accept for their own courses the kinds of constraints that are still widespread in secondary schools. Indeed it is one of the paradoxes of the British as of many other European systems that great pressure is exerted on secondary schools through examination boards which are heavily influenced by the expectations of university teachers even though the vast majority of pupils passing through these secondary schools never undertake any higher education. This paradox can be explained away but only by producing thoroughly unconvincing arguments about the special virtues of the academic as a curriculum decision-maker.

(*c*) The case for school-based curriculum development is not merely an abstract one, based on contentious notions of freedom, democracy and the dismantling of some of our treasured hierarchies. It is in part also a reaction against what is widely felt to be a failure in practice of the descending models of control and dissemination which are still prevalent in many different kinds of countries to produce a satisfactory educational system. There are two points here. First, in the United Kingdom there is a deep distrust amongst teachers or at least amongst their official representatives of anything suggestive of national curriculum control. As already stated, control of a kind certainly is exerted through the examining boards, and in a number of other ways, but these boards are not governmental agencies, and they are teacher-dominated even if the major single influence is often the university teacher. Resistance to national syllabus making was most obviously displayed during 1963–64 when it was felt by the teachers' associations (and by the local authorities) that there was a threat in the then Ministry of Education's proposal to set up for itself a curriculum study group somewhat along the lines of the highly successful Buildings and Architects Branch. What eventually emerged as the Schools Council took great care in its terms of reference to affirm that it was a supporting and facilitating body . . . After ten years of highly productive activity, there is growing evidence that the Schools Council sees its future less in the generating of ready-made curriculum packages than in the support of local and regional initiatives, and in various other systems which will sustain teachers as at least participants in curriculum development . . . The second point to make about dissatisfaction with descending models has perhaps more relevance to American than to British experience. It is the claim which is frequently made that the model has not worked, or, more precisely, that the massive investment in national projects dominated by scholars from the disciplines and by management strategies has paid inadequate dividends in the form of changed schooling. Some truly remarkable attitudes were engendered by this managerially dominated movement, including that which treated the teacher as a functionary in a technically bureaucratic system whose alleged incapacities could be sur-mounted by that system's producing 'teacher-proof' learning packages. This was sophistry more rampant and overweening than was witnessed in Classical Greece or other periods of history such as seventeenth and eighteenth century Europe, when pedlars of systems enjoyed a great success. As against this view, it is now being argued that ways must be found to involve the teacher in fundamental decisions concerning every aspect of the curriculum. It is a curious quirk that the same educational system which engendered the 'teacher-proof' mentality also gave rise to the most fully documented and possibly the most successful ever, large-scale experiment in school-based curriculum development, namely the Eight Year Study.

In the United Kingdom the resistance to descending models does not imply a dismantling of many of the existing control structures, such as examination boards. However, so far as the Schools Council is concerned, there is a shift in focus, following the Council's stated intention to devote more of its resources to problems of evaluation at the users' level, to dissemination and to supporting programmes for the education of teachers in the use of materials. These emerging emphases will have many implications for teacher-education policy and practices, since the teacher will be expected to perform tasks of adaptation, evaluation and development which, while familiar enough to many primary teachers, are less so in secondary education.

(*d*) Further points in the case for school-based curriculum development are

closely related to the disparate theories of teacher self-actualization, achievement motivation, and professionalization. Teacher involvement in the
processes of curriculum making is more consistent with a professional self-
image, with a sense of professional achievement and with a more complex
sense of personal value and worth than is the functionary image. The
remarkable upsurge in recent years of the phenomena of power-sharing,
participatory decision-making, populist resistance to technocracy, and other
aspects of the so-called counter-culture which directly challenge the values,
assumptions and procedures of hierarchy, all provide a congenial climate for
school-based curriculum development. They indicate deeply felt needs and
wishes for involvement and engagement in social action which are peculiarly
attractive to teachers who have the mental and emotional power to become
engaged but are restrained by tradition, the demands of office and, possibly, a
deeply-seated sense of inadequate social recognition. This analysis suggests
that in the future school-based curriculum development will become a
movement which engages the energies not only of teachers but even more
dramatically of pupils, parents and a large variety of social groups. There is
evidence of this already in the spread of student militancy from higher
education into secondary schools, the growth of parent action groups, etc.
(*e*) A final argument to be adduced in favour of school-based curriculum
development is that it provides more scope for the continuous adaptation of
curriculum to individual pupil needs than do other forms of curriculum
development. Learning systems dominated by national and international
textbooks, by pre-specified 'ground to be covered', by external examination
syllabuses, and by development projects may be effective in guiding teachers,
stimulating their teaching, and establishing a standard of sorts (although just
what that standard is constitutes a problem, not a solution, as the
achievement studies of the IEA [International Evaluation of Achievement]
demonstrated). These systems were by their nature ill-fitted to respond to
individual differences in either pupils or teachers. Yet these differences, of
experience, social class, intelligence, motivation, interest, learning style and
so forth are of crucial importance in learning. Furthermore, the establishment
of an interpersonal relationship as a setting and context for learning is greatly
facilitated by opportunities to structure learning tasks according to the needs
of the individual learner. At the very least, schools need greatly increased
scope and incentive for adopting, modifying, extending and otherwise re-
ordering externally developed curricula than is now commonly the case.
Curriculum development related to individual differences must be a
continuous process and it is only the school or school networks that can
provide scope for this.

School-based curriculum development and other forms of curriculum development

So far I have mentioned some of the arguments that favour school-based
curriculum development and some of the trends that seem likely to strengthen

it in the year ahead. We shall come later to some of the criticism, objections, and difficulties. But it is still not altogether clear just what school-based curriculum development entails and how it is to be related to other kinds of curriculum development. For example, we might ask in what sense *school-based*: the whole curriculum process, or only parts of it, as in the recent French and Swedish innovations of zones of free time? What kind of support does the school need, and what can it realistically expect to receive? What kinds of non-school-based curriculum development should there be and what agencies other than the school will have their part to play? These questions are pertinent to any consideration of a *system* of curriculum development, as distinct from a philosophy by which greater freedom and spontaneity for the school might be elaborated and justified. In this paper, it is not possible to explore these system-level questions in any depth . . . It will have to suffice here to say that school-based curriculum development does not presuppose system anarchy; it is in no way a negation of national policy-making including the setting of national goals as in Sweden and many other continental countries; its proponents do not minimize the need for local, regional and national support structures such as teachers and resource centres, regional and national centres for curriculum development, national textbooks and publishing agencies and so forth. Essentially what supporters of school-based curriculum development seek is a recognition of the need to incorporate fully and deliberately into the emerging national structures for curriculum development a carefully worked-out role for the school as a creative, developmental agency, and to design and establish support systems including teacher-education systems which will encourage and nurture school enterprise. These support systems must include guidelines for curriculum development and advice and assistance on problems of design and implementation.

The curriculum-development process: a model for school use

It is common to start discussions of the curriculum-development process with objectives. This, at any rate, is what the technology of educational decision-making encourages practitioners and theorists alike to do.

Curriculum objectives may be formulated at the national level as part of government policy for education, or at the state or regional level, or left to the school itself. Whatever the pattern, and it differs in detail from country to country, it is important to be clear about the source of the objectives, which may be very different from what it appears to be. One of the fundamental weaknesses of the so-called behavioural-objectives model of curriculum planning is that within it objectives are necessarily treated as given; similarly the famous 'Tyler rationale' provides no adequate account of the source and origins of curriculum objectives. It is curious and disturbing that few of the models for curriculum development available in the published writings of curriculum theorists in Anglo-Saxon countries handle this problem adequately. They all either start with the objectives stage, or precede it with a very partial source, such as 'the pupils'. This is odd, since the objectives model as used in government and business though without any great success, it appears, does propose a prior stage to the defining of objectives. This is PPBS [Planning Programming Budgeting Systems] which assumes an initial, complex situation which has to be changed, or 'managed'. One of the startling consequences – for theorists at any rate – of school-based curriculum development is that it immediately forces a reconsideration of the whole question of the context within which and for which objectives are to be defined (if indeed they are to be defined at all in the sense intended by behaviourists). The fundamental curriculum questions, what is to be taught, and why, become a stark reality when the teacher has to answer them rather than having them answered for him by detailed syllabuses, study guides, examination boards, inspectors and other parts of the paraphernalia of control. He must look again at the situation he and his pupils are in, the learning situation, the social situation of the school, the context in which his activities are carried out. His objectives, as a teacher and a curriculum developer, cannot be simply deduced from subjects, or accepted from high officialdom, or intuited from a sense of what the child needs, or inferred from his knowledge of learning theory, although all of these elements have a part to play in the judgments he makes about what are the appropriate objectives. According to the conception of curriculum as experience and as communication between teacher, learner and environment which was adumbrated earlier in this paper, curriculum development at the school level must start, not with given objectives or objectives drawn up abstractly, but with a critical appraisal of the situation, the learning situation as it exists and is perceived at the school level. It is into this situation that curriculum is to be inserted, as a means of extending or transforming it, and it is with this situation that the teacher must start his analysis. This, at any rate, is the alternative school-based curriculum development offers to the system of importing objectives, syllabuses and learning materials into the school and requiring pupil and teacher to fit themselves to these externals.

A model for curriculum development, which accepts much, but not all, of the recent thinking about planned change, is now outlined in Table 1.

Clearly the scope of any systematic, comprehensive inquiry the school might itself undertake along the lines suggested by stage 1 of this model is enormous. Some of the decisions will be made for the school, for example by law, decree, administrative controls, guidelines, etc.; others will come naturally to a competent professional; many could only be reached after some specially initiated inquiries had been undertaken. The model attempts to outline the scope of possible action and to some extent the inter-relatedness of parts; it would be the task of any school curriculum group to map out a curriculum development programme for the school – or for sections of the school – within this framework, proceeding only so far in certain directions (e.g. data collection on community assumption) as was practicable. The model may be used for purposes of designing a curriculum, for observing and

Table 1

	1 Situational analysis
Review of the change situation	Analysis of factors which constitute the situation
(a) external	(i) cultural and social changes and expectations including parental expectations, employer requirements, community assumptions and values, changing relationships (e.g. between adults and children), and ideology;
	(ii) educational system requirements and challenges, e.g. policy statements, examinations, local authority expectations or demands or pressures, curriculum projects, educational research;
	(iii) the changing nature of the subject-matter to be taught;
	(iv) the potential contribution of teacher-support systems, e.g. teacher training colleges, research institutes, etc.;
	(v) flow of resources into the school;
(b) internal	(i) pupils: aptitudes, abilities and defined educational needs;
	(ii) teachers: values, attitudes, skills, knowledge, experience, special strengths and weaknesses, roles;
	(iii) school ethos and political structure: common assumptions and expectations including power distribution, authority relationships, methods of achieving conformity to norms and dealing with deviance;
	(iv) material resources including plant, equipment, and potential for enhancing these;
	(v) perceived and felt problems and shortcomings in existing curriculum.

2 Goal formulation

The statement of goals embraces teacher and pupil actions (not necessarily manifest 'behaviour') including a statement of the kinds of learning outcomes which are anticipated. Goals 'derive' from the situation analysed in 1 only in the sense that they represent decisions to modify that situation in certain respects and judgments about the principal ways in which these modifications will occur. That is, goals imply and state preferences, values and judgments about the directions in which educational activities might go.

3 Programme building

(a) design of teaching-learning activities: content, structure and method, scope, sequence;

(b) means-materials, e.g. specification of kits, resource units, text materials etc.;

Table 1 Cont'd

---

3 Programme building

(c) design of appropriate institutional settings, e.g. laboratories, field work, workshops;

(d) personnel deployment and role definition, e.g. curriculum change as social change;

(e) timetables and provisioning.

---

4 Interpretation and implementation

Problems of installing the curriculum change, e.g. in an on-going institutional setting where there may be a clash between old and new, resistance, confusion, etc. In a design model, these must be anticipated, pass through a review of experience, analysis of relevant research and theory on innovation, and imaginative forecasting.

---

5 Monitoring, feedback, assessment, reconstruction

(a) design of monitoring and communication systems;

(b) preparation of assessment schedules;

(c) problems of 'continuous' assessment;

(d) reconstruction/ensuring continuity of the process.

---

assessing curriculum systems in use, and for a more theoretical analysis of the nature of the task of curriculum development. In this paper, it is not possible to present its many components in more than an abbreviated fashion.

There is a temptation to suppose that there is a logical order in the five stages of this model, and in designing a system, whether for manual or computer use, this temptation can easily be succumbed to. It is certainly possible to produce elaborate systems diagrams of the curriculum process. Yet there may be sound institutional and psychological reasons for intervening first at any one of the stages not for following the arrows on those increasingly elaborate diagrams. Furthermore, in a practical planning operation, the different stages can be developed concurrently. There is plenty of evidence that despite the enticements of the technological approach, teachers do not, in fact, proceed in a linear fashion from goals to evaluation. The model outlined does not presuppose a means-ends analysis at all; it simply encourages teams or groups of curriculum developers to take into account different elements and aspects of the curriculum development process, to see the process as an organic whole, and to work in a moderately systematic way.

This model differs from the numerous models available in curriculum publications deriving from the Tyler rationale in at least these respects:

(a) It identifies the learning situation, not materials production and change strategies, as the major problematical area of curriculum development; encourages developers to think educationally about the situation which is

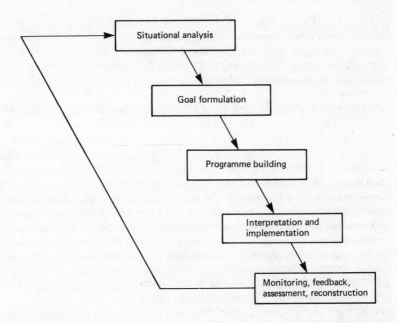

to be changed, not about how to implement pre-designed models and techniques of change; and suggests, in a preliminary way, a number of relevant categories in the situation, to which teachers ought to be attending.

(b) It accepts that practitioners do not readily accept the command to 'specify your objectives', and encourages them to enter the model at whatever stage they wish, e.g. the real problem as perceived by the teacher may be inadequate examinations, or poor text materials – either can be the starting point of developmental thinking.

(c) It is not committed to means-ends reasoning but accepts that an end – an objective, for example – is only meaningful in and through activity.

(d) It makes no assumptions about the depth and scale of school-based inquiries into any one of the stages identified beyond the basic point that effective and justifiable school-based curriculum development requires that criteria be formulated and schools assisted in their endeavours to satisfy these criteria.

School-based curriculum development: objections and difficulties

Part of the process of understanding what school-based curriculum development is consists of recognizing the difficulties and problems to which it will give rise . . . The problems in this section are all of a kind which pose a challenge to teacher education. The question to ask, therefore, is how far does teacher education policy and practice recognize the pressures that are operating increasingly on teachers, as their roles in the curriculum development process are extended.

(*a*) The model, of course, makes a number of assumptions about the teacher. These may be summarized in an idealized description of the role that is presupposed for him. He is conceived as a change agent, diagnosing a situation, preparing objectives, designing schemes of work, devising implementation procedures, implementing and evaluating the effects of his treatment. He understands the processes of curriculum development and is competent in carrying them out. He will be provided with the necessary resources and support structures. This description, it will be rightly pointed out, does not match what we know about teachers and teaching. The level of expertise, motivation and resource are inadequate; the traditions in many countries 'point' in quite other directions; and all kinds of pressures militate against the extension and development of teachers' professional roles. Teacher-role analysis and a realistic appraisal of the changing demands being made upon him are needed in the teacher education institutions.

(*b*) As has been stated already, school-based curriculum development does not centre all curriculum decisions in the school. It does, however, acknowledge or confer upon the school the right to design curricula, utilizing whatever outside resources are available to them, e.g. syllabuses and teaching materials prepared by national committees and project teams. It also confers upon schools responsibility for assessing pupil performance, again drawing upon such external resources as national guidelines, standards and so forth. These rights and responsibilities, in order to be realised in practice, require a high level of organization and organizational skill which do not exist in most schools. Thus, it may be objected that school-based curriculum development cannot be introduced or extended except by taking into account and in many cases re-defining the responsibilities of other agencies.

(*c*) Re-defining organizational responsibilities would not be enough since successful school-based curriculum development would depend upon a substantial infra-structure of support. This is an argument for proceeding slowly, or across a broad front, not an objection to school-based curriculum development as such.

School-based curriculum development requires various support structures and a developed capacity in teachers to use the structures that are available to them. It cannot be introduced as an isolated reform and it cannot be introduced as an effective reform unless other structural changes take place, for example the provision of teachers' resource centres. Even quite modest, small-scale development activities at the school level will be messy and damaging to all concerned if they are not adequately supported. How far lack of resources in a period of financial stringency will constrain the build-up of support services it is impossible to say. It is a task for administration to analyse needs and to draw up and cost alternative support structures. It would be reasonable to attempt to cost school-based curriculum development, though not in absolute terms as a supposed addition to but as a substitute for some parts of the national apparatus of curriculum making, and this cannot be done easily. In the United Kingdom it is within the power of the Schools Council to deflect some of its expenditure from national projects, of which many observers feel there are far too many already – to the support of school-based curriculum development, but we lack information at present on how cost-effective this might be.

(*d*) Another objection which might be raised to school-based curriculum development is that it seems to confer excessive power on the teacher and take insufficient note of the participatory principle which requires a much greater diffusion of power, to pupils, parents, community groups and so forth. In the diagram [Table 2, p. 30] the manner in which different groups and agencies might participate in school-based curriculum development is indicated. There need be no concentration of power in teachers' hands, if levels and types of decision-making are so specified as to indicate precisely the roles to be exercised by other agencies. Effective school-based curriculum development requires that some such analysis be undertaken and so far from centralizing power in the teaching profession, this type of inquiry might help to make education a more participatory process than it commonly is at present. Of course, the distribution and sharing of responsibility themselves pose major educational tasks. We should not be talking merely about the education of teachers but of all those who are to be involved in the curriculum process. In the United Kingdom, until relatively recently, there were very serious deficiencies in the educational provision for administrators and many gaps are still very apparent. Nobody would suppose that educational resources have been adequately deployed to facilitate rational participation at all levels in the curriculum development process, a point which probably holds true of all countries.

(*e*) Another objection to school-based curriculum development is that it will produce an atomization of schooling: disunity in policy, lack of uniform provision, varying standards and opportunities. Of course, this objection would be stronger if it could be shown that any educational system has been able to achieve uniformly high standards. Furthermore, there is an artificiality about national standards, syllabuses, examinations and textbooks which is reflected in the enormous gulf between what is believed, provided and stated, on the one hand, and actual achievements on the other. The fact of a common syllabus does not, given the complexity and diversity of cultural environments, in any way guarantee common learning experiences and it is a *function*, not merely an artifact, of national standards to codify differences. The myths surrounding national standards of provision, opportunity and attainment in curriculum matters ought themselves to be exploded instead of being used as a self-justifying means of undermining the case for school-based curriculum development.

Arguments for a common curriculum which have been advanced in recent

Table 2   Curriculum process: decisions

Process	Agency	Role
Situational analysis	Teachers, heads of school departments, school principals	Decision, discussion
	Pupils	Discussion
	Parents	Discussion
	Consultants (local authority) . . . . . . (college and university) (other schools) (research agencies)	Advice
	Administration	Support
Objectives	Teachers, etc.	Decision
	Pupils	Discussion
	Parents	Discussion
	Consultants	Advice
	National governments and government departments	Advice
	Project teams	Support, advice, discussion
	Administration	Support
Design	Teachers, etc.	Decision
	Pupils	Discussion
	Parents	Discussion, support, advice
	Consultants	Advice
	Project teams	Support, advice, discussion
Implementation	Teachers, etc.	Decision
	Pupils	Discussion
	Administration	Support
Evaluation	Teachers, etc.	Decision
	Pupils	Discussion
	Consultants	Advice
	Government departments	Support, advice
	Administration	Support

Note: For simplification this diagram does not specify either the full range of agencies or of development roles. Agencies include: teachers' and resource centres (Administration; Government departments); examination boards (Administration; Government departments); inspectors (Administration; Government departments); employers; parent-teacher associations; trade unions, etc.

philosophical studies, even if they were accepted, do not destroy the case for school-based curriculum development. There are other mechanisms than standardized syllabuses, textbooks and examination for developing common learning experiences and attaining a reasonable homogeneity of attainment. By far the most powerful of these mechanisms is teacher education, especially at the in-service stage. It is to the implications of school-based curriculum development for teacher education that we now turn.

Teacher education

(a) Some policy issues

A policy for teacher education must assume or express views about responsibility for curriculum. To take an obvious example: where teachers exercise responsibility for all major curriculum decisions, even if under various kinds of constraints, the task of teaching for which the training institutions prepare them is very different from that where major decisions are taken for the teacher. In the former case, unless teacher education does equip the teacher as a curriculum developer there will be a serious gap between training and classroom reality; in the latter case, that particular gap will not occur. From this point of view, there is an intimate connection between curriculum development and teacher education, and the connection is being increasingly recognized in those countries where school-based curriculum development is part of the present system. The connection is also recognized, sometimes rather belatedly, in those systems where massive investment in curriculum materials production have not paid off because of implementation failures. It is coming to be realised that dissemination is more than just an apparatus of communication and persuasion, like advertising or political propaganda. Teachers at the very least must be trained to use the new materials and in some institutions they are being trained on and in the use of these materials in such a way that they are contributing to the further development of the curriculum package – hence the so-called open-ended curriculum.

Traditionally, teachers have not been trained as curriculum developers even though, without benefit of training, many of them have acquired the necessary understanding and skills as part of their formation as classroom practitioners. Indeed, there have been virtually no training programmes anywhere for curriculum developers, except in the United States – and even they were largely by-passed in the curriculum reform movement of the fifties and sixties. A first requirement of policy for teacher-education, in the context of a discussion of school-based curriculum development, is to recognize that this movement exists, it is growing, and it places very heavy demands on the competencies and commitment of teachers. Questions of strategy and resource allocation are secondary since we must know for what responsibilities, roles and relationships we are educating our teachers before deciding where are the gaps in our present system. It is unfortunate that, despite its avowed commitment to teacher professionalism and its excellent proposals for teacher in-service education, the James Committee so presented its findings as to give minimum prominence to the tasks which teachers are being educated to carry out as distinct from the stages of their preparation, and the institutions which are to play a part. This is essentially strategy-type thinking; what is equally needed is the analysis of problems and issues in teaching – of which curriculum development is one. Consequently, the James Committee has little of interest to offer to the continuing debate on the content of teacher education.

(b) Initial courses: self-selection and curriculum orientations

School-based curriculum development is so radical in its longer term implications for schooling that re-thinking of every stage of the teacher-training process is required, from initial selection to certification and subsequent in-service treatment. Since teacher self-image, motivation and professional commitment are involved, the selection process should aim to take into account those characteristics of students that seem to correlate with the kind of professionalism outlined in this paper. Our present procedures are very inadequate and we can have little confidence that they will be significantly improved in the years ahead. A more practical way of looking at this problem is to accept that selection for initial training is not a scientific process at all, and that self-selection through professional engagement is more effective. Since, in the United Kingdom at least, a substantial proportion of people trained to teach seem to have left the profession within five years of qualifying, it may be better to accept that the teacher who is to act as curriculum developer is the one who stays on beyond the initial stages and has become a career teacher by his or her late twenties. The younger, more mobile and less committed teacher must accept a role as member of a curriculum development team, under the direction of someone akin to the master teacher. This suggests a corporate approach to curriculum planning, which could be justified on many other counts than expediency, and correspondingly a form of training that prepares the young teacher for group decision-taking, committee work, group assessment and related procedures which run counter to the individualistic tradition of closed-door class teaching. Course structures which divide 'subjects' from each other and from 'education', and which treat 'education' as a series of discrete sub-disciplines, are all too prevalent, and reflect a feeble academicism rather than imaginative and forward-looking assessments of the tasks and responsibilities of the teachers . . .

(c) Curriculum studies in post-experience courses

Much may be done to develop a curriculum expertise in the pre-service course, through units of study in curriculum design, team-teaching, classroom-interaction studies, assessment and evaluation, inter-disciplinary teaching, and so forth. Nevertheless, the sense of need for systematic training in curriculum development cannot be expected to emerge strongly in students when their primary fears have to do with self-image, ill-disciplined classes and the basic capacity to survive in a school situation. The more practical concepts and techniques of curriculum development are more congenial to experienced teachers, for whom also the philosophy of school-based curriculum development, despite their disenchantment with some aspects of teaching and schools, is more acceptable than it is for the pre-service student. The primary focus of teacher education for school-based curriculum development should be the post-experience or in-service stage of his training. [. . .]

[. . .] In a system where already in most primary schools, and in many secondary modern and comprehensive schools, teachers have a wide measure of curriculum control, these in-service programmes will include a considerable element of curriculum theory, design and development. However, much work remains to be done in designing appropriate courses and other learning experiences corresponding to the different needs of teachers: subject specialists, heads of department, counsellors, directors of study, school principals, and so forth. School-based curriculum development does not imply a uniform role and not all teachers need or are ever likely to become expert in all aspects of curriculum development.

[Skilbeck recognises that his conception of school-based curriculum development makes great demands on the teaching profession, and lists some of the problems which might be anticipated if teachers were to be brought more into the process of decision-making.]

a A sense of low self-esteem and inadequacy in staff, and lack of relevant skills, e.g. in analysing objectives, constructing tests, working in planning groups, etc.; failure of authorities to provide advisory and specialist consultancy services.
b Lack of interest or conviction in staff, particularly in sustaining change processes over a period of time; careful planning is hard work.
c Inadequate allocation of resources (time and personnel as well as money); rigidity and bureaucracy in control of resources.
d Conflicting priorities on part of teacher, e.g. planning, teaching, assessing, private study, increased leisure and recreational interests; lack of incentive to teachers to engage in planning and evaluation.
e Rapid staff turnover.
f Reconciling what may be conflicting demands e.g. Ministry requirements, external examination, parental pressures, pupil interests, teachers' educational values.
g Inadequacy of theoretical models – teachers tend to reject what they cannot easily apply.
h Complexity of issues and of managerial problems e.g. designing, and implementing individual study programmes within a common core curriculum.

i Failure to appreciate subtleties of group interactions when the balance of power in an existing institution is threatened.

j Tendency of institutions to revert to earlier forms of organization and control if the pressure for change is not continuous.

k Discontinuance of new practices before they have been fully implemented and diffused.

l Neglect of the diversity of successful teaching styles and range of possible strategies of change (premature selection of one set of procedures in preference to possible alternatives which either singly or in combination may be more effective.

m Failure to carry out optimizing studies e.g. what is the distinctive contribution to curriculum development of schools, national project teams, universities, colleges, national and regional administrations!

1.5 Authority and participation

Terry Moore and Denis Lawton

Talk about authority and participation might be regarded as setting out exclusive alternatives with the implication that we have to choose either the one or the other, that educational practices must be based either on the pronouncements of authority or on some shared participatory activity. Such a view would seem to be oversimplified if not incorrect. [. . .]

It will be argued that we are not presented simply with a polarity of incompatibles, but with two concepts, both of which have a proper application in an educational context, although in different ways.

To develop the thesis we may begin with the notion of 'pupil-participation'. It is possible to distinguish between two separate senses in which this term may be used in connection with education:

1 Pupil-participation in education in the sense of participation in the business of *being educated*, participation in what is going on in an educative experience.

2 Pupil-participation in education in the sense of participation in decision-making *about what goes on* in an educational situation, about procedures and arrangements in schools and elsewhere.

It will be argued that pupil-participation in sense 1 is justified by logic, in that this sort of participation is necessarily involved in education. Participation in sense 2 is justified, where it is so, by moral rather than by logical considerations. It will be maintained that in both cases there is connection with *authority*, but that only in sense 2 may the pupil be said to have a justified claim to exercise authority, and even then only in a limited way.

Education, in any normative sense of the term, involves initiating pupils into various aspects of knowledge, understanding and skill. This must involve the pupil in *learning* something, coming to understand what he is taught. Now, no one can be *initiated* into anything unless he actively takes part in the initiating proceedings. This is participation in the business of being educated. Participation involves a sharing in an enterprise, with others, taking one's part and knowing that one is doing so. So participation in the business of learning, trying to come to understand, is a necessary condition of being educated. Pupils *must* participate in this sense or education isn't taking place at all. This is the point made in 1 above, participation by the pupil in what is going on, is required by the logic of the term 'education'.

But there is another side to this. In this business of initiation there are *teachers*, who are supposed to be in possession of the knowledge and skills being passed on. Pupils are not in possession, not fully so. It is because they are not

Source: LAWTON, D . *et al.* (1978) *Theory and Practice of Curriculum Studies*. London: Routledge and Kegan Paul, pp. 261–71.

fully in possession that they are pupils. This means that initiation involves a transfer, from the teacher to the pupil, the initiation of one by the other, into a public tradition. Thus the enterprise rests on the prerequisite that teachers are, to some extent, *authorities* on what they teach, that they have a right to be listened to. They don't have to be absolute authorities, nor infallible, but they must be authorities relative to those they are trying to educate. Pupils are not authorities in this sphere, since if they were they would not be pupils. There is thus a conceptual connection between *educating* someone and being *an authority*. It simply would not make sense to say the teacher was *educating* his pupil unless he knew what he was talking about, and moreover, knew more about the subject than his pupil. Therefore, in so far as there is an *educational* situation both participation *and* authority are conceptually involved; participation by the pupil in what is going on, the exercise of authority by the teacher. These are conceptual points, matters of logic not matters of empirical fact.

Now let us turn to the other aspect, i.e. participation in decision-making *about* what goes on, *about* educational arrangements. An institution, a school for example, has, as a condition of being an institution, a rule-structure to organize its efforts. The rules have to be made, interpreted and maintained, if the institution is to continue as such. Those who have the right to make, interpret and enforce the rules are *in* authority, authority *de jure*. Those who are in such authority in schools are so, in the vast majority of cases, because they are older, more mature, more experienced than their pupils. They are adults whereas, in most cases, the pupils are children. But, those who are in actual authority *de jure* in schools are not in the logically, superior position *vis-à-vis* those they govern, that the teacher, as *educator* must be *vis-à-vis* his pupils in an educational situation.

Before a teacher can *educate* his pupils he must be an authority, i.e. know more than his pupils know about the matter in hand. He must exercise academic authority, which his pupils, as pupils, can't do. But he doesn't have to be wiser, more tactful, more sympathetic, than his pupils to be in authority in the rule-making and rule-enforcing sense. It is just a matter of fact that he usually is so, a contingent matter, not a matter of logic. There is nothing logically sacrosanct in the notion of the teacher alone being in authority, and nothing in logic which keeps the pupil out of this position.

Now, the decisions that people in authority make and the rules they enforce have an impact on the lives of those affected by them and this is particularly the case in schools. In respect of this impact pupils will have as much knowledge and awareness as anyone else. They will know how rules, decisions, even teaching methods affect the quality of their lives. So, it can be argued, there is a moral case for saying that pupils should have some say in the decision-making that affects them, through consultation, representation or whatever other means are appropriate. [. . .] For in *this* sphere they too can be authorities, in that they have appropriate knowledge, and so can have the right to be heard.

[. . .]

But a note of caution is needed here. To say that participation is appropriate is not to say that all children are capable, ready or willing to share in policy decisions. Age, maturity, a sense of responsibility are also relevant considerations. What is being said is that there is a moral case against any *a priori* attempt to rule out pupil participation merely on the grounds that they are pupils. There is also an educational case, namely that it is through such participation that pupils may come to acquire virtues like tolerance and rationality in decision-making virtues essential to a democratic society.

[. . .]

What would be wrong would be to permit pupil-participation in decision-making where, since they are pupils, they have no right to be heard or consulted. Teachers would throw up their essential authority if they asked pupils what they thought they should be taught. For here, academic authority is crucial, and pupils, as pupils, do not have this authority. What would be equally wrong would be to deny pupil participation where pupils *do* have a right to be heard, i.e. in cases where, with reservations, they too can be said to be authorities on what goes on. Here they do have a claim, a moral claim, to participation, and it is as well to recognize this claim for what it is.

The nature of authority

Max Weber (like many other sociologists) was interested in the question of *social action* (how individuals react towards each other in a relationship), and one aspect of this question of social action is 'why do some people do what others tell them?' One answer would be *power*, and in this section we are concerned with that kind of power regarded by the recipients as *legitimate*, i.e. authority. Weber defined power as 'the possibility of imposing one's will on the behaviour of others'. In those social relations where power is *recognized* as 'legitimate' this may be described as *authority*. This distinction between 'power' and 'authority' is a useful and important one.

Weber wrote a great deal about authority and domination and used a typology of three kinds of authority: 1 traditional authority, 2 legal-rational authority, 3 'charismatic' authority.

Traditional authority

This mode of legitimation of a power relationship consists of an acceptance of authority of 'masters'. The legitimation is based on custom. The authority has been acceptable or valid for a long time. 'We have always obeyed this kind of person' (maybe a king or chief). [. . .]

Legal-rational authority

This mode of legitimation of power depends on the existence of good reasons for accepting the authority. The authority is part of an institution which is beneficial in some way to those obeying the authority. It is in accord with more general rules such as fairness or justice, or the need for order.

Charismatic authority

This kind of authority is 'legitimated' (if that is the right word) by the special gifts and purpose of the individuals possessing charisma. Such individuals might include such diverse personalities as Christ and Hitler. The authority depends on a belief that the wielder of authority has sacred or super-human qualities. His followers are disciples. Charisma can, however, be transmitted institutionally: for example, the ordination of Roman Catholic priests [. . .] Bierstedt (1967), writing about the connection between social control and authority, maintains that the *order* essential in social life is maintained by various expressions of institutionalized authority. But authority is not the same as *competence* (which is closer to R. S. Peters' distinction of '*an* authority' which is different from being *in* authority), and it is not the same as *leadership*. Bierstedt's definition is 'Authority pertains to the exercise of social control through clearly defined status arrangements between those in super-ordinant positions and those in positions below.' This underlines the important distinction between *authority* which is the legitimate institutionalized exercise of *power*, and *leadership* which is about *influence* (or persuasion) (Peters, 1959). This would imply that Weber's category of charismatic authority was not really authority at all but a kind of leadership. [. . .]

Both views (i.e. Weber's and Bierstedt's) would agree on the distinction between legitimate authority and coercive control. Power is regarded as coercive control rather than legitimate authority when it acts contrary to the rules established for its legitimation. Thus authority can lose its legitimation *either* by failure to behave justly (i.e. according to the rules) *or* failure to do what it is there for: e.g. if it fails to maintain order.

We should also make a distinction between the basis of authority which is in terms of an institution, and what one has to do as an individual to *maintain* a position of authority: this may involve questions of competence and leadership (and there is some psychological evidence about this – what it is and how to get it). A headmaster or a teacher is presumably a legitimate authority figure because he is part of an institution – the education system. He is entrusted by society to transmit certain kinds of knowledge. What he has to do to exercise authority, to get respect, etc., is another question.
[. . .]

Authority and education

Superficially there is a similarity between the liberal humanitarian kind of rational movement against injustice and the demand for participation by pupils or students (but see R. S. Peters' opposing point of view in Hirst and Peters, 1970). There may be arguments against some kinds of participation, but in a non-traditional kind of organization based on legal-rational bureaucratic criteria it is inevitable that questions of authority will be mixed up with questions of competence. Pupils are encouraged to ask *why*, and teachers must not only know the answers but be prepared to discuss them.

I have already said that authority is different from competence, and one view of authority is that the person in authority does not have to possess competence (i.e. to be *an* authority). The authority figure is simply given a certain status in order to preserve order: e.g. a policeman does not have to be particularly good at directing the traffic, but he has authority to do so which motorists do not; the treasurer of a society does not have to be better at signing cheques than the other members but he has the authority to do so, etc. But there is a weakness in this argument (especially when applied to education): authority of some kinds does depend *to some extent* on competence: e.g. a football referee needs to know the rules otherwise bottles with begin to fly; teachers much have something worthwhile to teach and be able to communicate otherwise their authority may be questioned.

Another difficulty is that education is compulsory. Sociologists are fond of making distinctions between voluntary associations and involuntary associations. In a voluntary association authority tends to rest upon consent (in a club or a debating society a member accepts the authority of the chairman even if he thinks he is a fool; he can leave if he wants to). But in an involuntary association, e.g. the army or a prison, there is no question of consent. Schools are *in fact* involuntary associations but we often act as though they were not. We value liberty so highly that we pretend it exists even when it does not. There is a difficult borderline between manipulation of the pupils and genuine participation, i.e. ultimately we may decide that pupils have to do certain things whether they want to or not, but we will begin by trying to persuade them that they have some choice. (This is of particular relevance, of course, to the current debate on a 'compulsory' core curriculum.)

Yet another problem is that teachers may regard it as part of their job to make themselves and their authority redundant. The authority of a judge or an army officer is static, but the authority of the teacher has to be gradually reduced: part of a teacher's job is gradually to reduce the competence gap between himself and his students. The more he succeeds the less justification for the continued existence of his authority.

Summary

So far we have outlined some of the reasons which might explain both confusion about the nature of authority and the uneasiness many now have in exercising authority.

Authority is often treated as a dirty word in education and is not distinguished from being authoritarian. . . . [We wish] to indicate that there is nothing wrong with authority as such although there may be much wrong with the way it is still exercised in some schools.

The relation between authority and competence is also important for teachers. Any teaching-learning situation involves authority in terms of the competence gaps: but this is likely to be fairly specific and should not be confused with general superiority-inferiority of a social or moral kind.
[. . .]
Finally, although a teacher is inevitably in an authority position he still has to persuade his students to behave accordingly. He has to negotiate with them. He must have something worthwhile to offer but they must also see it as worthwhile – they must participate in some way. To be a teacher in the days of traditional authority was much easier; to be entirely rational is extremely difficult; many schools seem to have settled for an intermediate position – manipulation.

References

BIERSTEDT, R. (1967) 'The theory of authority', in ROSE, R. (ed.) *The Study of Society*. New York: Random House.

HIRST, P. H. and PETERS, R. S. (1970) *The Logic of Education*. London: Routledge and Kegan Paul.

PETERS, R. S. (1959) *Authority, Responsibility and Education*. London: Routledge and Kegan Paul.

WEBER, M. (1947) *The Theory of Social and Economic Organization*. Oxford: Oxford University Press.

1.6 The notion of the ethos of a school

John Dancy

Experienced teachers have long claimed not merely that each school has its own ethos but that they themselves can identify (even feel or smell) it quickly and unerringly. The concept has sometimes been given a quasi-metaphysical status: the cliché phrase is 'an indefinable ethos', a kind of 'definite *je ne sais quoi*'. Rutter (1979) begins to produce a bony structure for this ectoplasm. More precisely, he produces some bones; I want in this paper to suggest a conceptual skeleton to articulate them.

The relevant *Shorter Oxford* definition of ethos is 'the prevalent tone of sentiment of a people or community'. 'Tone of sentiment' does no more than change the metaphor. 'Prevalent' and 'community' are more suggestive. 'Prevalent' implies that the tone

(i) is more powerful than other competing 'tones', and will go on being so – indeed it can hope soon to become ennobled as 'tradition';
(ii) holds sway in the sense of being shared by *either* most members of the community *or* the most powerful or influential *or* some weighted mixture of the two.

This second point immediately raises the question of the extent to which in a hierarchy the tone is set by each level for the one below it: to put it differently, how much contribution is made to it in a school by the pupils. The HMI *Secondary Survey* (1979) adopts a model of provision (namely by the staff) and response (namely by the pupils). Rutter (1979) also usually speaks as if the role of the pupils is to accept or reject, rather than to modify, that which is set before them by the staff (pp. 186, 194–203; but see also p. 181).

The same point is raised by 'community'. In spite of its slightly smug overtones (King, 1976, p. 192), community is the right word to use in this context. Schools may not be, but they do in this country aspire to be, communities, and the aspiration is an important part of their ethos. But a school may contain sub-communities (notably boarding-school houses) whose ethos, within its own confines, is stronger than that of the school.

For purposes of this paper, however, I must follow the simpler model whereby a school's tone or ethos is essentially set by the staff. And indeed it is a situation where over-refinement can misrepresent. Whether they or anyone else likes it or not, teachers are in the influencing business – they must take the horse to water *and* make him drink. Therefore the correspondence between the (presumed) intentions of the staff and the (actual) outcomes in pupil behaviour does constitute a reasonable, if rough, guide to a school's effectiveness.

I propose to analyse school ethos in terms of values, aims, attitudes and

Source: DANCY, J. (1979) *Perspective I.* Exeter: University of Exeter School of Education.

procedures. *Values* I take to be the ultimate in the sequence, that is the criteria by which in the last resort one grades one's various aims. *Aims* fall into two classes, intrinsic and extrinsic. The intrinsic aims of a school are those which inhere in the concept of education itself, for example the acquisition of desirable knowledge, skills and attitudes, whether in academic or social spheres. Extrinsic aims are those which have no logical connexion with the concept of education *per se*, though they do inevitably arise in our school system: for example the reputation – indeed the survival – of the school, the social advancement of its pupils, the maintenance of discipline as an end in itself.

Between the intrinsic and extrinsic aims there is some disputed territory, because education can never in practice be as 'pure' as most teachers would like it to be. For example it is not easy to say where the intrinsic aim 'to fit them to do a job of work' (Callaghan at Ruskin, 1975) verges over into the extrinsic aim of social advancement. Or take the case of exam successes. Rutter treats them as a good indicator of a school's effectiveness. The HMI secondary survey is 'purer'. It asserts – and few teachers would dissent – that a concern for exam success often distorts the teaching. In truth the difference between Rutter and the HMIs is more apparent than real. Exams, like profits in business, make a good criterion but a bad objective. Exam results, together with discipline and career success, lie on that sensitive frontier between intrinsic and extrinsic aims. At present the public spotlight is focused on that very frontier, and the map of it may need to be redrawn in places. But that does not undermine the main distinction between the two kinds of aims.

As to the *attitudes* that go to make a school's ethos, Peter Mortimore suggested in seminar discussion that they fall into two groups: attitudes to people and to school work. Under the heading of 'attitudes to people', I distinguish further between attitudes to individual people and attitudes to the school itself as a social entity or community. I make this distinction because of experience. Many issues in schools, particularly those involving one or two pupils, resolve themselves into a balance between the claims of the individual and those of the community. Many staff line up regularly on one side or the other in such issues; and the way in which the balance is held between them constitutes a most important ingredient in the school's ethos. Attitudes to these three objects can then be classified according to their correspondence with either intrinsic or extrinsic aims. Thus:

attitudes towards:	*intrinsic aims* lead to *concern for*:	*extrinsic aims* lead to *concern for*:
community	social development of individuals	administration and organisation
	order, cohesion, commitment	reputation and PR
	fair distribution of resources	economical use of resources
individuals	growth as persons (staff too!) with individual differences	discipline and control
	concept of 'personal best'	competition
school work	mastery of skills and knowledge	success in exams and career

This table brings out more clearly a fundamental difference between the two classes of aims. The extrinsic aims are those which a school has in common with any other organisation, especially a business. Employers understand such aims and not surprisingly wish to see them given more prominence in schools. But teachers are equally committed to the intrinsic aims – and these are the moral aims. Hence the agony of spirit into which many teachers are being thrown by current pressures upon that sensitive frontier-land.

Values order aims, aims inspire attitudes. Attitudes issue in, and are exemplified by, *procedures*. (A procedure is a pattern of actions, where an attitude is a pattern of felt thoughts.) Most of the Rutter 'process variables' are procedures, and it is procedures above all which turn out to be significantly associated with outcomes. Like attitudes, I put them in three classes, according to whether they relate to the community, to individuals or to school work.

Community procedures cover a wide range. At one end of the scale is the school prospectus, designed solely for the maintenance of the organisation. Next comes the school prize day, rightly regarded by staff and pupils as having no intrinsic link with education. Then, after the school play or concert, which is partly a PR exercise, comes the school assembly. Of all the school's procedures this is perhaps the one that most betrays a school's (at least a head's, and often also a staff's) values, aims and attitudes; and it is not surprising that to the pupils it is a more honest occasion than a public prizegiving. Honesty is one of the virtues proper to community procedures.

Another such virtue is fairness in the treatment of sub-groups, particularly of children with special needs. The distribution of resources between the different ability bands (and between sixth form and main school), the system of options in years 4 and 5, the criteria for grouping children in years 1–3 – all these procedures contribute much to the ethos of a school, though Rutter was not able to take account of them.

Procedures relating to individuals are management procedures. To management of staff the virtue proper is consultation, to management of pupils it is consistency. Rutter is particularly good on consistency (p. 192 ff.) and its importance in persuading pupils to accept staff values.

But there is something even more important in schools than the acceptance of staff values. One of the most frightening features of Auschwitz was the way in which some prisoners came to adopt the values of the guards; in that way they ensured their physical survival at the expense of their humanity. If Langford (1973) is right that the central concept of education is that of 'becoming a person', then certain attitudes and procedures acquire a new importance. Chief among these attitudes is respect – the exact opposite of the attitude cultivated at Auschwitz – and an important part of respect is trust. Bryan Wilson (1969) has written wistfully of trust in a paper about the ethos of universities.

In advanced societies we rely less and less on personal trust – trust in individuals as such – and more and more on technical competences and role performances. . . . Trust is mechanized, but thereby loses its intrinsic human quality. . . . It seems to me that trust and love belong to *communally* organized societies, and that the search . . . is for community, sustained face-to-face relations. . . . To that community I do not know whether we know the way back.

A community is indeed marked by trust between its members. Of course schools fall short of the community ideal, that is their members fall short of trusting each other. But many a teacher has implemented his belief that 'children become trustworthy by being trusted'. And now Rutter finds that desirable outcomes are correlated with keeping the school in good decorative repair and with other procedures which show that pupils are trusted, for example to look after their own resources, to take a responsible part in assemblies and house or year meetings, and to hold positions like form captain. Connected here is also the staff's readiness to see pupils 'at any time' and to arrange school outings. Rutter finds a further correlation between pupil outcomes and procedures which show that staff themselves are trusted, for example the provision of clerical help. What he has not done (yet) is to comment on one's expectation that trust is contagious, that is the more the staff are trusted, the more they in turn trust the pupils (and even, perhaps, each other!).

The final group of procedures is those relating to work. They include the organisation of work, the teaching styles, and the curriculum itself. The organisation of work is straight-forward enough: the setting and checking of homework, the punctuality of lessons and the proportion of the lesson time spent 'on task' – all these are matters crucial to what one might call the work ethos of the school. And they represent the clearest instance of the stability of ethos. A new recruit to the staff finds it, in Rutter's words, 'much easier to be a good teacher in some schools than others'. (For this stability compare the way that in the human body each cell is said to be replaced every seven years, yet the whole remains recognizably the same.)

Of teaching styles Rutter has less to say. Successful outcomes are associated with praise, as exemplified in the display of children's work on walls and also in high expectations on the part of teachers. One might guess that such procedures (together with others, noted above, for encouraging pupils) would have proved to be further associated with the more open styles of teaching. But on that, as on most other aspects of classroom interaction, the team collected no evidence.

There remains the curriculum itself. The HMI *Survey* links the concept of ethos particularly with the school's provision for the personal and social development of its pupils, whether within or without the formal curriculum (9.1.2). Here again, one would expect to find a high correlation between a school's general treatment of its pupils and its formal curriculum in such matters as health, careers, religion/morals. But that still leaves out the bulk of the classroom subjects. The contribution which classical studies could once make to the ethos of a selective school *can* now be made by a strong tradition in for example environmental science, music and drama or European studies – any subject area, in fact, which can both capture the young imagination and form the focus of an adult philosophy of life.

But if excitement of this kind is part of a school's ethos, so also is its antithesis, the deadening or even alienating curriculum, which is the school's equivalent of repetitive work at the factory bench. In between those two extremes lies a middle position where the content of the curriculum is, so to speak, neutral: it is there to be got through, nobody quite knows why, it is just part of the 'system'. Such a curriculum makes little impact either way upon the thoroughness with which people approach their work, and even less upon what is still the core of the school's ethos, namely the way people treat each other.

I have attempted to analyse school ethos in terms of values, aims, attitudes and procedures, the attitudes and the procedures being those relating to the community, to individuals and to work. If the distinctions have creaked at times, that is partly because in a school almost everything is interconnected. A factory exists for work, a family for community and personal growth, a school for all three together. Many school procedures exemplify at one and the same time attitudes to the community, to individuals and to work: this is true for example of school assemblies, of staff meetings, and of all procedures relating to the discipline of work. For this reason it is not in the least surprising that 'good *behaviour* should be a consequence of praising good *work* in the school assembly or vice versa'. Public praise encourages a commitment to the school, with all that this implies both for behaviour and for work.

It is indeed this very interconnexion of factors which suggests to the theorist the logical construct of 'ethos'. Such at least seems to be the sequence of thought in Rutter (p. 183): 'the importance of the separate school process measures may lie in their contribution to the ethos or climate of the school as a whole'. The cautious researcher can here take comfort from the fact that he is speaking a language which makes sense to the practitioner.

Two final points. First, it is obvious that the concept of ethos is morally neutral – compare 'the ethos of Auschwitz'. Nor is there any moral or educational merit in what one might call strength of ethos. Too strong an ethos can prevent a child from developing as himself, prevent him even from ever really leaving school. We all know the phenomenon of the retarded 'old boy', still wearing nappies but in the school colours.

The second point is related. It concerns what Rutter calls the 'importance of a sense of direction' (p. 192). A sense of direction is sometimes provided by external circumstances for example reorganisation or involvement in a major curriculum project or strong neighbourhood links with a particular industry. Sometimes again it derives from the academic or social tradition of the school – for instance a girls' grammar school strong in science. But in a school that attempts to meet a wide range of needs and to prepare children for life in a mobile, pluralist society, any simplistic clamour for a sense of direction needs to be carefully scrutinized. On this, Rutter's comment is typically useful, not to say encouraging and (I hope) provocative of further research: 'the greater the group agreement on crucial issues, the greater the tolerance which is possible for individuality and idiosyncrasy on other matters'.

References

Her Majesty's Inspectorate (1979) *Aspects of Secondary Education in England*. London: Her Majesty's Stationery Office.

KING, R. A. (1976) *School and College*. London: Routledge and Kegan Paul.

LANGFORD, G. (1973) 'The concept of education', in LANGFORD, G. and O'CONNOR, D. J. (eds) (1973) *New Essays in the Philosophy of Education*. London: Routledge and Kegan Paul.

RUTTER, M. *et al.* (1979) *Fifteen Thousand Hours: Secondary schools and their effects on children*. Shepton Mallet, Som.: Open Books.

WILSON, B. R. (1969), in NIBLETT, W. R. (ed.) (1969) *Higher Education, Demand and Response*. London: Tavistock Publications, pp. 24–6.

1.7 Leadership in middle management

Denys John

Middle managers (department/faculty, house/year heads)

The task of middle managers is to provide leadership to teams of class or tutor-group managers. For the first part of this section the term 'department' will be used for convenience to cover faculties as well as pastoral units (house or year). If discussion about objectives and syllabuses appears inappropriate to pastoral units, it is because the latter have too often been regarded as having no learning objectives. It is the argument of a later chapter on pastoral and curricular sub-systems that both serve the purpose of pupil learning, only differing in the composition of the pupil groupings and the nature of the learning objectives [(John, 1980)].

Middle managers, like all leaders except those at the summit or at the base of an extended hierarchy, have a dual role. They are both members of a higher-echelon management body and leaders of their own sub-systems. As members of a general management team they contribute their particular skills and expertise to questions concerning the whole institution (such as the general aims of the school). As managers of their own sub-systems they provide the members of their groups with the leadership required for the effective internal organization of the sub-system concerned.

The leadership of middle managers in the first place consists in gaining the commitment of the members of his group to a set of clearly understood objectives. He or she may exercise this leadership in a variety of ways . . . The mode of leadership, to be effective, should be consistent with the one normally exercised in the institution by other levels in the structure and by other middle managers at the same level. All teachers are members simultaneously of a number of different task groups. Management exercised by any of the recognized modes, if consistent, is likely to be more effective than if it is fluctuating and unpredictable. The drawing up of objectives must be the first task; and ensuring that they are understood and will be pursued by the whole team of teachers is the second. Once objectives have been defined for the whole course there is a tendency to assume that the task is finished for an indefinite period into the future. It is in itself such a long and complex job. Nevertheless the good middle manager will keep a copy of the department's objectives in a loose-leaf file and always open on his or her desk so that notes can be made and questions raised about items which were unsatisfactory. Syllabus objectives and methods must be open to continuous reappraisal.

The head of a large department is responsible for all the work of all the teachers in the department and all the classes which he or she has delegated to

Source: JOHN, DENYS (1980) *Leadership in Schools*. London: Heinemann, pp. 52–6.

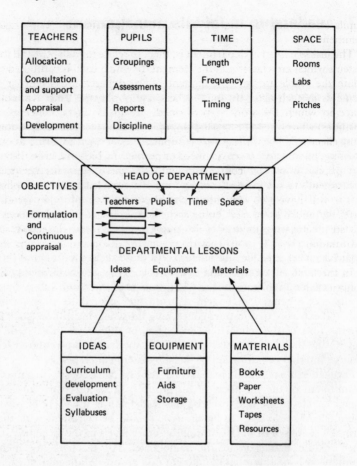

Figure 1   The management of a department
The task is to relate the elements together and to the environment

them. In a school of 1,000 pupils a mathematics head of department may be responsible for 8,000 mathematics lessons each year. All these 8,000 lessons have to be related to each other and to the environment of the department consisting of the work going on in the rest of the school. It is probable that in the past heads of department have been better at co-ordinating the work in their own subject than at co-ordinating it with what went on elsewhere. Subject departments are so often castles surrounded by a moat that teachers sometimes forget that the inhabitants of the castles move regularly from one to another every time the bell rings. One small piece of research revealed that 12-year-old pupils in a certain school were 'doing' coal mines in the same year simultaneously in science, geography and history. There was no co-ordination between any two classes about how the topic was treated. Only the pupils knew until the enquiry revealed the information. They made no comment!

The task of a head of department is, then, to relate to each other all the task systems which are classes and the elements of which each is composed and to relate the whole to the environment of the department (Figure 1). The elements in each class are the teachers, the pupils, the time available, the space in which the work is performed, the ideas (facts, concepts, skills, attitudes) which are to be learned by pupils and the ideas about how they can most effectively learn them, the equipment to be used to bring about this learning, and the materials acquired or prepared which are to be the basis of the pupils' work. In connection with all these elements the head of department's task is to select, acquire, make accessible. In all these spheres he or she will have two overriding considerations constantly in mind: first, fostering the skills and developing the effectiveness of the teachers concerned so that their management of their classes may be enhanced, second, seeking information about what other departments are doing and informing them of what his or her department is doing.

In the light of this wide and heavy responsibility it is possible to list the qualities most likely to help the head of department fulfil it.

1   *Contribution* as a middle manager to the formulation of school goals.
2   *A sense of purpose*: commitment to school goals and clarification of departmental objectives.
3   *Confidence* in self and in subordinate colleagues.
4   *Unselfishness*: readiness to share by delegation.
5   *Openness and availability*: communication with departmental colleagues, other staff, pupils, parents, head, primary schools, governors, advisers and inspectors.
6   *A sense of interdependence*: readiness to co-operate with other departments; support, encouragement, advice, appropriate action to help subordinate colleagues; staff development and instigation of in-service training.
7   *Awareness of role*: recognition of all aspects of the task, readiness to discharge it without status consciousness.
8   *Judgment*: ability to appraise the work of subordinate colleagues in a helpful way so that intervention presents an opportunity rather than a threat.
9   *Broad interests* in the work of other departments.
10   *Resolution, decisiveness*: establishing policies and explaining reasons for them.
11   *Personal teaching skills*: effectiveness as a teacher of all ages and abilities of pupils as a means of providing an example for imitation by junior teachers.
12   *Orderliness and method*: in storage and listing of books and apparatus and in keeping accounts and records.

The common theory is that curricular departments are to do with teaching and learning and that house or year groups are to do with caring and social activities. As a result middle managers in the pastoral system are in danger of being stereotyped as soft-hearted, or even as 'soft'. By contrast heads of subject departments may be saddled with the image of being tough or hard. This kind of polarization is echoed in the supposed division between affective and cognitive education, child-centredness and subject-centredness, and even within the curricular area, between rigorous 'disciplines' like mathematics and physics, and soft options like art, literature and biology. Such mythological oversimplifications bear little if any relationship to the truth. In fact softness and hardness are inseparable opposite faces of each coin. Since pastoral teachers are as much responsible for discipline as curricular teachers, and mathematics teachers are as much concerned with their pupils as people as are art teachers, the images are plainly not reflections of the facts. Nevertheless the idea that pastoral heads are experts in understanding children and in providing them with recreational activities is not easily dismissed unless a more plausible reason for their existence can be found. This question is pursued [elsewhere]. At this point the intention is limited to indicating that the separation of the roles of departmental and house or year heads along the dimension of caring and demanding presents a danger to both as limiting their roles as teachers responsible for both.

Reference

JOHN, D. (1980) *Leadership in Schools*. London: Heinemann, chapter 6.

1.8 Ideology and management in a garbage can situation

Kristian Kreiner

[In this extract we will discuss] different techniques of management in an organization characterized as being a direct democracy. The organization is an experimental free-school in Denmark ... No formal authority-differentiation exists; all adult members (parents and teachers) of the organization are invited to participate in the decision-processes as equals. Our aim was to examine management success and failure in an ideological organized anarchy. Despite the ideology of the organization, we found little apparent correlation between the legitimacy of the form of management and the apparent success of the attempt.

The organization

Formal structure

During 1971–72 we made observations of the decision-making processes in an experimental free-school in Copenhagen, Denmark. One of the decisions made during this period was to change the pedagogical structure of the school, and it is this decision which is the focus of this [reading]. During the course of this decision, the research group was present at every important meeting except one, conducted extensive interviews, and drew upon a detailed questionnaire completed by parents and teachers.

The decision was made by the *open assembly* – the formal governing body of the school. All 170 parents and 10 teachers of the school were invited to the open assembly's monthly meetings. A chairman was elected each time, but there existed no rules for the procedure of the meetings. Subject to the approval of the participants present, the assembly could discuss and decide upon everything. Normally, the meetings were structured by an agenda, put together by the school board and mailed to all members.

The six members of the *school board*, all of them parents, were elected by the assembly. They served for two year terms. Normally, the elections were not contested, the usual problem being one of finding enough candidates willing to serve rather than choosing from among competitors. The main function of board members was administrative, but they also served as a link between the assembly and the board of teachers.

A system of collective leadership existed among the teachers. In order to exercise this, the *board of teachers*, consisting of all teachers, met once a week.

Source: MARCH, J. G. and OLSEN, J. P. (eds) (1976) *Ambiguity and Choice in Organizations*. Bergen: Universitetsforlaget.

The planning of teacher activities was to take place here. In day-to-day matters, individual teachers had considerable autonomy. During the observation period there were six grades, among which the approximately 110 children were distributed according to age. Most teachers were assigned to a specific grade. The parents from each grade met occasionally with the teacher(s) in order to discuss class-specific problems. These *class meetings* had no formal authority to make decisions.

Pedagogical structure

The children were divided into six different grades. Most of the time was spent in these groups. Although a time schedule did not exist officially, most grades seemed to follow some plan of activities. Subject to a few limits, children were allowed to leave the group in order to take part in outdoor activities. During two afternoons each week the grade-structure was replaced by a workshop structure: every teacher offered an activity, and the children could choose among these according to their own desires – at least in principle. In practice, due to an overwhelming interest in the cooking class, children were distributed among the workshops by the teachers.

The ideology

The school was founded by a group of parents in reaction to the public school system. The founders believed that:

(a) The hierarchical structure of the public schools resulted in a situation in which parents had little influence on the kind of education provided for their children. This dissatisfaction developed into the concept of a parent-governed school, which further developed into a direct democracy. An attempt was made to avoid status and authority differentiation.

(b) The high priority given by the public schools to intellectual development produced more harm than good for the children. In the view of the founders the children would, by their own drive, demand such education when they were ready for it. To force them to learn to read before they themselves demanded it would disturb their natural development, or at least be a waste of energy. This idea manifested itself in a high priority for playing, as play was believed to develop creative and social abilities. In the application form to the school it was clearly stated that the children should not be expected to read as early as children in the public schools.

The ideologies were real, but they were not completely fulfilled in practice. Even though the formal authority distribution was eliminated, there existed clear differences among the members with regard to their influence on the development of the school. This was the perception of the members as well as the observers. Of the approximately 200 members, only 27 members were mentioned in our questionnaire as being influentials. Further, of these 27, a group of six was mentioned on the average ten times more often than the remaining group on the average. Thus, there seemed to be a high degree of consensus in the perception of a power-distribution. In addition, even though the official policy was not to force the children to acquire intellectual abilities – and this policy was often praised at the assembly meetings – quite a few parents felt unhappy about it. Their complaints were aired to the teachers privately or at the class meetings.

Description of the choice-situation

. . . The school could be described as an organized anarchy (Cohen, March and Olsen, 1972). By this we mean:

1 No consistent set of preferences existed to be applied to actual choices. Instead, a number of highly valued symbols (e.g. democracy, Marx, children's right to self-determination) were used. However, the implications of the symbols for any choice were uncertain and subject to much interpretation from the participants.
2 The knowledge about the technology, in the realm in which decisions were to be made, was vague. Thus, questions about which solutions solved which problems, or which consequences should be taken into consideration, were matters of individual judgment.
3 The participants were not assigned to different decisions through rules or obligations. Although there were fairly stable differences in participation, it was hard to predict who would participate in a given choice. Whether a member would participate was at least partly a result of outside time and energy demands (e.g. childcare, work).

Normally about 40 parents participated in an assembly meeting. In our questionnaire, only a few stated that they never participated (mainly parents with no children in the school at the moment) and only a few stated that they always participated. The series of meetings, which we will describe shortly, attracted about 80 parents on the average. They were well-attended. Attendance varied within single meetings; typically quite a few participants left before a meeting was concluded.

In general, the decision-structure and the access-structure placed few limitations on the way in which problems, solutions, and participants were connected to choices. In fact, the ideology encouraged members to participate and encouraged the participants to air their concerns in open debate.

The load these meetings put on the members' energy was not very high. Almost no preparation was required. The amount of written material distributed in advance was usually modest. In our case, three meetings were held within one month. There were numerous requests for more meetings.

The dynamics of the decision-process

We expect a decision-process to exhibit some kind of dynamic by which it moves toward a conclusion. This may be through the solution of problems, or through some other logic by which the decision process produces a decision. The process secures its major meaning from the outcomes it generates. In contrast, choice-opportunities in the school we studied seemed to contain little of these dynamics.

We think that there are at least three reasons for this:

(a) Many of the problems were highly discussable but hardly solvable. A long ideological discussion of creative training may serve as an example. Creative training had always had a high priority among the educational goals for the school. At one point, however, one of the members persuaded the participants to focus on the fact that industry made use of exactly such abilities. Since presumably none of them wanted to educate children for capitalist society, the concept of creativity needed some kind of reformulation. The ensuing discussion was long, but without conspicuous results.

(b) Members of the school were urged to participate. Intrinsic in the democratic ideals was the idea that as many as possible should make the decisions. Furthermore, the assembly was perceived not only as an arena for discussion, but also as a social centre for the school, a place to meet each other, and in some important respects, a church.

(c) Status and power-reputation were distributed according to activity at the assembly meetings. It appeared to be more virtuous to have one's definition of the choice accepted as definitive than to make compromises. Thus, there were disincentives for participants, seeking status and power-reputation, to sacrifice a preferred definition of the situation, even if the symbolic intransigence limited the chances of a decision.

The main participants

We have already mentioned that six members of the school were commonly perceived to have more power than other members. . . .

(a) All of them had high seniority in the organization. In fact all but one had participated in the founding of the school.

(b) Each attended the assembly meetings every time or almost every time.

(c) All but one rated themselves as belonging to the most active third of the participants at the assembly meetings.

(d) All but one rated themselves as belonging to the most radical group in the school.

(e) Their circles of private acquaintances were dominated by other free-school members (from 50 per cent to 85 per cent with an average of 75 per cent), rather than outsiders.

One of the six was a teacher at the school. The others were a psychology student, bookbinder, architect, artist, and public school teacher. The four last mentioned parents all had children in the third grade; and the public school teacher and the bookbinder were members of the school board. All of them seemed to be well trained in meeting behaviour and to be in the possession of some oratorical gifts.

These six members seemed to agree on most issues. Often the 'enemy', whom they fought at meetings, was not easy to discover. In particular, they were concerned with 'the conservative parents who force the school in the direction of intellectual over-emphasis'. Often their meeting activity seemed to be a kind of educational performance in which public virtue was demonstrated and reinforced.

At times, however, confrontations did occur. The usual opponents in these confrontations belonged to a rather unstructured group, the members of which could be described as fairly active at the meetings but without great power-reputation. Often they seemed to be regarded as less radical than the leadership, but whether this was a result of real differences or just derived from the fact that they opposed the leading radicals, we are unable to answer. In such confrontations, many (maybe most) participants played on-looker roles. They did not participate in the debate, but only in the voting procedures.

The events

The decision

By 69 votes to 6, the assembly decided to change the pedagogical structure. The main idea was to dissolve the existing grades and to have a considerable proportion of the teaching take place in workshops. . . . A lot of questions were still not settled: How much time should be spent in workshops? How much freedom should children have in their choice of activity? What should the workshops contain? All these questions were to be worked out in seven small groups as specified in the school board's plan for the implementation. These groups were to consist of teachers as well as parents.

The antecedents

The situation, in which this choice-opportunity appeared, was from all sides described as a crisis. The teachers had major troubles with their collective leadership, as well as personal problems among themselves. Some parents were dissatisfied with the school. Some of the children were playing outdoors most of the time; others complained of being bored. The teachers were too busy with their own problems to do much or anything about them.

The problems among the teachers led to a discontinuation of the normal collaboration between the two teachers in the third grade. Consequently, a newly-hired teacher was left alone in what was generally regarded as the most difficult grade. At a class meeting for the third grade, parents tried unsuccessfuly to persuade the teachers to reallocate some teacher hours back to the grade.

In the course of this process the idea of a new pedagogical structure was born. Dissolution of the grades would also solve the problem for the third grade. One of the parents from this grade wrote a paper, in which he discussed different pedagogical goals and structures. He submitted the paper to the school board. Using the construction of a new school as the occasion, the assembly leaders placed the paper on the agenda for the regular meeting in the assembly on 8 October 1971.

Highlights of the process

The main events we wish to consider took place over a period of about one month in 1971. It was a relatively crowded month, as the following table (Table 1) suggests:

Table 1   Time-line of decision

Date	Arena	Agenda	Events
1971 8 Oct.	Assembly	Paper on pedagogical goals and structures	1 general discussion of the paper 2 airing of dissatisfaction over teachers and structure 3 teachers complaints of cross-pressure regarding the priority of intellectual education 4 vote on the priority of intellectual, social, and creative training. By 31 votes to 16 the meeting refuses to make any priority at that time
11 Oct.	School board	The cross-pressure on the teachers	1 it is decided to cancel all class meetings for a period of three months 2 the members agree to draft a proposal for a new pedagogical structure and to present it in the assembly as soon as possible.
21 Oct.	Extra-parliamentary meeting	The crisis of the school	1 due to the autumn holidays not all invited show up in the home of the originator 2 the teachers present attack the meeting, which they say is violating basic, democratic principles in the school 3 exchange of viewpoints
29 Oct.	Assembly	School board's proposal for a pedagogical structure	1 presentation of the proposal 2 general discussion, no agreement on whether to discuss goals or structure 3 group discussion. The groups can decide themselves what to discuss

Table 1 Cont'd

Date	Arena	Agenda	Events
			4 school board demands final decision on their proposal. Many objections. The school board threatens resignation
			5 a vote shows a small majority in favour of a final vote
			6 a guiding vote shows near unanimity for the proposal
			7 the school board agrees to postpone the final vote one week
2 Nov.	Extra-parliamentary meeting for 'the silent majority'	Meeting with head of another free-school with workshop structure	1 initiative taken by four couples from the third grade; approximately 30 members attend
			2 the speaker has positive experiences with the structure, and he is thus able to relieve worried parents
5 Nov.	Assembly	Final decision on the proposal	1 school board presents the implementation plan
			2 general discussion, in which all concerned are referred to as being taken care of by the group
			3 final decision; the proposal is accepted by 69 votes to 6

Efforts at management

[. . .]

We . . . consider five efforts to manage the process leading up to the vote to change the pedagogical structure in the school. They were the five identifiable occasions on which an initiative was taken during the time period covered by this report:

1 A proposal to vote on the priority of pedagogical goals (8 October).
2 The school board decision to cancel class meetings for three months (11 October).
3 The meeting of a group of parents and teachers to reach private agreement (21 October).
4 The development of a new implementation plan (29 October).
5 The imposition of a deadline under threat of resignation (29 October).

A vote on goals

At the end of the first meeting in the assembly (8 October) a vote on the priority of different educational goals was proposed. The idea was to assert whether intellectual, social, or creative goals should be given precedence. The proposal was made in a situation which was characterized by confusion. The preliminary paper contained two different topics, one concerning the goals and the other the pedagogical structure. While nobody objected to a change of the structure, one group of parents felt that the goals had to be considered and probably changed prior to any change in the structure. Thus, not only was there no consensus about what to do; no consensus existed about what to discuss, either.

The immediate occasion for the priority proposal was a challenge from the teachers. Following rather sharp attacks by some parents, the teachers answered by claiming that parents made inconsistent demands on them. While the low priority for the intellectual training was never doubted at assembly meetings, teachers reported receiving many complaints at class meetings and privately from parents on their children's inadequate performance on intellectual subjects. An unidentified group of 'reactionary parents' was accused by the teachers of having forced a departure from the school's ideals.

The priority proposal was more or less a codification of existing ideology. One of the original reasons for the foundation of the school was to escape the (in the founders' view) over-emphasis on intellectual training in the public schools. To give this a lower priority than social and creative training was not something new. An acceptance of it would probably reinforce some basic beliefs and attitudes of the parents.

Almost no effort was made to argue in favour of the content of the proposal. The discussion was entirely about whether or not to vote on it at all. The prime argument for taking a vote was that this was a way of ensuring that equality was maintained. A recent issue in the assembly had been that very few people participated in the debates. This was perceived as contradictory to the democratic ideals of the school. Voting had become a recognized way of ameliorating the situation and inhibiting the development of inequality in power.

The proposal was more or less a codification of an already accepted ideology; popular reasons were given for taking the vote; the proposer was an important leader in the school; and the proposal was supported not only by most teachers but also by the most high-status parents. Nevertheless, there was opposition to taking a vote. Indeed, the assembly ultimately refused to vote on the priority proposal.

The only expressed reason for the opposition was that the three goals were so much inter-connected that it made no sense to make priorities among them. The argument, of course, has merit in principle; but it is not the kind of argument that normally was persuasive in the group. What appears to be true is that this proposal had a context. It was seen in connection with another proposal which was made (but never came to a vote either). It had for some time been believed that a group of parents wanted a division of the school. In their view, the school had grown too big. Consequently, since no members could be excluded, they had adopted a strategy of attrition. The idea was that the assembly should be induced to make radical enough decisions so that the school would become unacceptable to the more conservative parents. For example, one of the members of this group proposed that instead of making a ranking of the goals, all intellectual training should be abandoned for a period of three months. At least some participants saw the priority-proposal as connected to the desire for a division of the school. Such an interpretation was facilitated by the attack on the 'reactionary parents' by the teachers.

In this context, the assembly refused to vote to establish a goal priority. The management attempt, which could have led to a less complex definition of the choice by excluding some ideological concerns, failed to succeed apparently because of circumstances which had less to do with the proposal itself than the context in which it was made and the supporters it attracted.

The cancellation of class meetings

Three days after the refusal of the assembly to vote on priorities the school board met. At this meeting, two things were decided. First, the members of the board agreed to draft a proposal for a new pedagogical structure, and to seek its approval in the assembly as soon as possible. Second, the board agreed to cancel all class meetings for a period of three months. The cancellation was an implicit bargain. Although the 'terms of trade' were never clearly specified, we think that the cancellation of the class meetings was an attempt by the board to make an exchange with teachers.

While the number of teaching hours in the school was fixed through legislation, the number of hours the teachers were expected to use on meetings with the parents (both at class meetings and assembly meetings) was determined internally and informally. Normally, four or five class meetings were held during a year for each grade. During this period, where many assembly meetings were held and where the teachers met frequently to work on their own collaboration problems, teachers felt a heavy overload. Cancellation of class meetings was viewed as a relief.

Just what the board expected to receive in return was never made explicit. One possibility, however, is the removal of an 'extraneous' concern. Since parental cross-pressure on teachers was most conspicuous in class meetings, the cancellation made the pressure less obvious. Teachers would be less likely to keep that garbage in the can at the next meeting. Since the issue of cross-pressures had diverted attention from the pedagogical structure, the implicit side bargain was to permit it focus on pedagogy in return for avoiding further parent–teacher confrontation in class meetings. The cross-pressure issue was in fact not mentioned again in the assembly. If our interpretation is correct, the teachers kept their part of the bargain.

By making the decision to cancel class meetings without consulting the assembly, the board violated some widely-shared norms in the school. The decision was never made public as an explicit decision. Instead the board suggested to the teachers that no class meetings should be held for three months. Since teachers were responsible for calling meetings, they simply were not scheduled. No protest was recorded from the parents. Apparently, they did not know about the decision. The lack of class meetings elicited no comment. The high activity level in the assembly, in combination with the background of irregularity in timing of class meetings, obscured the management-attempt.

The trade was successful. A move that in spirit (implicit bribe) and in style (secret) violated the norms of the group appears nevertheless to have modified the flow of problems into the choice situation.

The extra-parliamentary meeting

On 21 October the originator of the discussion in the assembly (the architect) gathered all teachers and a few parents to an informal meeting in his home. This meeting was called after the first, rather chaotic, meeting in the assembly. In the assembly the teachers had shown little interest in discussing the pedagogical structure. In fact, they had agreed privately to neglect this discussion and to concentrate on their own problems of internal collaboration. Their reluctance to participate was a source of concern. It was widely believed that the teachers' commitment to the decision was of great importance. They were acknowledged publicly as the experts and several times were urged to state their opinions and preferences. They resisted.

We view this extra-parliamentary meeting as an attempt to change the arena in which the actual decision was to be made. Only a few parents (mainly rather high-status members and mainly third grade parents with a supposedly relatively homogeneous view of the situation) were invited. As a result, the possibility of reaching a conclusion among the parents was much higher in this group than in the assembly. The pressure these parents, in turn, could put on the teachers for changes was consequently much stronger. If the extra-parliamentary meeting had reached some kind of an agreement, the discussion in the assembly would probably have been different. A proposal supported by the teachers and the high-status parents would be very likely to be adopted.

In order to persuade the teachers to participate in the meeting, the crisis-nature of the situation was stressed. Something had to be done soon, and the teachers had to do it. The unusual situation justified the unusual procedure. This seemed to be the reasoning of the architect, who justified his action in terms of 'honest concerns about the future of the school'. Although the teachers to a certain extent agreed, they nevertheless defeated the effort by arguing emphatically that the meeting violated basic democratic principles in the school, symbolized by the assembly. It was asserted that such concerns should be dealt with in an assembly meeting and not in informal groups. The appeal to legitimacy made it impossible for the group to operate. The arena of the choice was still the assembly where the teachers still refused to participate.

In order to understand this outcome, we have to consider what was happening in the board of teachers. The immediate problem the teachers faced was a conflict between the third grade teacher on the one side and the rest of the teachers on the other. What started out as a collaboration-problem between two teachers in the third grade, increased during the autumn to a crisis. Several of the teachers were looking for jobs at other schools. Feelings were high. The teacher in the third grade was isolated. In fact, during this period all the other teachers were working to get rid of her.

In an organization where symbols like 'reason', 'solidarity', and 'tolerance' were highly valued, this was not an easy task. The conflict seemed to be based more on personal antipathy than on pedagogical inconsistency. Since they could not expect to get any help from the parents with this problem, they refused to inform anybody about it. They needed time to work out this problem (i.e. to find good reasons) without involvement of the parents.

Teacher participation could come only at the cost of other things. They were not generally opposed to a change of the pedagogical structure; but the work in the board of teachers was so much more vital for them, that no attention could be paid to the decision process in the assembly. That the reason for the teachers' resistance was one of timing rather than lack of concern is suggested by the fact that as soon as the third grade teacher was fired, the teachers immediately started working on a new pedagogical structure.

The attempt to change the arena for the choice failed. The conflict between the teachers distracted them and left little time for participation in the political manoeuvring and post-decision implementation that the extra-parliamentary meeting would have required. In their resistance, they appealed to major symbolic themes of the school. As a result, an illegitimate effort at management was unsuccessful.

The implementation plan

At the 5 November meeting in the assembly, the school board presented its plan for implementation of the proposed pedagogical structure. Part of the plan called for the formation of seven small groups of parents and teachers. Since the proposal was a framework only, quite a few questions remained to be settled. The official task of these groups was to work out the details.

In fact, the groups appeared to be designed to provide seven new, specialized-access garbage cans. Almost all of the concerns expressed during the process were referred to the small groups for discussion. The action was a log-roll. If the school board proposal were accepted, the resistant parents would have their concerns considered in more attractive arenas. For two reasons, these new arenas were more attractive than the assembly:

(a) The groups had restricted access and decision structures. The different groups had names that identified specific questions they were to consider. Participation was specialized. No one could participate in more than one group. Individuals were likely to get a favourable result in the areas they most cared about, at the risk of losing out in less important areas.

(b) The number of participants in each group was small. One of the acknowledged disadvantages in the assembly was that many individuals felt uneasy about addressing such a large audience, particularly when there was conflict. Consequently, a large 'silent majority' was believed to exist. For them the new arenas must have seemed more attractive.

The design of these alternative arenas was a part of the decision on the pedagogical structure. It preserved the illusion of assembly policy making, but would have the actual decisions highly decentralized. In the former sense it supported the ideology; in the latter it was not consistent with the general belief in the doctrine of collective discussion and decision.

Imposing a deadline on the choice

By a vote on 29 October, a deadline of one week was imposed on the decision. The action was demanded by the school board members as the price of avoiding their collective resignation. Even then it was approved by only a very small margin. The management technique was the overt threat of withdrawal.

The threat by the school board and the time limit were neither very popular nor perceived as legitimate. A good deal of protest was raised. It was, however, futile. The realities favoured the board. Election to the school board was not very attractive (as suggested by the difficulties in finding candidates for the seats). The work was time-consuming. The present members did the job well. The threat was effective despite its illegitimacy.

The imposition of a deadline enforced by the threat of resignation and in conjunction with a log-roll, produced the final decision almost without resistance. Only one participant protested strongly against the procedure used by the school board at the 5 November meeting when the decision was made formally.

Discussion

We have described decision making in a standard garbage can situation. Various symbolic and substantive problems were exercised. Participants wandered in and out. The definition of what was being decided changed over time. The process was guided by the often casual temporal connections among problems, solutions, participants, and choice opportunities.

In the midst of this, there were efforts to direct the process. Individuals and groups, particularly the leaders of the school, tried to control the process by various moves. These attempts varied significantly in terms of their consistency with widely-shared norms of legitimate decision behaviour.

We have examined five such efforts (Table 2) and have tried to indicate for each attempt how it related to the ideology of the school and whether it was successful.

The data are thin enough and subjective enough to make any interpretation problematic. Nevertheless, it is hard to see in this sequence of management attempts any sign that the likelihood of success of the attempts is positively related to their ideological purity. The ideology was real. The complaints about violations were intense. The commitment to the ideas was important. But the flow of events in the process dominated the rationality and ideology of

Table 2   Five attempts at management in an ideological organization

Attempt	Management method	Ideological legitimacy*	Outcome
1 Vote on goals	Priority setting	High	Failure
2 Class meeting cancellation	Private trade	Low	Success
3 Extra-parliamentary meeting	Caucus	Low	Failure
4 Implementation plan	Log-roll	Intermediate	Success
5 Deadline	Threat	Low	Success

* As assessed by the writer on the basis of comments made by participants and consistency with the explicit ideology of the organization.

the stages. The efforts at intentional management and the debates over their legitimacy were educational. They provided a serious training in the values of the group. But the connections between legitimacy and effectiveness were tenuous and confused by the ways in which the process confounded attempts to understand outcomes as intended.

Our observations, moreover, seem to suggest that the time perspective is important. Individual phases of a decision-process might be described as fairly intentional in the short term; but the process taken as a whole is better described in terms of a garbage can model. Within the time frame of our study, the broader the time perspective, the better does the garbage can description fit. Indeed, our story has no end. Class meetings were resumed after less than two months, and the decision to change the pedagogical structure was never implemented.

References

COHEN, M. D., MARCH, J. G. and OLSEN, J. P. (1972) 'A garbage can model of organization choice.' *Administrative Science Quarterly*, Vol. 17, No. 1, pp. 1–25.

COHEN, M.D. and MARCH, J.G. (1974) *Leadership and Ambiguity: The American College President.* New York: McGraw-Hill, Carnegie Commission on the Future of Higher Education.

1.9   Aspects of accountability

East Sussex Accountability Project

Three points deserve to be borne in mind by the reader in working through the arguments we shall now rehearse. The first is that accountability can have a positive as well as a negative aspect. It need not be seen simply as a burdensome necessity in meeting external obligations. If properly designed and implemented, an accountability policy can also provide a defence against outside attempts to limit autonomy and the enjoyment of legitimate rights and powers. Such attempts might take the form of political encroachments on freedom, or the unjustified erosion of financial entitlements, as well as campaigns to undermine reputation through the media or to destroy it through libellous gossip.

Second, accountability – as we have come clearly to recognise in the course of our study – is a two-way process. Any LEA [Local Education Authority], in satisfying its external obligations to maintain proper educational standards, must also see itself as answerable to its teachers and its schools, and must strive actively to sustain its supportive relationships with them.

The third point leads on from these. It is possible to approach accountability as a process of mutual negotiation, in which something is conceded – say, some professional prerogative which contemporary values call into question – and something gained – perhaps a firm declaration of public trust, a renewed guarantee of essential autonomies, or an insurance against future encroachment. Such an approach must call for a gradualist and long-term strategy, based on careful consultation between the Authority and its schools. It could be expensive in time and effort, and could risk exasperating public patience. But the alternative, of imposing an apparently cheap, quick and easy solution, against the wishes of the schools, might in the end prove a hollow victory. It would at best achieve conformity without conviction; at worst it could lead to the general debilitation which now characterises many school systems in North America.

Six modes of accountability

In the attempt we now make to knit together the diverse strands of our analysis and to give them a coherent shape, we have inevitably had to oversimplify or sharpen a number of familiar distinctions as well as to

Source: EAST SUSSEX ACCOUNTABILITY PROJECT (1980) *Accountability in the Middle Years of Schooling: An analysis of policy options*. Brighton, Sussex: University of Sussex, mimeographed paper, pp. 96–100.

introduce some new ones of our own. We wish to acknowledge the crudity and occasional artificiality of the barriers which we have found it necessary to erect in marking out the terrain for further exploration. We recognise and welcome the fact that they will be transcended by the subtleties of future political debate.

As we noted [previously], it is possible to distinguish three facets within the broad meaning of the term accountability: (1) *answerability* to one's clients ('moral accountability'); (2) *responsibility* to oneself and one's colleagues ('professional accountability'); (3) and *accountability* in the strict sense to one's employers or political masters ('contractual accountability').

These distinctions are exemplified in different ways by schools on the one hand and Education Committees on the other. Schools are primarily answerable to parents, but legally accountable to the LEA (in some circumstances directly, in others via their managers). Education Committees are answerable to their schools, but constitutionally accountable to the electorate (either directly, or via their governing Council). Both have also to acknowledge certain responsibilities to their own professional consciences and to their peers.

We have earlier remarked that accountability must meet two basic, interconnected demands: (1) the preservation and, where possible, enhancement of overall levels of performance through *maintenance* procedures; (2) the detection and amelioration of individual points of weakness through appropriate *problem-solving* mechanisms. [. . .]

Taking these two sets of considerations together, we can distinguish six different modes of accounting, as follows:

1 Answerability for maintenance
2 Answerability for problem-solving
3 Responsibility for maintenance
4 Responsibility for problem-solving
5 Strict accountability for maintenance
6 Strict accountability for problem-solving

Between them, these six modes serve to draw attention to the demands which might – in principle if not always in practice – be made on schools and LEAs. We shall accordingly use them as the basis for our subsequent discussion. First, we shall look at the pattern of possible expectation as it relates to schools, taking this to be a matter of legitimate interest also to the Education Committee and its officers.

The elements of school-based accounting

. . . There is a variety of possible ways (see East Sussex Accountability Project, 1980) in which the schools might elect to meet their answerability to parents for the maintenance of standards – the first mode in our list. The parents' awareness of what their children's schools are doing may be promoted through regular communication on individual pupils' progress, or by allowing ready parental access to classrooms and teachers, or by encouraging a general atmosphere of open enquiry. . . . Other forms of provision would include explanations of curricular aims and teaching methods, accounts of overall policy, and reports on general standards of performance . . .

The second mode concerns the school's potential problem-solving strategies, and especially its means of responding to matters of parental concern. These may include early disclosure of problems – whether affecting individual children or relating to wider issues – where this seems appropriate in averting later crisis; and the prompt acknowledgment and investigation of – and subsequent response to – expressions of parental grievance . . . All parents have a right to know what the appropriate procedures are within the school if they wish to raise a complaint.

The professional responsibilities which might be exercised by schools in the course of their own internal maintenance – the third mode in our list – could be expected to include the development of good relationships with parents on the one hand and the Authority on the other, alongside various forms of domestic monitoring of standards and the regular review of staffing, curricula and teaching arrangements . . . Schools may also – insofar as their reputations are interdependent – be called upon to exercise professional responsibility towards one another. Junior and Middle schools must, moreover, share responsibility with the Infant and Secondary schools to which they are linked, for the long-term interests of their pupils.

The fourth mode, relating to internal problem-solving, would include – on the institutional front – being aware of and taking steps to rectify incipient points of weakness, and the vigilant anticipation of potential crisis (East Sussex Accountability Project, 1980, section 3.3); and – in relation to individual children – the sensible use of screening procedures (such as pupil records and diagnostic tests) to identify and give remedial help to those at risk . . .

The fifth mode – strict accountability for maintenance – is concerned with the accountability of each school to its LEA for overall quality of provision. Here, one might note its explicit obligation to observe mandatory and constitutional accounting procedures and to meet centrally-agreed specifications. Implicit expectations would include the school's openness to informal visitation by authorised representatives of the Authority, its readiness to justify (if reasonably called upon to do so) its curricular goals and methods and its overall policies, and its similar readiness to account for below-average levels of pupil performance . . .

The sixth and last mode focuses on the ways in which the schools do or should account to the LEA with respect to problem-solving. In this context, they have a clear duty to report on all such grievances or complaints deriving from external sources, and all such internal difficulties, as they are not themselves able to resolve satisfactorily within a reasonable period of time.

Fig. 1 Elements of schools' accountability

	Answerability (to parents)	Responsibility (to self and peers)	Strict Accountability (to LEA direct or via managers)
Maintenance	1 - Regular communication on individual children's progress (via written reports, etc.) - Accounts of overall policy (via prospectus, etc.) - Explanation of curricular aims and methods - Reports on general standards of performance, academic and other (via open days, speech days, etc.) - Encouragement of better parental awareness of school's activities and endeavours (via ready access to classrooms and staff, atmosphere of open enquiries and discussion)	3 - Domestic monitoring of standards - Regular review of staffing, curricula and teaching arrangements - Promotion of good relationships with parents (via school social occasions, etc.) - Promotion of good relationships with feeder and receiving (secondary) schools - Promotion of good relationships with managers, Advisers, and LEA as a whole	5 - Observation of mandatory and constitutional procedures - Meeting of centrally agreed specifications - Openness to authorised visitation - Readiness to justify curricular goals and methods and overall policies - Readiness to account for pupil performance standards

Problem-solving	2
	- Notification to all parents of complaints procedures
	- Prompt acknowledgment and investigation of parental complaints, confirmation of action taken
	- Early disclosure to parents, where appropriate, of problems
	  (i) relating to individual children
	  (ii) involving wider issues
		4
		- Screening of individual children at risk (via internal reporting, pupil records, tests, etc.)
		- Provision of remedial help to children in need
		- Awareness of incipient points of weakness
		- Anticipation of potential crises
			6
			- Reporting of unresolved external complaints and grievances
			- Reporting of unresolved internal difficulties
			- Development of effective means to deal with problems arising

NB The entries above are not intended to be comprehensive. They are meant only to indicate possible expectations or demands in each category. They should *not* be taken as indicating policies which are necessarily feasible, desirable or deserving of priority at the school level.

They would also properly be expected to develop, on their own initiative, appropriate means of anticipating and dealing with such problems as may in fact arise . . .

These various elements of school-based accounting are summarised in Figure 1. We have not attempted to mark out the distinctions between those items which are universally applicable, those which are common practice, and those at present observed by few schools or none. We have not made any of the subsidiary differentiations between informal and formal, mandatory and constitutional procedures. Nor have we attempted to single out those particular policy options which remain presently available to schools. All such categories are dependent on context: the demarcation lines between them will vary from one time and one place to another. Any reader who wishes to define them for his own purposes will, we hope, have no difficulty in doing so.

Note

The implications of this study are more fully discussed in:
BECHER, T., ERAUT, M. and KNIGHT, J. (1981) *Policies for Educational Accountability*. London: Heinemann.

Reference

EAST SUSSEX ACCOUNTABILITY PROJECT (1980) *Accountability in the Middle Years of Schooling: An analysis of policy options*. Brighton, Sussex: University of Sussex, mimeographed paper.

1.10 Keeping the primary school under review

Inner London Education Authority Inspectorate

Foreword

The process of self-appraisal, of looking at what you are doing, why you are doing it, whether you are doing it well, whether you ought to be doing something different is, or should be, a continuing one in every school. Now that we have reached a point of greater stability of staffing and shortages are being overcome it is easier to take stock and plan for the future with a clearer indication of where we want to go. The idea of a check list of questions the staff of a school might seek the answers to, giving a framework to support a more systematic form of self-assessment, originated in a discussion between the Chief Inspector and some head teachers. As a result, the Staff Inspectors for Primary and Secondary Education met with a group of head teachers to see what they could produce. This pamphlet is the result of their work and a subsequent trial run in a number of schools.

What this paper offers is not a blue-print or questionnaire to be rigorously followed or answered in its entirety every year. It is presented as a basis for the development of a school's own form of self-assessment, to be modified or extended to suit the intentions and interests of the individual school. The object of applying some form of systematic self-appraisal is to assist in the clarification of objectives and priorities, to identify weaknesses and strengths and ensure that due attention is given in turn to all aspects of school life. To examine all aspects in a single year would be an impossible task. Improvement of the quality of education, and that I hope is the basic aim of all of us, can only come when current practices are examined in detail, questions are asked, the answers are examined and consideration is then given to appropriate action. This is a time-consuming task, not to be undertaken lightly. It will involve many and at times the whole staff. If a school undertakes this kind of course it must plan to proceed at a pace that is reasonable and within its resources. It must decide what are the areas that most need attention and deal with these first.

There is a danger in any form of self-assessment that people do not always see themselves as others see them. To overcome this it is hoped that schools who take into use a form of self-assessment such as is outlined in this paper will be prepared to discuss the outcomes with colleagues in the inspectorate so that they may have the benefit of an external viewpoint to put beside their own. Additionally, the possibility of some form of cross-moderation through linking

Source: INNER LONDON EDUCATION AUTHORITY INSPECTORATE (1977) *Keeping the School under Review: A method of self-assessment for schools devised by the ILEA Inspectorate*. London: Inner London Education Authority.

at departmental or school level in relation to different aspects of assessment might be worth considering.

Guy Rogers
Deputy Chief Inspector
Summer 1977

The primary school

This self-assessment paper is designed to assist a school to examine its organisation, its resources, its standards of achievement and its relationships. It suggests facts to be sought and questions to be discussed. It does not attempt to be comprehensive or detailed, and it is for individual schools to elaborate upon any of the suggested sections that are of particular relevance and to work out their own priorities.

An exercise in self-assessment must take into account what in the school's view the primary stage of education is about. This view is usually put in the form of a series of broad aims concerned with the growth and personality of the child and generally makes reference to aspects of intellectual, physical, emotional, social, spiritual and moral development.

Further aims normally reflect the way in which the school functions as a community.

In most schools there is a continuing dialogue about aims which are understood and accepted by the staff although they may not always be set down in precise terms. It could be that they may need to be redefined and that from them will grow a set of more detailed objectives relating to the everyday working of the school.

Although this paper is essentially concerned with practical issues relating to the smooth running of a school it is hoped that the ensuing discussions will take account of those deeper issues that reflect fundamental principles, aims and objectives.

A *The children*

1   In considering the needs and interests of individual children what provision is there for:
    gifted children?
    children who are slow to learn?
    children with behaviour problems?
    children for whom English is a second language?
    children from different ethnic backgrounds?
    children who have a specific skill or talent?
2   What opportunities are given for the development of initiative and responsibility?
3   What initiatives does the school take about getting to know the children coming to the school for the first time?

i.e. from home?
> from a nursery?
> from another school?

4   Who is responsible for promoting continuity for individual children and in the areas of the curriculum
   (*a*) from home to school (including reference to play groups, etc)?
   (*b*) from class to class?
   (*c*) from one school to the next   (from nursery to infants;
   > infants to junior;
   > junior to secondary)?

   (*d*) from a different school?

5   What attention is given to
   (*a*) the children's previous experience at home and school?
   (*b*) the records of the programmes of work and whatever tests may have been made?
   (*c*) the use of individual apparatus and materials?
   (*d*) differences in learning and teaching styles?

6   What records are passed from stage to stage
   e.g. folders of work?
   > children's books?
   > annual records?

7   In the school are there any serious obstacles to achieving continuity?
   > What are they?
   > How are they being tackled?
   > What further steps might be taken to promote educational development at each of the above-mentioned stages?

8   Does the school have adequate information about children's health and physical development?

9   What use does the school make of agencies such as the Educational Welfare Service and the Schools Psychological Service?

B   Parental and community involvement

1   What initiatives are taken to introduce the school to parents?

2   How is the school developing links with the neighbourhood?

3   What opportunities are made to give parents an understanding of what the school is trying to do and of their child's part in it?

4   How are parents helped and encouraged to be interested in helping their children to learn?

5   What opportunities are there for parents to discuss their children's development and progress with the teacher and the head teacher?

6   Are there any prepared leaflets of explanation or information for the parents to consider?

7   Is there a parent/community association?
   Is it effective?

8   Is there a parents' room in the school?

How is it used?

9   How are non-English speaking parents helped to participate in the life of the school and community?

10   How and for what purpose does the school co-operate with:-
   (*a*) secondary schools (preparation for parenthood/community studies)?
   (*b*) adult education service?
   (*c*) colleges of further education?
   (*d*) neighbouring special schools?
   (*e*) colleges of education?
   (*f*) other primary schools?
   (*g*) the teachers' centres?

11   In what way and how often does the school account to the parents for the child's progress and development
   (*a*) by interview?
   (*b*) by interview preceded by letter/report?
   (*c*) by standard report?
   (*d*) other ways?

C Managers

1   What are their contacts with the school?
2   How are they informed of what the school is trying to do?

D Programmes (schemes) of work or guidelines

1   Has the school programmes of work or guidelines in all or any of the following areas of the curriculum:
   (*a*) physical education?
   (*b*) language and literacy?
   (*c*) mathematics?
   (*d*) aesthetic developments, e.g. music, art and crafts?
   (*e*) environmental studies, e.g. geography, history, social studies, physical and natural sicences?
   (*f*) religious and moral education?

2   When were the programmes drawn up?
     By whom were they made?
     When were they last revised?
     What advice was sought from any learning support agencies?
     Which programmes now need revision?

3   Do all members of the staff possess copies of all of the school programmes?
4   Do new teachers receive copies of the school programme as a matter of course?
5   What help is given to teachers to help them to understand and follow the programmes of work? For example is there staff discussion on the content and pattern of the work?

6   In which programmes of work is it of particular importance to stress continuity of development in teaching methods throughout the school?

7   Has there been an opportunity for teachers to attend appropriate in-service training courses?
    Are there opportunities for them to comment on these courses on return to school?

8   To what extent is the head teacher involved in implementing the guidelines and in the development of work within the school?

9   Do the teachers keep a regular record of their plans of work?
    At what intervals are these compiled?

10 Are visits and school journeys a normal part of the curriculum?
    Are they designed to fit in with children's interests and stage of development?
    Is there a review of the number and types of visits undertaken during the past year?
    Is the distribution of resources balanced so that all classes of children have a suitable opportunity for participating in these visits?

11 What opportunities are there for children to develop talents and interests beyond the normal curriculum?
    What clubs and societies have been organised?

12 In what way does the school assembly contribute to the children's development?

E Class organisation

1   On what basis are children arranged in classes or home base groups?

2   Are children grouped within a class? If so, on what basis and for what purpose?
    What degree of flexibility is there in this grouping?
    When are revisions made?
    What degree of freedom has the teacher in organising or arranging these groups?

3   In a given period (e.g. a week or a month) how much of the teacher's time is given to each of the major areas of the curriculum?
    In a similar period approximately how much time is given to class teaching, group teaching and work with individuals?

4   Are any children extracted from their classes?
    For what reasons?
    Does the class teacher know what work they do?
    Is there consultation between teachers to ensure general educational development of the children?

5   Do the children experience a range of activities over a period of time?
    How much choice does an individual child have?
    What guidance is given to him?

6   Does the organisation of the day and the grouping of the children enable

the programme of work to be effectively interpreted and the needs of the individual children sensitively met?

If not, what changes are needed?

F Attainment

1   Do teachers make their own continuing record of children's progress in physical, intellectual, social, emotional and aesthetic areas of development as a basis for completing the Authority's annual records?

2   Does the school have a common basic pattern for this recording?

3   To what extent are the school's current methods of recording successful:
   (a) in guiding a teacher's observation of children in the different areas of their development?
   (b) in identifying needs of individual children?
   (c) in assembling information that is relevant to another school or for discussion with parents?

4   In assessing progress in literacy and mathematics is any use made:
   of standardised attainment tests?
   of a published diagnostic test or procedure?
   of internally devised tests and procedures?

5   Are tests and/or recorded observations made of other aspects of the curriculum in order to ascertain standards of attainment?

6   Who is responsible for judging the validity and value of the testing/ diagnostic procedures?

7   When was the nature and the timing of these last reviewed?
   To whom are the results available?

G Staffing

1   What human resources are available?
   Full-time teachers
   Part-time teachers
   Technicians
   Ancillary helpers
   Other adults

2   Are there any vacancies?

3   If any full-time teachers do not have regular responsibility for a class how is their teaching strength used?

4   How are the part-time teachers used?
   Do their responsibilities relate to their particular skills and interests?
   Do their responsibilities and those of the teachers without classes meet the stated needs of the school?
   When was their deployment last reviewed?

5   What are the duties of those teachers who have posts of responsibility?
   Does the staff generally know of these duties?

Are these duties revised from time to time?
Do they meet the needs of the school?
Is there a policy for training and developing the skills of post holders?
Who is responsible for the care of probationary teachers?
6   What are the duties of the ancillary staff?
(a) Around the school?
(b) In the classroom?
(c) With the children?
Who is responsible for training the ancillary staff in their duties and for reviewing their relationships within the school?

H Staff meetings

1   What meetings of the full-time staff (all sections) have been held during the last three terms?
    Why were they held?
    Who initiated them?
    Who attended them?
    Did anyone seem to be left out for any reason?
2   Was an agenda produced in advance?
    How was it originated?
3   What matters were discussed at these meetings?
    Were the decisions minuted?
4   What procedure was adopted when matters could not be agreed?
5   Is there general satisfaction with the variety of the timing and mode of staff meetings and the implementation of decisions reached?

I Simple statistics

The following details may be of importance particularly if they represent a trend or a marked difference from the previous year's figures.
At the end of the academic year:
1   What was the number of full-time staff that left the school for:
    retirement?
    promotion?
    family reasons?
    other?
2   How many teacher-days absences due to sickness were recorded?
3   Other than normal nursery/infant transfer and statutory enrolment how many children joined the school from another school?
4   Other than the normal infant/junior or junior/secondary transfer how many children left the school?
5   How many accidents to pupils were recorded?
6   What were the results of the comparability tests in the last three years?

J *General environment*

1   Who is responsible for ensuring that the school is kept in a state of workmanlike tidiness?

  Can the storage arrangements be improved?

  Are there displays of material and work to stimulate interest amongst the children, adults about the school, parents and visitors?

2   Who ensures that displays in the halls and corridors are well mounted and frequently changed?

3   Is the school in good repair?

  e.g. in the classrooms?

    in the halls?

    in the cloakrooms?

    on the staircases?

    in the playgrounds?

  Do the school keeper and his staff make a satisfactory contribution to the maintenance of the school?

4   Is the way to the Head's room and the Secretary's room clearly indicated?

5   Can anything more be done to improve the use of the outside play areas?

6   What procedures are there for a regular review of the provision of materials and resources in all of the major areas of the curriculum?

  This is to include a review of past expenditure on various items,

  e.g. consumable art and craft materials

    consumable stationery

    textbooks, library and resource materials

    musical instruments

    physical education apparatus

    maths and science apparatus

    school visits

    AVA [Audio Visual Aids] apparatus and software

7   How is waste of materials and resources avoided?

8   How are decisions about AUR [Alternative Uses of Resources] reached? Is there full staff consultation?

K *Action*

1   Are we clear what we have been trying to do? How far are we meeting those intentions?

2   What are the priorities for action

  (*a*) next term?

  (*b*) in the coming year?

3   Who will initiate this action?

4   Do we need any outside support and advice? If so, what?

L Questions for the headteacher to ask himself or herself

The head will, of course, be involved in the answers to all the other sections. It may also be helpful for heads to keep a detailed diary for a given period, say a fortnight and then to ask themselves the following questions:

Time

1 How often did I
   (a) go into all classes on one day?
   (b) greet parents at the beginning or end of the school day?
   (c) teach?
2 What time did I give to meeting staff individually or in groups?
3 How much time did I spend out of school
   (a) at County Hall?
   (b) at Divisional meetings?
   (c) in other schools?
   (d) at conferences or inservice courses?
   (e) elsewhere?
   Was this time
   (a) necessary?
   (b) useful to the school or to the service?
4 How much time did I spend on adminstration?
5 How much time did I give to visitors including parents, inspectors and ILEA officers?
6 Do I need to try to change the time distribution revealed by the answers to questions 1–5?

Objectives and organisation

1 What do I see as the priorities for the school in the next term/year/five years?
2 To what extent is my view shared by others?
3 What constraints exist?
4 Am I satisfied with the curriculum?
5 Which areas of the curriculum need attention and who can give it?
6 How do I ensure that resources are distributed in a balanced way?

Staffing

1 How available am I – formally and informally?
2 Do the staff feel that I am interested in their professional development and advancement and their personal welfare?
3 How accurate is my awareness of the load carried by different individual teachers
   (a) on the timetable?
   (b) in voluntary activities?
   (c) in helping pupils and colleagues?
4 How accurate is my awareness of the load carried by non-teaching staff?

M *Questions for the individual teacher to ask himself or herself*

1 My work in the classroom

Do I prepare adequately? What do I think of the presentation of my work? What improvements can I make in class organisation? How satisfied am I with my class control and relationships? Do I spend enough time in talking to children about their work? What kind of comment do I make on it?

2 Knowledge of the children

Do I really know all the children in my class including those who do not make obvious demands on me? Do I take account of individual differences between children in my relationships with them and in making educational provision for them? How successful am I in keeping records of children's development and progress? In what ways do I try to ensure continuity between my stage and the one before and the one after?

3 General

How do I contribute to the development of good relationships with children, colleagues, parents and other adults connected with the school? Do I contribute to discussion in staff meetings?

N *The acid test!*

Each member of staff asks the following questions:

1   Would I recommend a colleague to apply for a post in the school?
2   Would I recommend the school to friends for their children?

1.11   The methods of evaluating

Robert E. Stake

No one method of evaluating educational programmes is suitable for all situations. The information needs will vary. The audiences will have different expectations and standards. The evaluators will have different styles, which in turn are more or less useful to different clients. The purpose of this [reading] is to examine some of the differences in existing evaluation methods.

1 The most common dimensions for classifying evaluation designs

The writing of Michael Scriven has been influential in identifying basic dimensions of evaluation. His paper 'The methodology of evaluation' (Scriven, 1967) identified six dimensions, starting with a distinction between the goal of evaluation (to indicate 'worth') and the roles of evaluation (the different reasons and circumstances for which we need to know the 'worth'). Blaine Worthen and James Sanders (Worthen and Sanders, 1973) created a more elaborate taxonomy of evaluation designs. For this report ideas are borrowed from both these sources but presented in a simpler and less thorough way.

Formative–summative

The most pervading distinction Scriven made was one between evaluation studies done during the development of a programme and those done after the programme has been completed. Obviously, a developing programme has components that are completed day by day. It is difficult to distinguish between the summative evaluation of a completed component and the formative evaluation of a part of the programme. The distinction is not clear-cut.

The most useful distinction here may be between the users of the evaluation findings. Elsewhere I have noted that when the cook tastes the soup it is formative evaluation and when the guest tastes the soup it is summative. The key is not so much *when* as *why*. What is the information for, for further preparation and correction or for savouring and consumption? Both lead to decision-making, but toward different decisions.

Source: STAKE, R. E. (1976) *Evaluating Educational Programmes: The need and the response*. Paris: CERI/OECD, pp. 18–28.

Formal–informal

It would be foolish not to recognise the distinction between formal and informal studies, even though in this report only formal evaluation studies are being considered. Informal evaluation is a universal and abiding human act, scarcely separable from thinking and feeling. Formal evaluation is more operationalized and open to view, and less personal. It is needed when the results are to be communicated elsewhere. Of the two, the formal evaluation study is under an obligation to pass tests of accuracy, validity, credibility, and utility.

Case particular–generalisation

A most important distinction is between the study of a programme as a fixed and ultimate target, or the study of a programme as a representative of others. Most research is expected to be generalised in some ways: over time, over settings or over subject matters, for example. Evaluation research may be done essentially to discover the worth of a particular programme, or the worth of the general approach. Studies are perceived very differently in this regard, both by investigators and their audiences; and a large misperception is possible.

The more the study is expected to be a basis for generalisation the more the need for controls, controlled variation, or careful description of uncontrolled variation. Description is needed of the changes in time and place and persons, and in many of the ways in which generalisation may be directed. The case study undertaken for either knowledge of the particular or for generalisation is a more useful document when it provides the reader with a vivid portrayal of the setting and context of the teaching and learning.

Product–process

Another dimension on which evaluation studies vary is as to whether they give primary attention to the outcomes of the programme or to its transactions. A study of the 'product' is expected to indicate the payoff value; a study of the 'process' is expected to indicate the intrinsic values of the programme. Both are needed in any effort to get at a full indication of the worth of the programme, but in any actual study only a small portion of either can be examined. Much of the argument as to preferable methods depends on the beliefs held as to which is more measurable and useful.

Descriptive–judgmental

Many evaluators coming from a social science background define the evaluation task largely as one of providing information, with an emphasis on objective data and a de-emphasis on subjective data. Those coming from the humanities are likely to reverse the emphases. One will find some studies highly descriptive of students and settings, providing careful reports of differences and correlations, but with little direct reference to criteria of worth and value standards. And elsewhere one will find evaluation studies probing into the pluralism of values to be found in any educational setting. As with any of these dimensions, any particular study is not likely to be at one pole or the other, but to make some combination the compromise. The extremes identify a dimension on which some variation is apparent from study to study.

Preordinate–responsive

Studies differ considerably as to how much the *issues* of evaluation are determined by observation of activities and by realisation of concerns of participants in the programme. Preordinate studies are more oriented to objectives, hypotheses and prior expectations, mediated by the abstractions of language. Preordinate evaluators know what they are looking for and design the study so as to find it. Responsive studies are organised around phenomena encountered – often unexpectedly – as the programme goes along. (There are ways of being prespecified and responsive other than these, of course.)

In a preordinate study a relatively large portion of resources is spent on getting objectives specified in writing and developing instruments; and sometimes in providing for or controlling variation to yield more dependable statements of relationship among variables. In a responsive study a relatively large portion of resources is spent in preparing and placing observers on the scene.

Wholistic–analytic

Studies differ also as to how much they treat the programme as a totality, recognising conceptual boundaries common to non-technical audiences. The more common social-science research approach is to concentrate on a small number of key characteristics. A case study is often used to preserve the complexity of the programme as a whole, whereas a multivariate analysis is more likely to indicate the relationships among descriptive variables.

Internal–external

An obviously important difference in evaluation studies is whether they will be conducted by personnel of the institution responsible for the programme or by outsiders. They differ as to how formal the agreement to evaluate, as to how free the evaluators are to raise issues and interpret findings, and as to how changes in plans will be negotiated.

The eight dimensions above do not result in 256 different evaluation designs. Many of the dimensions are correlated, both conceptually and in frequency-of-use. For example, an 'internal' evaluation study is more likely to be formative than summative, more likely to be descriptive than judgmental. These characteristics and correlations might be particular to the places where evaluation has been most common. In new evaluation situations the key dimensions and combinations might be quite different.

2 Nine evaluation approaches

Another way to look at the different ways educational programmes are evaluated is to look at typical approaches. The differences between the approaches can partly be described in terms of the dimensions just discussed, but more subtle characteristics become apparent when models or prototypes are examined (Stake, n.d.).

In this section, nine approaches will be considered. The first two are very common. In any one year at least 10 per cent of American teachers and pupils are involved, at least for a few minutes, in student achievement testing or institutional self-study, as part of a formal evaluation effort. Some of the others are typical as part of informal evaluation, but uncommon as formal studies. The last two are much more rare, but increasingly mentioned by evaluation consultants. Particularly helpful in this context is the OECD document *Case Studies in the Evaluation of Educational Programmes* which is available free on demand from CERI/OECD. References in the text to case studies are to those in that document.

Student gain by testing

The approach usually suggested by measurement specialists and educational psychologists is 'testing to measure student gain in performance' (Bloom *et al.*, 1971). It relies on tests developed to match prespecification of objectives or on standardized tests that match or cover programme objectives (or their correlates). Many studies are undertaken using tests developed primarily for counselling and guidance purposes. Educators in favour of highly structured curricula prefer criterion-referenced tests as a basis for measuring student gain or mastery of the task. Control groups are sometimes used. Analysis of regression or covariance is sometimes used to identify variance in student scores attributable only to the teaching. The method is found weak by some critics because the tests under-represent what education apparently does for school children and because the identification of poor learning is often not much help in identifying or correcting deficiencies in teaching. [. . .]

Institutional self-study by staff

Mostly because schools in America have, by law, a great deal of autonomy, their officers have looked for ways of evaluating them, to avoid federal and state control. Long ago they formed regional alliances, a network of schools, for the purpose of accrediting each other. A number of special professional organisations, such as the American Association of Medical Colleges and the National Council for the Accreditation of Teacher Education, moved in the same way to provide self regulation and to avoid state regulation.

The principal method of evaluation adopted by these organisations has been *faculty self-study*. This is not to say that the final word on any matter was left to the school's faculty, but the primary gathering of data, interpreting of problems and recommending improvements has been via the initiative and hard work of the faculty. Review by visiting committees and adherence to specifications adopted by member schools has also been common to the self-regulation process.

The self-study is sometimes used by an institution under internal pressure, without any external requirement, such as when students are protesting or when major budget changes are imminent. It is a procedure which honours the *status quo*, establishmentarian values. It takes a heavy toll in staff time, and is a subject in contract negotiations with some unions. It has the great value of keeping problem-solving responsibility at the site of the problem. [. . .]

Prestige panel or blue-ribbon panel

A third common evaluation approach used by governments and organis-ations of all kinds is the panel of leading citizens, usually people without expertise in education (or whatever the focus is), but who are held in high esteem, who have a strong sense of social responsibility, and who are respected for outstanding achievement of some kind. A group of several such people is asked to study a problem. They may follow their intuitions, or be guided by an experienced counsel or staff member. They are expected to make a very formal report, usually in a matter of weeks or months.

A well-known example of this approach is the British [Plowden] report on *Children and their Primary Schools.*[1] In some countries such studies are often used as grounds for the enactment of corrective legislation. The blue-ribbon panel, also, is often the first choice among evaluation methods when matters are 'in extremis' – seized upon by leaders when the institution has been greatly injured, or is immobilized by crisis.

Less sensational instances are common in the schools when a new curriculum or student policy or staff organisation is needed. A prestigious group is asked to investigate. It almost always is expected to make recommendations. In these instances the method becomes similar to the self-study approach mentioned previously. It should be noted that the distinction of the panel members permits them to use personal experience and judgment as an adjunct to and sometimes in lieu of more objective and definitive data.

Transaction–observation

In contrast to the student-testing approach as a (sometimes) disciplined study focusing mainly on educational outcomes, the transaction observation approach is a (sometimes) disciplined study of educational processes. Here the activities of the programme are studied, and with special attention to settings or milieu (Parlett and Hamilton, 1972). Issues are often drawn from the proceedings rather than from theory or from goal statements.

Disciplines from which the methods of observation come include anthro-pology, ethnography, history and journalism. Some of these disciplines emphasize the crucial importance of reporting as well as of measuring. This evaluation approach follows that lead.

The transactions emphasized are not those between evaluator and educator, although it is the evaluator with this approach who seems to be especially sensitive to professional role relationships. [. . .]

In the transaction–observation approach one often will find an attention to the pluralism of values in education. This is consistent with the plea made by François Hetman in a 1973 OECD document (Hetman, 1973). He first extracted a sentence from a Report of the (U.S.) National Academy of Sciences (1969):

'Whatever improvement might be made in assessment systems, therefore, it is important to remember that the products of such systems ultimately represent no more than inputs into the complex network of decision-making processes, private and public, economic and political, that together mold the growth of technology and channel its integration into the social structure.'

But is this duty to fall only and exclusively to the central decision-making authorities? In a pluralistic society, such a monopoly in formulating and assessing alternative future options and courses of action may be regarded as a contradiction if not as a real danger to democracy. Hence the idea of a 'competitive assessment', in other words, of such an institutional set-up as would allow different sectors of activity, organisations, groups of interest and affected parties to make assessments of their own, on the basis of their proper standpoint and scale of values.

It is not unusual to find populistic sentiment in the transaction–observation methodology.

Instructional research

When many educational researchers are asked to recommend an evaluation approach they speak of an experimental design, with comparison of randomized treatments under controlled conditions, or as close an approximation as possible (Campbell, 1969; Stanley, 1972). They urge the investigator not to pass up the chance to contribute to the general knowledge about teaching and learning, sometimes paying little attention to whether or not the study is useful to the people involved in the programme.

Some authorities believe that the experimental approach is essential even to an understanding of the particular programme.

. . . the small differences [educational programs] are likely to make can easily be either overestimated or missed entirely by comparing the treatment group with a non-comparable group. The only truly satisfactory way of dealing with this problem, of course, is through randomly assigned treatment and control groups (Evans, 1974).

There is a great respectability to this approach, but it has come increasingly under criticism for its poor record of assistance to practitioners and policy setters.

Management analysis and social policy analysis

The next two approaches blend into each other but represent differences in the urgency of the findings and audiences. When an evaluative study is done to assist programme managers (to make immediate or repetitive monitoring decisions) the approach might be called *Management Analysis*. When the same study is done to assist policy-making, perhaps with a longer time-span, perhaps for a wide constituency or for governing board members (rather than managers) the approach might be called *Social Policy Analysis*. But they are similar in many respects. They both draw upon the social sciences not usually involved in educational research, management perhaps more often raising economic issues, policy-setters perhaps more often raising socio-political issues. They both draw up such economic concepts as cost-benefit analysis and productivity coefficients, and such sociological concepts as opportunity costs and work ethic (Cohen, 1970; Weiss, 1972).

Goal-free evaluation and adversary evaluation

These two approaches are newcomers to the educational research scene. Michael Scriven introduced goal-free evaluation (Scriven, 1972) [. . .] To avoid co-option he stressed keeping distance between evaluator and programme staff, even to the extent of not knowing what the staff goals were. Scriven's evaluator is aware of what goals are usually pursued and is supposed to be sensitive to a great range of indications that attainments were made, so the approach is not goal-free in that sense. A highly structured checklist of evidences is utilised.

The Adversary approach has several champions, most prominently Murray Levine, Thomas Owens and Robert Wolf (Levine, 1973; Owens, 1973; Wolf, 1974). The resources for evaluation are divided in two; part to show the shortcomings of the programme, the rest to show merit. In some cases the court of law is taken as the model, with the testimony shaped, the case made, and with cross-examination by counsels for the prosecution and the defence. The approach has an unusual command of the use of real time for decision-making, an asset that few other approaches can match.

These nine prototypes are over-simplifications of the approaches evaluators actually use. Most actual studies draw upon several styles, varying as the programme, the issues and the audiences change.

[Below], a grid summarises the features of these nine approaches. . . .

Like evangelist preachers and high pressure salesmen, evaluators promote their methods. There is good and bad in each of them. The task for the consumer is to pick the method for which the things it does well are important and for which the things it does poorly are unimportant. But there is all too little agreement, all too little evidence, as to what each method does accomplish under which circumstances.

[Two columns omitted]

Nine approaches to educational evaluation

Approach	Purpose	Key elements	Purview emphasized	Risks	Payoffs
STUDENT GAIN BY TESTING	To measure student performance and progress	Goal statements; Test score analysis; Discrepancy between goal and actuality	EDUCATIONAL PSYCHOLOGISTS	Oversimplify educ'l aims; Ignore processes	Emphasize, ascertain student progress
INSTITUTIONAL SELF-STUDY BY STAFF	To review and increase staff effectiveness	Committee work; Standards set by staff; Discussion; Professionalism	PROFESSORS, TEACHERS	Alienate some staff; Ignore values of outsiders	Increase staff awareness, sense of responsibility
BLUE-RIBBON PANEL	To resolve crises and preserve the institution	Prestigious panel; The visit; Review of existing data & documents	LEADING CITIZENS	Postpone action; Over-rely on intuition	Gather best insights, judgment
TRANSACTION-OBSERVATION	To provide understanding of activities and values	Educational issues; Classroom observation; Case studies; Pluralism	CLIENT, AUDIENCE	Over-rely on subjective perceptions; Ignore causes	Produce broad picture of program; See conflict in values
MANAGEMENT ANALYSIS	To increase rationality in day to day decisions	Lists of options; estimates; Feedback loops; Costs; Efficiency	MANAGERS, ECONOMISTS	Over-value efficiency; Undervalue implicits	Feedback for decision making
INSTRUCTIONAL RESEARCH	To generate explanations and tactics of instruction	Controlled conditions, multivariate analysis; Bases for generalization	RESEARCH METHODOLOGISTS	Artificial conditions; Ignore the humanistic	New principles of teaching and materials development

SOCIAL POLICY ANALYSIS	To aid development of institutional policies	Measures of social conditions and administrative implementation	SOCIOLOGISTS	Neglect of educational issues, details	Social choices, constraints clarified
GOAL-FREE EVALUATION	To assess effects of programme	Ignore proponent claims, follow check-list	CONSUMERS; ACCOUNTANTS	Over-value documents & record keeping	Data on effect with little co-option
ADVERSARY EVALUATION	To resolve a two-option choice	Opposing advocates, cross-examination, the jury	EXPERT; JURISTIC	Personalistic, superficial, time-bound	Info impact good; Claims put to test

Of course these descriptive tags are a great over-simplification. The approaches overlap. Different proponents and different users have different styles. Each protagonist recognises one approach is not ideal for all purposes. Any one study may include several approaches. The grid is an over-simplification. It is intended to show some typical, gross differences between contemporary evaluation activities.

Note

1 A report of the Central Advisory Council of Education (England), 2 volumes. London: HMSO, 1967.

References

BLOOM, B. S., HASTINGS, J. T. and MADAUS, G. F. (1971) *Handbook on Formative and Summative Evaluation of Student Learning.* New York: McGraw-Hill.

CAMPBELL, D. (1969) 'Reforms as experiments.' *American Psychologist*, 24, pp. 409–29.

COHEN, D. K. (1970) 'Politics and research – evaluation of large-scale programs.' *Review of Educational Research*, Vol. 40, No. 2, pp. 213–38.

EVANS, J. W. (1974) 'Evaluating educational programs – are we getting any where?' *Educational Researcher*, Vol. 3, No. 8, p. 9.

HETMAN, F. (1973) *Society and the Assessment of Technology.* Paris: Organisation for Economic Co-operation and Development.

LEVINE, M. (1973) 'Scientific method and the adversary model: some preliminary suggestions.' *Evaluation Comment*, Vol. 4, No. 2, pp. 1–3.

OWENS, T. R. (1973) 'Educational evaluation by adversary proceedings', in HOUSE, E. (ed.) (1973) *School Evaluation: the politics and process.* Berkeley, Calif.: McCutchan.

PARLETT, M. and HAMILTON, D. (1972) *Evaluation as illumination: a new approach to the study of innovatory programs.* Centre of Research in the Educational Sciences, Occasional Paper 9. Edinburgh: University of Edinburgh October 1972.

SCRIVEN, M. (1967) 'The methodology of evaluation.' *AREA Monograph Series on Curriculum Evaluation*, No. 1. Chicago, Ill.: Rand McNally, pp. 39–83.

SCRIVEN, M. (1972) 'Pros and cons about goal-free evaluation.' *Evaluation Comment*, December 1972. (also in: POPHAM, W. J. (ed.) (1974) *Evaluation in Education: current applications.* Berkeley, Calif.: McCutchan.)

STAKE, R. E. (ed.) (n.d.) *Case Studies in the Evaluation of Educational Programmes.* Paris: CERI/OECD.

STANLEY, J. C. (1972) 'Controlled field experiments as a model for evaluation', in ROSSI, P. H. and WILLIAMS, W. (eds) (1972) *Evaluating Social Programs.* New York: Seminar Press, pp. 67–71.

WEISS, C. H. (1972) *Evaluation research: methods of assessing program effectiveness.* Englewood Cliffs, New Jersey: Prentice-Hall.

WOLF, R. L. (1974) 'The application of select legal concepts to educational evaluation.' Unpublished Ph.D. Dissertation, University of Illinois.

WORTHEN, B. R. and SANDERS, J. R. (1973) *Educational Evaluation: Theory and practice.* Worthington, Ohio: Charles A. Jones.

Part Two

Teachers, learners and the curriculum

Part Two contains extracts and articles which deal with curriculum in classroom terms as opposed to the institutional concerns of Part One.

So it is particularly fitting to start the section with the Michael J. Dunkin and Bruce J. Biddle extract (2.1) as these writers offer a model which attempts to deal with the actual behaviours that take place in the classroom. One of the major problems of such an undertaking is, of course, the difficulty of dealing with the sheer *complexity* of what goes on, and they do not pretend to offer an exhaustive or definitive explanation. What they do offer, however, is a very useful model of teaching consisting of presage, context, process and product variables, terms which embrace characteristics of teachers, the environments to which they must adjust, the actual activities of classroom teaching and the outcomes of that teaching.

David Hamilton and Sara Delamont (2.2) raise a number of questions about the issues involved in classroom research. They describe the advantages and disadvantages of two major research traditions, interaction analysis and anthropological classroom research. So, for example, interaction analysis typically uses an observation schedule and aims at being 'objective', whereas the anthropological tradition typically employs participant observation and attempts to discover how the subject sees the world. The article ends with a discussion of the future development of classroom research.

In the third paper Neville Bennett tackles the thorny problem of teaching styles, starting with a re-analysis of the terms 'progressive' and 'traditional'. He reviews questionnaire research in this field before going on to describe a piece of his own research carried out in Lancashire and Cumbria. Basing his comments upon his findings, he paints a picture of life in British primary schools, proceeding to discuss the range of teaching styles adopted. He identifies twelve teaching types or styles, arguing that the progressive-traditional distinction is inadequate, as most teachers adopt a mixed style. The validity of the typology is discussed, and Bennett gives two case-study examples of differing teaching styles.

In the fourth extract we move on to the question of objectives. The main thrust of the Hilda Taba extract is to suggest a case for an *organized* statement of objectives using types of behaviour (as opposed to the content of behaviour) as a fundamental rationale for curriculum development. Her objectives are eclectic and far-ranging. She discusses the acquisition of knowledge (of facts, of principles, and of concepts which relate groups of principles), the development of critical thinking, values and attitudes, sensitivities and feelings, and the development of skills both academic and social in an *organized* approach to the basis of curriculum development.

In the next reading, Ralph W. Tyler discusses different ways of stating objectives such as in terms of the activities of teachers, in terms of content (topics and concepts, for example), and in terms of generalized patterns of behaviour. He maintains that the most clear formulation of an objective must contain both a *behavioural* and a *content* aspect. Objectives should express the kind of behaviour to be developed in the student and the area of life in which this behaviour is to operate. Tyler gives an example from secondary school Biology. His second major point deals with the ways in which objectives can be attained. Learning experiences in this context can be looked at under three headings: characteristics, organization and evaluation. Learning experiences must be satisfying to the student and within his range, and it must always be remembered that any one experience can bring about several outcomes. There are differing ways, too, of achieving the same effect. Continuity, sequence and integration are, Tyler argues, the criteria to be met if learning experiences are to be organized effectively. As regards 'evaluation', he stresses the importance of a clear definition of objectives and the creation of situations which are likely to evoke the behaviour under scrutiny as essential precursors of successful evaluation. The extract concludes with a discussion of the objectivity, reliability and validity of evaluation instruments, and comments upon possible uses of evaluation results.

After such global considerations F. R. Leavis's world (2.6) seems almost parochial, as he deals with the approaches to literature which should or should not be encouraged in a university School of English. He attacks the kind of literary criticism which is merely the collection of information or the imbibing of conventional wisdom. What is necessary, he argues, is the personal response aimed at capturing the whole poem: this should be fostered through a training in practical criticism.

In a brief extract (2.7) Jerome Bruner emphasizes that school curricula should be geared to conveying the basic underlying principles of each of the subjects taught. It deals both with some of the problems that arise when this is attempted and with some of the reasons for attempting it.

It is appropriate that the Lawrence Stenhouse extract (2.8) should follow the Bruner, as much of it concerns an examination of two curricula, *Man: A Course of Study* and the Humanities Curriculum Project, the first of which had Bruner as chief consulting scholar. What Stenhouse is really against is the Tyler-style objectives model because, he argues, such a model distorts the curriculum. What he offers instead is the process model, using the two curricula to discuss some of the issues involved.

John Elliott's paper (2.9) is similar in structure and content to the Stenhouse extract. Elliott, too, starts with an attack: this time it is not the objectives model but the process-product model as an approach to classroom research. Elliott attacks what he sees as the assumptions behind the model, such as the idea that there are general laws governing classroom behaviour. These assumptions, for Elliott, distort the curriculum, and he wants such studies replaced by educational action research. To argue the action perspective of curriculum developers (which he sees classroom researchers adopting) Elliott, as Stenhouse before him, uses *Man: A Course of Study* and the Humanities Curriculum Project. Elliott views educational action research as a movement away from a concern with the mechanical, where teaching is viewed instrumentally, to teaching for understanding, a communicative concern.

Bruce Joyce and Marsha Weil (2.10) are opposed to any search for a 'perfect' model for teaching. Students have different learning styles and there are many different kinds of learning. Considerations such as these mean, they argue, that no single model can ever be sufficient. What they suggest instead is a basic repertoire of twenty-two models grouped into four families of information-processing, personal, social interaction and behavioural models. They propose concepts for describing a model, and discuss the direct and indirect effects of choosing a particular model.

I. K. Davies (2.11) moves the argument in a different direction. For him, analysis of the nature of the task is essential before a successful educational programme can be established. It is not just a question of analysing the task into its component parts: the relationships between the parts themselves have to be determined. He suggests three types of task analysis: topic, job and skills analysis. After discussing sources of information for and isolating components of task analysis, Davies puts forward a method of writing up a topic analysis.

Change in the classroom can only be effective, argues Ian Westbury in 2.12, if tasks and resources are taken into account. The framework of Westbury's paper is the open versus conventional classroom debate. He maintains that the open classroom can only work if materials are available for much of the explicit instruction. If these materials are self-instructing, and, to a large extent, self-managing, the teacher is free to concentrate on more individual instruction and on management. Westbury discusses the nature of the open teacher's role, where such problems as coverage and mastery still have to be faced.

The short extract 'Meaning making' (2.13) is a eulogy of Ames's work on the nature of perception. By attempting to demonstrate, for example, that perceptions come from within the individual and that they are largely the product of his experiences, Ames has altered, Neil Postman and Charles Weingartner suggest, our conception of the student.

In extract 2.14, Carl R. Rogers offers a bleak and critical view of the education system. It is a system, in Rogers' view, where the intellect is welcomed but at the expense of the whole person. The answer to all this is a movement towards person-centred learning where self-evaluation on the part of the student is important. The rest of the extract deals with Rogers' efforts to move in this direction at a series of seminars at Brandeis University, Waltham, Massachusetts.

The section concludes with an article by Tim O'Shea dealing with the computer programming language, Logo. After describing some of his observations of children aged 11–13 using Logo in the classroom, he discusses some of the advantages and disadvantages of Logo as a learning environment.

2.1 A model for classroom teaching

Michael J. Dunkin and Bruce J. Biddle

[A model that will enable us to organize the findings of research on teaching must concern itself with properties of teachers and pupils.] Characteristics of the classroom must also be considered, together with those of its enfolding school and community. We must also consider the outcomes of education, those changes in pupils for which we are presumably conducting the enterprise. But most important, we must concern ourselves with the processes of teaching itself, with the actual behaviours of teachers and pupils as they play out the complex drama of classroom teaching.

A model reflecting these concerns is given in Figure 1. As may be seen, there are several 'regions' in the model. The central region is the classroom itself, symbolized, appropriately, by a rectangle. To the left of the classroom are three sets of variables that will surely have at least some influence on classroom events: variables associated with the teacher, variables associated with pupils, and variables representing the contexts of community, school, and classroom. To the right are some of the hoped for products of education.

Throughout the model appear arrows. Each presumes a causative relationship. Thus, we presume that teacher formative experiences occurred prior to, and tend to have a causative effect on, classroom – and not vice versa. Most of the arrows are laid in time (as would be true for teacher formative experiences, for example, which surely occurred prior to the appearance of classroom events). However, some of the arrows indicate causative sequences we presume, even though the events thus linked are nearly contemporaneous. Thus, we presume that school and community contexts affect the classroom, and not vice versa. Sometimes these latter presumptions will turn out to be in error, although they are usually made by those who think about or conduct research on teaching. For example, it is possible for a given teacher to become so excellent or so notorious that she generates a response in the community. Again, classroom activities also have an impact on the noise level of the school, on the reputation and career of the principal, on the economy of the school and community, on the status of the teaching profession. Thus, teaching has other functions than fostering pupil growth, and some of these may form feedback chains that will, in turn, affect the teaching process in the classroom. Most of these are ignored in classroom research, however, partly because they are too complex to study easily and partly because they are presumed to be remote from the basic purposes of education.

Each arrow is but a source of hypotheses, however, and not a symbol of invariant truth. Let us assume, for example, that a relationship has been

Source: DUNKIN, M. J. and BIDDLE, B. J. (1974) *The Study of Teaching*. New York and London: Holt, Rinehart and Winston, pp. 36–48.

established between a teacher formative experience and teacher classroom behaviour. For example, let us assume that teachers who come from middle-class backgrounds are known to approach pupils somewhat differently than those with lower-class backgrounds. Does this mean that social class 'causes' differential classroom behaviour? Indeed, this interpretation might be correct. But it might also be true that teachers who come from middle- and lower-class backgrounds are more likely to attend different colleges and thus to have had different experiences in teacher training; this latter factor, then, would be the actual cause of their different behaviour in the classroom. To establish a relationship of covariance between two classes of variables within the model is a first step, albeit a large one. To discover that the relationship is causative is quite another matter and generally calls for experimental research. . . .

Altogether there are some thirteen classes of variables suggested in the model of Figure 1. This list is neither exhaustive nor definitive. Other models with which the reader may be familiar will tend to cover the same ground, although they may present more or less detail than our model at certain portions of the paradigm. Given the present state of research on teaching, thirteen variable classes is too many for convenient review. Let us reduce these to *four* larger classes (see Mitzel, 1957). Following the terminology suggested by Mitzel (1960), we will distinguish *presage, context, process,* and *product* variables for research on teaching.

Presage variables

As we shall use the term here, *presage variables* concern the characteristics of teachers that may be examined for their effects on the teaching process – thus, teacher formative experiences, teacher-training experiences, and teacher properties. As a general rule, such variables have a potential for control by administrators or teacher educators. For example, teacher trainees may be selected or rejected for their profession in terms of known background experiences, the teacher-training program can be altered, or teachers may be selected or assigned to different jobs in the school depending on their properties.

Teacher formative experiences include every experience encountered prior to teacher training, and for older teachers subsequent experiences as well. Teachers, like other persons, will have been treated differently if they were born a man or a woman, if they are white or black, if they lived in a lower-class or upper-class home, if they came from a large city or a small town, if they lived in an ethnic ghetto, if they were an only child or the last child in a big family. Some of these experiences presumably terminated with the ending of childhood, although their impact may persist in the teacher's adult personality. For example, the fact that a teacher grew up in a lower-class home is not a contemporaneous experience faced by the teacher, since nearly all teachers are now paid lower-middle-class wages. Again, the fact that the

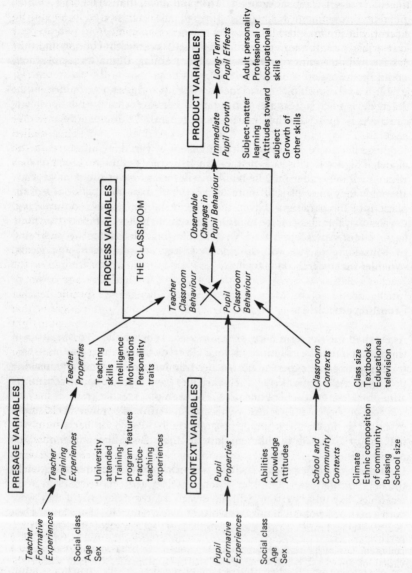

Figure 1   A model for the study of classroom teaching

teacher may have grown up an only child provided her unique experiences as long as she lived in her parental home, but these experiences will have passed for most teachers. However, other formative experiences lead to the classification of teachers into ascribed positions within the society which provide continuing pleasures or problems. Thus, teachers who speak with an accent, who are male or black,.or who have an obvious infirmity or a peculiar face or body are likely to be treated differently both within and without the school. Thus, some formative experiences are both historical *and* contemporaneous.

Teacher-training experiences include the college or university attended by the teacher, courses taken, the attitudes of instructors, experiences during practice teaching, and in-service and postgraduate education, if any. We should not be too surprised to learn that these variables are more often studied for their effects on classroom teaching than any others. After all, those who do research on teaching are likely to be teacher-educators themselves. For such persons not only are the conditions of teacher education convenient for study but often they can be manipulated, thus making experimental studies of the effects of new programs possible. Thus, presage research has appeared concerning the effects of 'new and improved' methods of teacher education, such as fifth-year programs, in-service training, model teaching programs, microteaching, the use of videotape for teacher training, or new curricula. Whether such variables can, in fact, be more influential in determining the teacher's classroom behaviour than, let us say, the teacher's age or sex or intelligence is moot. Most of the evidence 'favouring' specific teacher education programs is weak (Dunkin and Biddle, 1974), and it might be that as much improvement can be generated by recruiting and assigning the right teachers to the right jobs as by changing teacher training. The evidence is simply not available to answer the question yet, but on the assumption that formative experiences do influence teaching behaviour, teacher-education programs might be more successful if they were tailored to take account of these factors.

Training and formative experiences cannot affect the teacher's classroom performance unless she retains traces of these experiences in her attitudes or behaviour. Thus, we conceive of a third variable class, *teacher properties*, which consist of the measurable personality characteristics the teacher takes with her into the teaching situation. A legion of psychological traits, motives, abilities, and attitudes have been investigated for their potential effect on teaching.

Such properties have two features in common: they are hypothetical constructs in psychology, thus they are presumed to characterize the individual teacher in a consistent fashion, over time, and serve to explain her behaviour in response to a variety of situations. It is also presumed that such properties are laid 'within' the teacher and are not amenable to direct observation in the same way that behaviour can be observed. Contemporary American ideology [also] stresses the alterability of teacher properties. We know that warmth, authoritarianism, hostility – and even intelligence and physical aptitudes – are influenced by early learning and can be altered through appropriate educational experiences (including psychotherapy) in later life. (Biddle, 1964, pp. 9–10)

It is not clear why teacher properties such as authoritarianism, anxiety, attitudes toward pupils, personality inventory scores, and the like, should be studied more often than observable teacher characteristics such as age, sex, or race. One explanation might be the common view that teaching is largely a matter of personal relationships and personality, that such effects as teachers have are functions of their personalities (Nuthall, 1972, personal communication). Perhaps, too, there is joy in administering standardized instruments that purport to provide 'secret' information about respondents; perhaps the instruments for assessing personality characteristics have a mystique of their own. Although demographic variables have long been known to be major influencers of job performance in other contexts (see, for example, Helmreich, 1971), they have not often been studied by those interested in teaching.

Context variables

As we shall use the term here, *context variables* concern the conditions to which the teacher must adjust – characteristics of the environment about which teachers, school administrators, and teacher-educators can do very little. Normally the teacher, indeed the school administration, has little choice in its pupil population, inherits a well-used school building, must live within a budget, and must contend with the aspirations, angers, and beliefs of the community that supports the school. These, then, are the contexts of classroom education. Whether seen as a welcome challenge or an irrelevant annoyance, teachers must cope with contexts; and thus variables within the contextual sphere are likely to affect the processes of teaching.

Pupils have also experienced *formative experiences*. Like teachers, pupils will differ depending on whether they come from lower- or middle-class homes, have experienced socialization as a boy or girl, have suffered the loss of a parent, or come from a stimulus-rich or stimulus-deprived environment. Some of these events took place in the pupils' past lives. However, most of these conditions will continue to be present throughout the teaching year, thus modifying and in some cases defeating the efforts of the teacher. There can be few contextual experiences more disturbing to the teacher than a hostile, retarded, or withdrawn child, and much of the curriculum of educational psychology concerns strategies for meeting such problems. Teaching is also strikingly different in the urban ghetto and the affluent suburb, a fact that is now generating special curricula for those who are to teach in the ghetto. Pupils who speak nonstandard English or another language entirely, pupils who have physical or learning disabilities, pupils who are hyperkinetic or stout – all pose special problems. In part such problems are presented by the behaviours of these pupils, but in part they appear to be caused by the prejudices and expectations held by teachers and other pupils. Hostility among pupils representing different ethnic groups is only too common, of course, but teachers may also sort pupils into learning groups on the basis of social class backgrounds. . . .

Educators are even more prone to measure *pupil properties* than they are teacher properties. In fact, the periodic measurement of pupil abilities and pupil achievements by means of standardized tests is now a well-entrenched feature of most school systems. Such scores are used for various purposes, notably as an aid in deciding whether to promote or retain a pupil at his grade level, and for placing pupils within educational 'streams' or 'learning groups'. Thus, a 'fortunate' teacher might end up with a classroom of bright, well-scrubbed, highly motivated pupils, while another might have to contend with a classroom composed of the surly, stupid, and disruptive. Standardized measures of pupil achievement and pupil intelligence are both often used in research on teaching, usually for 'adjusting' or 'regressing' a subsequent achievement score so as to provide a measure of effect for a given classroom experience. But these measures were usually *not* designed for research, are known to co-vary with social class and ethnic background, and are generally employed improperly in the statistics used by researchers (see Cronbach and Furby, 1970). . . . Once again, surprisingly little use has been made of demographic variables concerning pupils in research on teaching. Those few researchers who have studied pupils on the basis of race or sex have nearly always uncovered substantial differences in treatment by teachers. One hopes that more research will be forthcoming on such variables in the near future.

Pupils are not the only context for teaching, of course. Additional contextual variables may be found within the *school* and *community*. Schools differ from one another in many ways, and some of these are now coming to be studied for their effects on teaching. In small, isolated schools, for example, teachers may have to contend with a multigraded classroom. Larger schools are more specialized, and their activities more expert, although pupils in them may experience less pressure to participate in those activities (see Barker and Gump, 1964). Schools differ depending on their physical facilities, the homogeneity of their teacher and pupil populations, the personalities and practices of their principals, the impact of their athletic programs (see Coleman, 1961), and so on. Schools are also constrained both by law and custom. One school system features a rigid curriculum imposed by an authoritative hierarchy, another a militant teachers' union, another a tyrannical and bigoted school board, still another a tradition of experimenting with both school architecture and classroom education. Each of these contexts is likely to affect the conduct and experiences of classroom participants.

The school also bears functional relationships with the larger community. School systems are expected to serve citizen needs ranging from entertainment, to the desire to learn, to the need for status advancement, to baby-sitting. . . . Further, the school interacts with other institutions in the community. It provides employment for a number of people, consumes certain kinds of goods, keeps 'wild youth' off the streets, provides an avenue for social service, and so on. The school building is sometimes stockpiled against the threat of tornadoes or nuclear fall-out. Often, particularly in small communities, the school may be the only institution attracting the attention of a majority of the citizenry; and observers have noted the demise of some small communities when their schools were consolidated with others. In low population areas a citizen may carry his community status into school settings, such as the PTA. Similarly, school personnel often may find their occupational positions carrying into the small community, such as when teachers are expected to lead in Sunday school or to be paragons of public virtue. Urban schools appear to be more isolated, and professional affiliation there may be easier to shed at the end of the day. (Biddle, 1964, p. 16)

Possibly because most classroom research is conducted by psychologists, or because it is expensive, few studies have investigated the relationships between either school or community variables and classroom teaching. A recent review of research on the properties of schools that might be relevant for their impact on teaching is provided by Biddle (1970), but we are unaware of more than a handful of studies concerned with the impact of community variables on teaching.

Fortunately, such is not the case with our final contextual category, *classroom contexts*. Classrooms also differ in size, and this variable has been investigated endlessly for its effects on the outcomes of teaching, with but indifferent success. Classrooms also differ in terms of lighting, equipment, and layout. Unfortunately, most of these variables have not yet been studied for their effects on teaching (although studies have been made of the impact of new educational media such as teaching machines and television). This is certainly too bad. One needs only to enter a crowded, poorly lighted, poorly equipped ghetto classroom to begin to understand why teaching is less successful in such an environment. Consider also the simple variable of classroom noise level. Most classrooms are quite noisy environments; with more than 70 feet, most of them restless, movable desks, excited voices, and with but minimal sound-absorbing surfaces, it is not surprising that teachers must often use a loud voice to command attention. Moreover, some less-talented school principals seem to evaluate the effectiveness of their teachers' efforts in terms of the low noise level of their classrooms. Some time ago one of the authors made videotapes of teaching in two carpeted classrooms and was struck by the quiet, order, attention, and relaxation they seemed to exhibit. Yet we know of no formal research that has been conducted on the effects of carpeting (and quiet) on classroom teaching. Other classroom contexts include the curriculum, the customs pertaining to conduct accepted by class members, the tasks promulgated for the group, and so forth. As these examples illustrate, some aspects of the classroom context are partially subject to the teacher's control. For instance, teachers may bring displays of wildlife or ship models to the classroom or set up conventions for conduct, entertainment, or competition that are not found in other classrooms. However, once these displays or customs are set, classroom participants, including the teacher herself, are likely to be affected by them. Once again, most of these effects have yet to be studied.

Process variables

As we shall use the term, *process variables* concern the actual activities of classroom teaching – what teachers and pupils *do* in the classroom. By 'actual activities' we mean to focus attention on *all* of the observable behaviours of teachers and pupils rather than upon only those that are productive of pupil growth or upon intangible or unobservable relationships between teachers and pupils. Some teachers appear incapable of keeping order in the classroom, some pupils engage in horseplay or whisper to others; as long as these events are observable they may be judged as components of teaching-process variables.[1] However, such factors as the teacher's like or dislike for a given pupil, or the classroom 'we feeling', or whether a pupil is actually paying attention to the lecture cannot be judged as process variables unless they can be measured by overt behavioural signs.

[. . .] It is convenient . . . to distinguish *teacher classroom behaviour* as a category. . . . Most systems for studying teaching have concentrated on teacher behaviour, assuming, reasonably, that much of the success of teaching is in the teacher's hands. Moreover, it is also assumed that the behaviours of the teacher must be primarily a function of presage variables – thus teacher formative experiences, teacher-training experiences, or teacher properties.

Are these presumptions adequate? Surely teachers not only induce but also react to pupil behaviour. (If they are incapable of responding to pupils, the act of teaching is debased. The wife of one of the authors once observed an elderly teacher who was nearly deaf. Her strategy in conducting discussions was to ask a question, then to call for a class vote on the answer, and then to announce the right answer herself. Thus, apart from the collective exercise of voting, these pupils were subjected to little more than the teaching display characteristic of educational television.) In some ways, therefore, teacher behaviour is also a function of pupil behaviour, and the success of the teaching enterprise rests with pupils as well as with teachers.

For these reasons many systems for studying teaching have also investigated *pupil classroom behaviour*. However, the study of pupil behaviour involves several problems not encountered for the teacher. For one, the classroom has 30 or more pupils, all of whom are 'behaving' at any given moment, although usually only one of them is actually speaking. Investigators have solved this problem in several ways. Some have confined their attention to the target pupil who is addressed by the teacher, ignoring the other, audience pupils. Others have studied the reactions of pupils as a mass audience, making judgments about the collective or average state of pupil behaviour for a given unit of time. Still others have studied the reactions of randomly selected pupils. . . . These solutions have reflected the particular interests and concepts of investigators and have led to somewhat different conclusions concerning the effects of teaching.

Another problem concerns the fact that pupils are constrained by the Rules of the Classroom Game to sit in silence much of the time. Hence their behaviour tends to be dull and uninteresting in comparison with that of the teacher, and much of what we hope is going on within the pupil is not exhibited externally. Most classrooms would be disturbed if pupils were to shout 'Eureka!' when suddenly seeing the point, although teachers strive valiantly to induce just such experiences in pupils.

Still another problem is posed by the rapid pace of teacher-pupil interaction. As anyone who has ever prepared a transcription of classroom interaction can testify, classrooms are wordy, and the words come thick and fast. Since the detailed analysis of transcriptions is costly, investigators have adopted several strategies that represent shortcuts. One of these is to develop concepts that are applied to units of time rather than to units of behaviour. In other analytic systems coders must ignore the distinction between teacher and pupil behaviour in favour of coding the 'content' or 'emotional quality' of the exchange, regardless of who was responsible for it. In still other methods, the distinction between teacher and pupil behaviour is maintained, but only a few categories are provided for judging each. Another type of solution to the problem involves the study of neither teacher nor pupil actions but rather their *inter*actions. Thus, the typical classroom sequence, teacher question – pupil response – teacher assessment, is noted whenever it appears, and judgments are made concerning properties of the exchange as a whole. None of these procedures is without its difficulties. Time intervals simply do not correspond to boundaries of teacher and pupil actions. To make judgments about interaction units requires us to ignore aspects of causative influence of teachers upon pupils.

Still another problem concerns the relationship between (prior) teaching activities and (subsequent) classroom events. As was suggested in Figure 1, it is possible to assume that observable changes in pupil behaviour are a function of teaching and hence evidence of the success or failure of the teacher's efforts. Such an assumption is involved in designs for various studies (for example, that of Kounin, 1970), and surely it is subscribed to by most teachers. After all, what can be more self-evident than the experience of working on dull Johnny for some minutes until he finally sees the point of the lesson? Such an assumption also appears in recent model teacher-education programs that emphasize performance criteria for judging the success of teaching. Yet are changes in pupil behaviour truly a function of teacher activities alone? Once again, it seems to us that this is a risky conclusion. It may be that pupils learn as much from other pupils as from the teacher, or that dull Johnny will get the point by himself if only given enough time. For this reason we must assume that conclusions concerning cause-and-effect relationships in the classroom are unvalidated unless checked with manipulative experiments.

Given these problems, it is not surprising that classroom processes have been conceptualized in many ways. . . .

Product variables

As we . . . use the term, *product variables* concern the outcomes of teaching – those changes that come about in pupils as a result of their involvement in classroom activities with teachers and other pupils. Although we normally think of these changes in positive terms, and label them 'growth' or 'learning', it is possible that pupils might actually be hampered or harmed by classroom experiences. For example, a teacher might be so punitive that she causes pupils to become disturbed, or so confused in her presentation that pupils come to doubt knowledge they have brought with them to the classroom. These too would be products of the teaching experience, however we might decry them.

The product variables most often investigated are subject-matter learning and attitudes toward the subject, both of which involve *immediate pupil growth*. Both variables seem obvious ones to choose for evaluating the success of teaching. Standardized tests are available for assessing pupil growth in most subjects, and measurement of pupil attitudes can be accomplished by means of one or two multiple-choice questions. Moreover, if education is successful, surely it results in increased subject-matter competence and positive attitudes. But there are difficulties. Most standardized tests measure knowledge of facts rather than ability to synthesize and use that knowledge. And most attitudinal questions require only superficial judgments. Above all, some of the grandiose claims made for the effects of really good teaching have not been researched at all. We, therefore, are very limited in our ability to measure pupils' creativity, their learning of adult roles, their ability to practise democracy, their values. Given these lacks, our research on the effectiveness of various kinds of teaching experiences has a strange, one-dimensional quality. For example, strong evidence has now accumulated demonstrating that pupils can learn from both teaching machines and educational television. But what is *not* known is how they react to the boredom and dehumanization of these experiences in comparison with classroom activities involving a live teacher. In her classic study Ann Roe (1953) discovered that students' decisions to become scientists resulted in part from close contact and identification with a scientist-teacher during their late-adolescent and young-adult years; and yet educational television, which precludes any direct contact between students and faculty, has had its greatest adoption in undergraduate courses in the large universities!

For these reasons and others some educators (and some classroom researchers) have abandoned the task of validating teaching in terms of product variables. As we suggested earlier, some educators seek changes in observable behaviour of pupils as the products of education. Jackson, for example, has questioned whether teachers themselves are primarily concerned with inducing measurable gains in pupil learning. Rather, teachers appear to be

> making some kind of an educated guess about what would be beneficial activity for a student or a group of students and then doing whatever is necessary to see that the participants remain involved in that activity. The teacher's goal, in other words, is student involvement rather than student learning. It is true, of course, that the teacher hopes the involvement will result in certain beneficial changes in the students, but learning is in this sense a by-product or a secondary goal rather than the thing about which the teacher is most directly concerned. (Jackson, 1966, p. 24)

Other educators appear to give teaching a high rating if it exhibits certain characteristics, regardless of whether these are ever found to lead to pupil change. Thus, teaching should be stimulating, democratic, or warm because of the obvious inherent superiority of these qualities. This latter position is generated by at least three arguments. For some people these desirable teaching objectives are too obvious to be worth further discussion. For others commitment is generated by psychological, social, or philosophic positions – for example, the nondirective philosophy of Carl Rogers, or popularizations of psychoanalysis. Still others, particularly adult educators, are beginning to see the classroom as a consummatory rather than an instrumental activity, as a desirable way of spending time, as a useful alternative to idleness or drug addiction. For these people, classrooms should be pleasant places to be in, regardless of whether one learns anything there or not.

Regarding all of these advocates we . . . here take the position that the traditional and continuing task of teaching is to promote learning. Thus, for our purpose, classroom activities can be deemed *successful* if they induce desired changes in pupils. Such a position requires us – eventually – to validate the practices of teaching with product variables.

The ultimate goal of education is not high test scores, although parents and educators sometimes appear to forget this fact. Rather, education is conducted for its *long-term effects on pupils*. Thus, we subject our sons and daughters to the tender mercies of classroom experiences in the hope that thereby they will become fit citizens, acquire the information and motivation needed to enter a profession, learn to meet the complex demands of a rapidly changing society, and contribute to the betterment of others. Unfortunately, the establishment of relationships between teaching and such laudable aims lies mainly in the future. Although anecdotal evidence may be found wherein an individual describes the signal influence a given teacher had on him, and although one can find the occasional master teacher who is known to have 'produced' several stellar pupils, to our knowledge no researcher has yet attempted to establish relationships between teaching variables and long-term product variables. Consider the difficulties one would face in such research. For one thing, the research would have to be longitudinal – unless one just happened upon a set of recordings or transcriptions for a large group of classrooms and teachers that was assembled, let us say, at least ten years ago. For another, the influence of a given teacher or classroom is inevitably mitigated by the teaching efforts of other teachers and other contexts. Even a master teacher can be defeated by the stultifying effect of a generally poor school, while pupils who truly succeed in later life are probably the products of many fine teaching efforts. It is wise to keep in mind the long-term goals of education, but we should not be too surprised if contemporary research in teaching does not tell us much about them.

Note

1 In making this distinction we part company with those who would restrict teaching to activities the teacher introduces 'with the intention that pupils will learn something' (Hudgins, 1971, p. 4; also see Gage, 1972, p. 18). We find it difficult to distinguish classroom events in terms of the teacher's 'intent' and are quite as interested in classroom events that are *un*intended or that occur when the teacher has nonlearning goals in mind.

References

BARKER, R. G. and GUMP, P. V. (1964) *Big School, Small School: High school size and student behavior*. Stanford, Calif.: Stanford University Press.

BIDDLE, B. J. (1964) 'The integration of teacher effectiveness research', in BIDDLE, B. J. and ELLENA, W. J. (eds) (1964) *Contemporary Research on Teacher Effectiveness*. New York: Holt, Rinehart and Winston.

BIDDLE, B. J. (1970) 'The institutional context', in CAMPBELL, W. J. (ed.) *Scholars in Context: the effects of environment on learning*. Sydney: Wiley.

COLEMAN, J. S. (1961) *The Adolescent Society*. Glencoe, Ill.: The Free Press.

CRONBACH, L. J. and FURRY, L. (1970) 'How we should measure "change" – or should we?' *Psychological Bulletin*, 74, pp. 68–80.

DUNKIN, M. J. and BIDDLE, B. J. (1974) *The Study of Teaching*. New York: Holt, Rinehart and Winston.

GAGE, N. L. (1972) *Teacher Effectiveness and Teacher Education: the search for a scientific basis*. Palo Alto, Calif.: Pacific Books.

HELMREICH, R. (1971) 'The TEKTITE II human behavior program.' NASA-ONR Technical Report No. 14.

HUDGINS, B. B. (1971) *The Instructional Process*. Chicago, Ill.: Rand McNally.

JACKSON, P. W. (1966) *Life in Classrooms*. New York: Holt, Rinehart and Winston.

KOUNIN, J. S. (1970) *Discipline and Group Management in Classrooms*. New York: Holt, Rinehart and Winston.

MITZEL, H. E. (1957) 'A behavioral approach to the assessment of teacher effectiveness.' Unpublished paper, Division of Teacher Education, College of the City of New York.

MITZEL, H. E. (1960) 'Teacher effectiveness', in HARRIS, C. W. (ed.) (1960) *Encyclopedia of Educational Research* (3rd edn). New York: Macmillan.

NUTHALL, G. (1972) in a personal communication to M. J. Dunkin and B. J. Biddle.

ROE, A. (1953) *The Making of a Scientist*. New York: Dodd, Mead.

2.2 Classroom research: a cautionary tale

David Hamilton and Sara Delamont

Educational research in Britain

Educational research in Britain is entering a new phase. As its preoccupations with mental testing, curriculum development and the effects of secondary school selection gradually diminish, a variety of other research interests seek to achieve pre-eminence. One area of increasing activity is classroom observation. During 1972, for example, grants totalling £¼ million were announced for studies in this field.[1]

To anyone outside education it may seem paradoxical that the classroom has been such a marginal preoccupation for educational research. Yet it remains the case that the classroom has customarily been a 'black box' for researchers – providing merely a vehicle for 'input–output' experimental designs or a captive population for psychometric testing programmes. Even the literature on 'teacher effectiveness' contains few studies which involve a direct examination of teaching processes. (Instead, it is full of studies of teacher attitudes and personality.)

Ten years ago Medley and Mitzel characterised the 'typical' research worker in this field as someone who 'limits himself to the manipulation or studying of antecedents and consequences . . . but never once looks into the classroom to see how the teacher actually teaches or the pupil actually learns' (1963, p. 247). This characterisation could still have been applied in Britain until the end of the 1960s.

More recently a shift of research emphasis has taken place: studies of the classroom have become more frequent.[2] It is not difficult to see why. Research workers in various areas have come to recognise that an understanding of classroom events is important to their endeavour. Thus, for example, the difficulties faced by curriculum developers in disseminating their products (e.g. Macdonald and Rudduck, 1971); the 'ineffectiveness' of much teacher training (e.g. Stones and Morris, 1972); and the survival of 'streaming attitudes' among teachers in organisationally unstreamed primary schools (e.g. Barker Lunn, 1970); have all pointed towards the classroom as a relevant setting for intensive research.[3]

Basically, classroom research aims to study – through direct observation or recording – the processes of learning and teaching which take place inside the classroom 'black box'. Hitherto such research in Britain has been small-scale: pursued largely by isolated individuals using *ad hoc* methods and patchwork theory. In the USA, however, classroom observation has been extensively funded and vigorously promoted for over a decade. Now that Britain looks set

Source: HAMILTON, D. and DELAMONT, S. (1974) *Research in Education*, No. 11, May 1974, pp. 1–15.

to fund large-scale programmes of classroom research, are there any lessons to be learned from across the Atlantic?

The American experience

Despite such widespread attention, classroom research in America has not been without its problems. While results have grown to voluminous proportion, their contribution to understanding has, unhappily, been disproportionately small. For instance, in reviewing the 'teacher effectiveness' literature Gage has concluded that 'here and there, in research on teaching methods, on teacher personality and characteristics, and on social interaction in the classroom, it might be possible to come up with more sanguine judgments about the meaning of research findings' (1971, p. 31). In his analysis Gage does not rate classroom research techniques as any better than those they were intended to replace.

In this paper our intentions are twofold: first, to describe 'interaction analysis' and 'anthropological' classroom research – the two major American traditions; second, to raise issues we feel are relevant to a successful development of classroom research in Britain.

Interaction analysis and anthropological classroom research differ in a number of important respects. In the USA they are clearly insulated from each other. Interaction analysis – for reasons cited below – has tended to ignore classroom studies conducted outside its own territory. Development of the 'anthropological' tradition has taken place in the middle and far west of the USA, away from the prestige universities of the east coast. By comparison its funds are limited, its access to formal outlets (journals and conferences) minimal and its findings difficult to obtain.[4]

In contrasting interaction analysis (the dominant tradition) with anthropological classroom research we hope to demonstrate that a wholesale and uncritical adoption of the former is perhaps premature, if not misguided.

Interaction analysis

Interaction analysis is a research style true to the behavioural core assumptions of American psychology. Characteristically it involves using an observation schedule to reduce the stream of classroom behaviour to small-scale units suitable for tabulation or computation. The interaction analysts' 'pharmacopoeia', *Mirrors for Behavior* (Simon and Boyer, 1970) details seventy-nine such systems. Some, for example, provide a set of general categories into which the interaction is coded ('teacher asks question' or 'pupil answers'), while others give check lists of more specific behaviours ('pupil using word-book' or 'teacher leaves room'). The majority (sixty-seven) of the systems are described as suitable for use in classrooms; fifty-nine of the systems are described as suitable for use with lessons in any school subject. While some of the systems require specialist audio-visual recording devices, fifty-two of them are suitable for coding 'live'.

Although all the systems in *Mirrors* were developed originally for research purposes, perhaps their most successful application has been in training programmes.[5] As such, they are used in a variety of ways as structured feedback. Indeed, according to Simon and Boyer, 'forty-seven of the seventy-nine systems have been transferred from research to training instruments' (1970, p. 27).

Interaction analysis has, of course, both strengths and weaknesses. On the credit side can be placed the simplicity of most of the observation systems. They are well tried, reliable and easy to learn. Also, they can be used to study large numbers of classrooms; they readily generate a wealth of numerical data suitable for statistical analysis. In essence, interaction analysis techniques are an efficient way of discovering the norms of teacher and pupil behaviour. Thus a particular teacher's 'score' from an interaction analysis study will 'place' her in relation to her colleagues; but it will supply very little other information about her as an individual.

In the debit column must be placed factors which impose restrictions upon the use of interaction analysis:

1   Most interaction analysis systems ignore the context in which the data are collected. They make no provision for data concerning, for example, the layout of the classroom or the equipment being used. Also, although this is not inherent in the method, most systems employ data gathered during very short periods of observation (i.e. measured in minutes rather than hours). Because they are divorced from the social and temporal context in such a way, the data may gloss over aspects of the interaction relevant to their interpretation.

2   Interaction analysis systems are usually concerned only with overt, observable behaviour. They take no account of the intentions which lie behind such behaviour. Thus whenever intention is relevant to an observational category (as with 'teacher praises or encourages') the observer has to impute the intention. No regard is paid to the actor's viewpoint; only the observer's interpretation is considered relevant. By concentrating upon such surface aspects interaction analysis runs the risk of neglecting underlying, but possibly more meaningful, features. A comprehensive understanding of classroom events may, for example, be dependent upon the translation of 'silent languages' (Smith and Geoffrey, 1968) or the uncovering of 'hidden curricula' (Snyder, 1971).

3   Interaction analysis systems are expressly concerned with 'what can be categorized or measured' (*Mirrors*, p. 1). But by using crude measurement techniques or ill-defined category boundaries the systems may well obscure, distort or ignore the qualitative features they claim to be investigating – e.g. in one system, for example, it is necessary to distinguish between the teacher's 'acceptance of student feelings' and 'use of student's idea' (see Flanders, 1970).

By ignoring context, emphasising the overt and concentrating on the measurable interaction analysis accounts for only a small part of the totality of classroom life. This narrow focus – a form of reductionism – is one reason why interaction analysis has not led to more significant discoveries about educational practice. There are, however, a number of additional reasons. These relate to more theoretical considerations.

4   Interaction analysis systems focus on 'small bits of action or behaviour rather than global concepts' (*Mirrors*, p. 1). Inevitably, therefore, they generate a superabundance of data. Yet to interpret such data it has to be linked either to a set of descriptive concepts – typically, the categories themselves – or to a small number of global concepts built up from the categories, (e.g. in Flanders' interaction analysis system the 'direct/indirect' ratio is calculated by combining scores in five different categories). This is, of course, a circular exercise. Since the original categories were devised to break down the global concepts to small bits of behaviour, combining the categories to reach global concepts does not provide new insights into the interaction! The potential of interaction analysis to go beyond the categories is limited. Necessarily this impedes its theoretical development.

5   By definition, the systems utilise pre-specified categories. If the systems are intended to assist explanation, then the explanations may be tautologous. That is, category systems may, in fact, assume what they purport to explain. To use Flanders' system as our example again: this system is founded on an assumption that successful teaching is akin to leading a group therapy session. The categories were constructed accordingly. It is only with difficulty that they can be used to demonstrate an alternative theory of teaching.

6   Finally, by placing firm boundaries on continuous phenomena, the systems create a bias from which it is hard to escape. Reality – frozen in this way – is often difficult to liberate from its static representation.

Some of these limitations, particularly the first three noted above, have been acknowledged by the originators of the systems (see, for example, Flanders, 1970, chaper 2), but they are sometimes forgotten when the techniques are used by other, less experienced researchers. The systems are seen as some kind of panacea and are endowed with interpretive powers with which they cannot, for the reasons we have given, validly be credited.

Despite the objections, interaction analysis lays strong claim to be 'objective'. Its proponents argue that compared to other forms of observation it provides unambiguous data uncontaminated by observer 'bias'.

However, the price paid for such 'objectivity' can be high. By rejecting as invalid, non-scientific or 'metaphysical' data such as actors' ('subjective') accounts, or descriptive ('impressionistic') reports of classroom events, the interaction analysis approach risks furnishing only a partial description. In justifying the abjuration of such data on operational rather than theoretical or even educational grounds, interaction analysis may also prematurely divert attention from the initial problem field towards a more 'technocratic' concern (e.g. the establishment of 'objectivity' and 'reliability').

In seeking to avoid 'bias', interaction analysis systems sustain a rigid distinction between the observer and the observed. (*Mirrors for Behavior* contains only one exception to this generalisation.) The observer is considered a 'fly on the wall', clearly separate from the people being studied.[6] By maintaining this strict 'distance', interaction analysis may again promote an incomplete appraisal. Louis Smith has pinpointed the recurrent defect of this approach.

Teaching must be seen as an intellectual, cognitive process. What goes on in the head of the teacher is a critical antecedent of what he does. The way he poses his problems, the kinds of goals and sub-goals he is trying to reach, the alternatives he weighs as he circumvents obstacles and barriers, the momentary assessment of potential rewards and costs are aspects of teaching which are frequently lost to the behavioural oriented empiricist who focuses on what the teacher does, to the exclusion of how he thinks about teaching. [Smith and Geoffrey, 1968, p. 96]

In much of interaction analysis aspects of teaching such as these are rarely considered. They are labelled as 'subjective' and placed beyond the bounds of the empirical world.

Finally, in the interests of 'objectivity', many interaction analysis research studies feel compelled to survey large numbers of classrooms. It is argued (correctly) that small samples may fail to provide statements relevant to the population at large. However, such an approach (even if it can achieve true randomness) may fail to treat local perturbations or unusual effects as significant. Indeed, despite their potential significance for the classroom or classrooms to which they apply, atypical results are seldom studied in detail. They are treated as 'noise', ironed out as 'blurred averages' and lost to discussion.

Besides a concern for 'objectivity', interaction analysis is also subject to a number of more deep-rooted theoretical and ideological constraints. Most American interaction analysis systems are based on a 'chalk and talk' model of the classroom. They imply a classroom setting where the teacher stands in front and engages the students in some kind of pedagogical or linguistic ping-pong (teacher asks question – pupil replies – teacher asks question . . .). Further, interaction analysis systems may reflect outdated models of teaching and learning unwittingly taken over with such categories. Many systems, for example, make a clear distinction between the cognitive and affective components of classroom interaction. Yet, *pace* Bloom *et al.* (1956), such a distinction dates back to Wolff (1697–1754), when it formed the basis of 'faculty' psychology – now largely disregarded (see O'Neill, 1968, pp. 24–5).

Ideological assumptions may also be involved in more subtle ways. Like much of the social psychological research conducted in the USA since the Second World War, interaction analysis has developed from certain premises concerning 'democracy', 'authoritarianism', 'leadership' and 'mental hygiene'. As noted, Ned Flanders has been expressly concerned with 'indirect' teaching. As a result, there is a latent evaluative residue in his observation system. It can be seen, for example, in his operational statement: 'Direct influence consists in those verbal statements of the teacher that restrict *freedom* of action, by focusing attention on a problem, interjecting teacher *authority* or both' (Flanders, 1965, p. 9; emphasis added). This fact may not always be appreciated.

In brief, we have argued with respect to interaction analysis that it is not an all-purpose method but, rather, one way of collecting survey-type data on the socio-psychological climate of the 'average' classroom. By their very nature, results from such techniques rarely provide new insights or theoretical developments; likewise they do not provide an understanding of aspects of classroom life not encompassed by their respective socio-psychological perspectives. In the next section we discuss a different type of observation: one that attempts to offset some of the problems thrown up by interaction analysis studies.

'Anthropological' classroom research

Outside the interaction analysis tradition in the USA there have been certain other important but widely neglected programmes of classroom research. Often described as 'anthropological',[7] this work has developed beyond the margins of mainstream psychology and relates instead to social anthropology, psychiatry and participant observation research in sociology. In the USA this tradition is perhaps better known for its work in higher education. (See, for example, Becker *et al.*, 1968; Kahne, 1969, and Parlett, 1969.) It contrasts strongly with interaction analysis and can be thought of as representing an alternative tradition: one that goes back to Malinowski, Thomas and Waller, rather than to Watson, Skinner and Bales.

While both interaction analysis and ethnographic classroom research are concerned with developing 'metalanguages' (*Mirrors*, p. 1) adequate to the complexity of the behaviour they countenance, the latter uses an approach based on ethnography rather than psychometry; and a conceptual framework which considers education in socio-cultural rather than, say, in 'cognitive' or 'affective' terms. Within each tradition, for example, 'knowledge', the 'curriculum', even 'learning' are regarded differently. Methodologically, ethnographic studies are based on participant observation. That is, they involve the prolonged presence of an observer (or observers) in a single or small number of classrooms. During that time the observer not only observes but also talks with participants (significantly, the 'anthropologist' calls them 'informants' rather than 'subjects') and immerses himself in their world, discovering how they see it.[8]

In addition to observing classroom life, the researcher may conduct formal interviews with the participants and ask them to complete questionnaires. Usually, to record his observations the observer compiles field notes or, more recently, field recordings. Compared to the results of the interaction analyst the primary data of the 'anthropological' researcher are relatively unsystematic and open-ended.

The 'anthropologist' uses a holistic framework. He accepts as given the complex scene he encounters and takes this totality as his data base. He makes no attempt to manipulate, control or eliminate variables. Of course, the anthropologist does not claim to account for every aspect of this totality in his analysis. Characteristically, he gradually reduces the breadth of enquiry to give more concentrated attention to the emerging issues. Starting with a wide angle of vision he 'zooms' in and progressively focuses on those classroom features he considers to be most salient. Thus ethnographic research clearly dissociates itself from the *a priori* reductionism inherent in interaction analysis.

Ethnographic classroom research, like interaction analysis, begins with description. But whereas the former is governed by preordained descriptive categories (e.g. 'verbal', 'non-verbal', 'praise', 'criticism') the latter allows and encourages the imaginative development of new categories. 'Anthropological' research can freely go beyond the *status quo* and develop new yet empirically based descriptive languages.[9]

Interaction analysis – unlike 'anthropological' classroom research – is typically concerned with generating normative data; that is, in extrapolating from sample to population. It is often argued against ethnographic studies that their results cannot be generalised to other settings in this way. However, statistical norms (e.g. 'teacher-talk percentages': Flanders, 1970) apply to the population *taken as a whole*, not to .its individual members. They apply to individual settings merely in probabilistic terms. Since classroom settings are rarely equivalent, such statistical generalisations may not always be relevant or useful. To an ethnographer the development of generally or universally applicable statements is quite a different task: one that is never achieved merely by surveying the field. Despite their diversity, individual classrooms share many characteristics. Through the detailed study of one particular context it is still possible to clarify relationships, pinpoint critical processes and identify common phenomena. From these, abstracted summaries and general concepts can be formulated which may be germane to a wider variety of settings. Case studies, therefore, are not necessarily restricted in scope. Indeed, unlike interaction analysis they can acknowledge both the particulars and the universals of classroom life.[10]

There is, of course, no inherent reason why the two types of classroom research should not be employed together. But as we pointed out earlier, in America this has not occurred. The two 'schools' of thought more closely resemble 'camps', each with its own entrenched position. In Britain this unenviable state has not yet developed. Dialogue still takes place. Recent conferences on classroom observation have included papers reflecting both interests, and British literature reviews (e.g. Delamont, 1973, and Walker, 1972) have considered the merits of both schools.

The future development of classroom research

In bringing our cautionary tale to a conclusion we should like to raise a number of issues which we feel are essential to an important yet largely unargued debate in Britain.[11] Although generally the issues relate to the practice of classroom research, they are particularly concerned with the theoretical and methodological substrate upon which it is founded.

1   In its search for the key to the classroom 'black box', there is a danger

that research will cease to consider the wider educational and social context of the classroom. As Walker (1971, p. 143) has clearly warned, 'any description of classroom activities that cannot be related to the social structure and culture of the society is a conservative description'. As noted above, interaction analysis explicitly excludes contextual factors and so must be 'conservative' in Walker's terms. While, for research purposes, it may be possible to regard the classroom as a social unit in its own right, it is only with difficulty that it can be regarded as self-contained. An adequate study must acknowledge and account for both the internal and the external aspects of classroom life.

2   While an elaborate technology can facilitate description of behaviour, it cannot furnish explanations for that behaviour. The methods themselves do not provide such a link, nor do they supplant the conceptual processes needed to generate explanations. In the past classroom research – particularly the interaction analysis tradition – has poured forth an endless stream of comparative studies in the hope, presumably, that some conceptual clarity would emerge. In a manner reminiscent of alchemy, it has produced an enormous corpus of experimental work now largely forgotten or disregarded.[12]

The recent development of audio-visual techniques makes this problem particularly acute. Much classroom research can now be based on the analysis of recorded rather than 'live' data. 'Technicians' can make recordings, thus allowing the 'researcher' to remain in his office. That is, 'observation' can now take place away from the classroom. While this is administratively convenient and allows for *post hoc* analysis, it has the disadvantage that much of the additional information available to the on-site observer is lost. It is not insignificant, we suggest, that at least two studies which have used visual and/or audio recordings have sought consciously to integrate them with the physical presence of an independent observer (see Walker and Adelman, 1972; Smith and Brock, forthcoming). Indeed, Walker and Adelman describe their observational approach as 'participant recording'.

It is for the above reasons, perhaps, that interaction analysis systems have proved more useful as training than as research tools. As training instruments they are used to give information directly to the people being observed. Indeed, when audio-visual systems are employed the observer and the observed can be the same person. Clearly, when used in this way the observer is more aware of the subjective processes involved and, at the same time, is sensitised to the temporal and social context. Thus he or she has the necessary data to reach a more powerful understanding of the interaction. In this respect interaction analysis as 'research' is fundamentally different from interaction analysis as 'training'. In that the latter necessarily incorporates a phenomenological understanding as well as a behavioural description of the situation it is much closer to the 'anthropological' model.

3   Much classroom description has been behavioural. It has tended to disregard the meaning(s) that such behaviour entails. As already suggested, such an approach may miss important differences that underlie such

behaviour. To the extent that classroom research claims to illuminate the processes associated with classroom life it cannot afford to divorce what people do from their intentions. If it treats teachers and students merely as objects, it can only obtain a partial analysis: one that falls short of explanation in terms of the subjective processes which inform a teacher's or student's actions. To inquire into subjectivity or relative truth is not, as is sometimes imagined, to accept solipsism or relativism. It can still be a central research theme. Thus as Harré and Secord (1972, p. 101) point out, 'to treat people as if they were human beings it must still be possible to accept their commentaries upon their actions as authentic, though revisable, reports of phenomena, subject to empirical criticism'.

4   Like any other research, each classroom study develops from certain premises, suppositions and interests held by the researcher. Typically, these reflect the intellectual ethos of his time. As noted, there is an insidious danger in an uncritical acceptance of techniques developed from different (and often forgotten) standpoints. The theoretical constructs used in classroom research are sustained by an equivalent set of research methods, empirical categories and statistical techniques. These too may bear the hallmarks, if not the scars, of an earlier and possibly outdated realm. (Perhaps the clearest illustrations of this phenomenon can be drawn from the history of mental testing.[13]) Educational research should always pay close attention to emergent themes in the social sciences, not merely cling to those which other disciplines have readily discarded.

5   One deep reflection of this methodological and empirical carry-over is the manic optimism with which much educational research is suffused. Absolute truth is heralded as just beyond the horizon.[14] This nineteenth-century belief in rational man and the power of science (with its implicit denial of the historicity of truth) has a number of consequences – not least for classroom research. In a field where instant solutions are at a premium there is a danger it will lead to premature closure (when an exploratory or heuristic stance would be more useful); to the presentation of cautionary notes dressed up as 'conclusions'; and to the pursuit of short-term reliability rather than long-term validity.

Conclusion

Although, for the purposes of this discussion, we have divided classroom research into two fields, we do not regard them *necessarily* as mutually exclusive. Indeed, in our own work both of us are concerned to go beyond this distinction. The task is not easy, as the respective positions are deep-rooted and the differences clear and well established. Ultimately, we suggest, significant advances will depend not on increased technological sophistication nor upon methodological convergence. Instead, it will hinge upon a reconceptualisation and transformation of the dimensions which divide the two traditions.[15]

While research awaits this advance it is still incumbent upon researchers to treat interaction analysis and anthropological classroom research for what they are. Confusion still exists as to their aims and objectives. Too often questions such as 'What are they for?' 'What can (or cannot) they do?' are not considered. A knowledge of their deficiencies is as relevant as an appreciation of their potential. As different tools they are better suited to different tasks. Thus for example, to criticise anthropological studies for not providing demographic information is as misplaced as it is narrow-minded. Likewise, to complain that interaction systems are not as sensitive as in-depth interviews is to forget that they were never intended as clinical devices. Their focus is the average rather than the individual classroom.

At the start of this paper we noted that classroom research is likely to become an important 'new' field in British educational research. There is a danger, we feel, that the American experience will repeat itself in Britain, with large amounts of money, time and energy being ploughed unilaterally into interaction analysis.

Research funding tends, preferentially, to reward research proposals strong on technology. Yet too often they are weak on ideas. This paper is offered as a warning. Accept no substitute! Let the buyer beware!

Notes

1 This estimate is a cautious one, but it must be seen as a substantial part of the £3 million spent annually on educational research. The funding agencies involved include the NFER, OECD, SED, SSRC and the Ford Foundation.

2 See, for example, Hilsum and Cane (1971), Barnes (1969) and Duthie (1970). One consequence of a neglect of classroom life is that teachers have remained largely indifferent, or even antagonistic, to the claims made for educational research. For insight into their daily lives they have turned elsewhere: to 'travellers' tales' (e.g. Holt, 1969); to 'non-fiction novels' (e.g. Blishen, 1955); or to the compounded folk tales, myths and mores of the staff room.

3 For a more extensive discussion of the origins of classroom research in Britain see Hamilton (1972).

4 For example, the AERA curriculum evaluation monograph on *Classroom obser-vation* (Gallagher *et al.*, 1970) contains no discussion or even acknowledgement of the anthropological literature related to curriculum evaluation (e.g. Russell, 1969; Smith and Keith, 1967; or Hanley *et al.*, 1969). Also, *Mirrors for Behavior* fails to acknowledge that there are (or even can be) '"metalanguages" for describing communication of various kinds' (p. 1) which are based on other than measurement of *a priori* categorization.

5 It is more correct, though perhaps tautologous, to say that all the widely used systems are simple. Of the remainder, five require four observers; one requires an extensive knowledge of psychoanalysis; and a third requires knowledge of the foreign language being taught in the classroom. Some systems are also restricted in the situations in which they can be used (e.g. a 'correctional institution for delinquents').

6 For example, in an observational study of English infant classrooms, Garner

(1972) devotes no discussion to the impact of the observer. More particularly, his check list makes no reference to infant behaviour directed towards the observer, though it is reasonable to assume that it did (or could) occur.

7 It has been described as 'microethnographical' (Smith and Geoffrey, 1968), 'naturalistic' (MacDonald, 1970), and 'ecological' (Parlett, 1969). Unlike the interaction analysis tradition, whose origins are clearly rooted in behavioural psychology, the anthropological tradition has no established roots. Some of its members are 'straight' anthropologists (e.g. Jules Henry), some are sociologists (e.g. Howard Becker), some are psychiatrists (e.g. Zachary Gussow) and some are 'converts' from behavioural psychology (e.g. Philip Jackson, Malcolm Parlett and Louis Smith).

8 Unlike the interaction analyst, the anthropologist does not make such a strong distinction between observer and observed. Indeed, this is one of the features that separates the traditions most clearly. Gussow and Vidich put the 'anthropological' case most clearly: 'When observers are physically present and physically approachable the concept of the observer as non-participant though sociologically correct is psychologically misleading.' (Gussow, 1964, p. 240.) 'Whether the field-worker is totally, partially or not at all disguised, the respondent forms an image of him and uses that image as a basis of response. Without such an image, the relationship between the field-worker and the respondent by definition does not exist.' (Vidich, 1955, p. 35.)

9 Not all anthropological research, however, is open-ended 'pure' research. Like interaction analysis, it has been used in curriculum evaluation (e.g. Smith and Pohland, 1973; Parlett and Hamilton, 1972) and in teacher training (e.g. Goldhammer, 1969).

10 Both interaction analysis and anthropological research are dogged by a tendency towards over-elaboration. Within interaction analysis this can be seen by the rapid increase of observations systems. For example, the second edition of *Mirrors for Behavior* (1970) contains three times the number of systems that appeared in the first edition (1967). In referring to this Barak Rosenshine has commented that 'it appears as if the creation of a new category system were a pre-requisite for graduation from some universities' (in Gallagher, 1970, p. 115). The same problem is exemplified in 'anthropological' research by the proliferation of case studies. Louis Smith has pointed out that 'most anthropologists define their cases so broadly and pursue them so intensively that they cannot cumulate cases. This inability . . . has some far-reaching and potentially tragic consequences for education and educational anthropology' (Smith, 1971). In both traditions the greater specificity gained by differentiation must be weighed against the diminished applicability of the findings.

11 Recently, there have been some signs in the USA of debate on these issues (see Smith and Brock, 1970; Westbury and Bellack, 1971). However, it is perhaps significant that the first of these was produced as a mimeographed researched report (not as a journal paper), and the second was produced following a *Canadian* conference.

12 Category systems are similar to intelligence tests. They can differentiate classrooms (instead of children). They can yield norms (of 'teacher-talk' rather than 'verbal reasoning'). They can produce demographic information (about 'teacher/pupil' rather than 'IQ/length of schooling' interaction). They can use similar statistics (e.g. factor analysis). To us this analogy is not misleading. We feel the present state of mental testing points to a potential future state for interaction analysis classroom research.

13 Classroom research is not alone in this respect. Computer-aided instruction and curriculum development are similarly affected. For example, millions of dollars have been spent in the USA developing 'drill and practice' computer programmes for maths, spelling and reading, when up-to-date research had already rejected 'drill and practice' in favour of other, more sophisticated models of learning.

14 Cf. 'A revolution in teaching is being fomented. If successful, it will overthrow the hegemony of the centuries-old pattern whereby one teacher and twenty to forty pupils engage for most kinds of instruction in a teacher-dominated discourse . . . If the revolution succeeds, the teacher will spend much less time each day with groups of students in time-honoured ways . . . In short, a spectre is haunting research on teaching – the spectre of programmed instruction' (Gage and Unruh, 1967, p. 358).

15 Drawing upon another field for an example, we could cite the discovery of the structure of DNA. As an event which transcended the (living/non-living) categories previously dividing biochemistry from genetics and cell biology, it helped to create the unitary field of molecular biology.

References

BARKER LUNN, J. C. (1970) *Streaming in the Primary School*. London: NFER.

BARNES, D. (1969) 'Language in the secondary classroom', in BARNES, D. *et al.* (1969) *Language, the Learner and the School*. Harmondsworth: Penguin Books.

BECKER, H. S. *et al.* (1968) *Making the Grade*. New York: Wiley.

BLISHEN, E. (1955) *Roaring Boys*. London: Thames and Hudson.

BLOOM, B. S. *et al.* (1956) *Taxonomy of Educational Objectives, Handbook I: The cognitive domain*. New York: McKay.

DELAMONT, S. (1973) Ph.D. thesis, University of Edinburgh.

DUTHIE, J. H. (1970) *Primary School Survey: A study of the teacher's day*. Edinburgh: HMSO.

FLANDERS, N. A. (1965) *Teacher Influence, Pupil Attitudes and Achievements*. Co-operative Research Monograph, University of Michigan (quoted in WALKER, R. (1971), p. 41).

FLANDERS, N. A. (1970) *Analysing Teaching Behaviour*. London: Addison-Wesley.

GAGE, N. L. (1971) *Teacher Effectiveness and Teacher Education: The search for a scientific basis*. Palo Alto, Calif.: Pacific Books (quoted by reviewer in *Harvard Educational Review*, XLII, 1972, p. 286).

GAGE, N. L. and UNRUH, W. R. (1967) 'Theoretical formulations for research on teaching.' *Review of Educational Research*, XXXVII, pp. 358–70.

GALLAGHER, J. J. *et al.* (1970) *Classroom Observations*. AERA Monograph Series on Curriculum Evaluation, No. 6. Chicago, Ill.: Rand McNally.

GARNER, J. (1972) 'Some aspects of behaviour in infant school classrooms.' *Research in Education*, No. 7, pp. 28–47.

GOLDHAMMER, R. (1969) *Clinical Supervision: Special methods for the supervision of teachers*. New York: Holt, Rinehart and Winston.

GUSSOW, Z. (1964) 'The observer-observed relationship as information about structures in small group research.' *Psychiatry*, XXVII, pp. 236–47.

HAMILTON, D. (1972) 'The genesis of classroom research as a legitimate field of educational research.' Unpublished paper, given to conference on classroom observation, University of Lancaster.

HANLEY, J. P. *et al.* (1969) *Curiosity, Competence, Community.* Cambridge, Mass.: Education Development Center.

HARRE, R. and SECORD, P. F. (1972) *The Explanation of Social Behaviour.* Oxford: Blackwell.

HILSUM, S. and CANE, B. S. (1971) *The Teacher's Day.* London: NFER.

HOLT, J. (1969) *How Children Fail.* Harmondsworth: Penguin Books.

KAHNE, M. J. (1969) 'Psychiatrist observer in the classroom.' *Medical Trial Technique Quarterly,* XXIII, pp. 81–98.

MACDONALD, B. (1970) 'The evaluation of the Humanities Curriculum Project: a holistic approach.' Centre for Applied Research in Education, University of East Anglia (unpublished).

MACDONALD, B. and RUDDUCK, J. (1971) 'Curriculum research and development: barriers to success.' *British Journal of Educational Psychology,* XLI, pp. 148–54.

MEDLEY, D. M. and MITZEL, H. E. (1963) 'Measuring classroom behavior by systematic observation', in GAGE, N. L. (ed.) (1963) *Handbook of Research on Teaching.* Chicago, Ill.: Rand McNally, pp. 247–328.

O'NEILL, W. M. (1968) *The Beginnings of Modern Psychology.* Harmondsworth: Penguin Books.

PARLETT, M. R. (1969) 'Undergraduate teaching observed.' *Nature,* CCIII, pp. 1102–4.

PARLETT, M. and HAMILTON, D. (1972) 'Evaluation as illumination: a new approach to the study of innovatory programs.' Centre for Research in the Educational Sciences, University of Edinburgh, Occasional Paper No. 9.

RUSSELL, H. (ed.) (1969) *Evaluation of Computer-assisted Instruction Program.* St Ann, Mo.: CEMREL.

SIMON, A. and BOYER, G. E. (eds) (1970) *Mirrors for Behavior* II. Philadelphia, Pa.: Research for Better Schools.

SMITH, L. M. (1971) 'Dilemmas in educational innovation: a problem for anthropology as clinical method.' Paper presented to AERA symposium 'Anthropological approaches to the study of education', New York.

SMITH, L. M. and KEITH, P. M. (1967) *Social Psychology Aspects of School Building Design.* Washington, D.C.: USOE Co-operative Research Report No. S-223.

SMITH, L. M. and GEOFFREY, W. (1968) *The Complexities of an Urban Classroom.* New York: Holt, Rinehart and Winston.

SMITH, L. M. and BROCK, J. A. M. (1970) ' "Go, bug, go!": methodological issues in classroom observation research.' St Ann, Mo.: CEMREL.

SMITH, L. M. and POHLAND, P. A. (1973) 'Educational technology and the rural highlands.' AERA Monograph Series on Curriculum Evaluation No. 7. Chicago, Ill.: Rand McNally.

SMITH, L. M. and BROCK, J. A. M. (n.d.) *Teacher Plans and Classroom Interaction.* St Ann, Mo.: CEMREL (forthcoming).

SNYDER, B. R. (1971) *The Hidden Curriculum.* New York: Knopf.

STONES, E. and MORRIS, S. (1972) *Teaching Practice: Problems and Perspectives.* London: Methuen.

VIDICH, A. J. (1955) 'Participant observation and the collection and interpretation of data.' *American Journal of Sociology,* LX, pp. 354–60.

WALKER, R. (1971) 'The social setting of the classroom – a review of observational studies and research.' M.Phil. thesis, University of London.

WALKER, R. (1972) 'The sociology of education and life in school classrooms.' *International Review of Education* XVIII, pp. 32–43.

WALKER, R. and ADELMAN, C. (1971) 'Towards a sociology of the classroom.' Research monograph, Chelsea College, London.

WESTBURY, I. and BELLACK, A. A. (eds) (1971) *Research into Classroom Processes.* New York: Teachers' College Press.

2.3   A typology of teaching styles

Neville Bennett

The first task of the study (see Bennett, 1976) was to break down the global terms 'progressive' and 'traditional' into their constituent elements before translating these elements into questionnaire items. One obvious approach was to review the many alternative conceptions of the teaching process which abound in the philosophical and psychological literature related to education. This was the first step taken, and included an examination of the theoretical and philosophical underpinnings of, to use Sherman's (1970) labels, the Platonic, instrumental approach versus the Rousseauian, naturalistic alternative; and a review of the differing psychological interpretations of the learning process, notably the behaviourist and cognitive theories, and of disputes such as that between Bruner (1961) and Ausubel (1963) concerning student motivation and creative growth. It also included an examination of the various educational reports, notably Hadow (1931) and Plowden (1967), both of which grounded their prescriptions on similar literature.

A purely theoretical breakdown was deemed insufficient, particularly since it would appear that teachers take little cognisance of such literature in determining their natural teaching style. This fact was noted in the Plowden report which considered that it was rare to find teachers who had given much time to the study of educational theory, even in their college of education days. It was therefore decided to complement the theoretical review with interviews with primary school teachers who, in the subjective opinion of the author, represented the range of teaching styles under consideration. Head and class teachers from twelve schools were interviewed to ascertain what teaching behaviours they considered differentiated progressive and traditional styles.

From these diverse sources eleven basic differentiating elements were isolated and are shown in Table 1. The elements were translated into classroom behaviours and then into questionnaire items. The final version of the questionnaire covered six major areas:

1   *Classroom management and organisation:* extent of freedom of movement and talk in the classroom, seating arrangements adopted
2   *Teacher control and sanctions:* degree of disciplinary rather than physical control
3   *Curriculum content and planning:* allocation of teaching time, extent of timetabling and homework, degree of pupil choice
4   *Instructional strategies:* type of teaching approach
5   *Motivational techniques:* whether intrinsic or extrinsic motivation is stressed
6   *Assessment procedures:* type and quantity of evaluation of pupil work

Source: BENNETT, N. (1976) *Teaching Styles and Pupil Progress.* London: Open Books, pp. 37–54.

Table 1   Characteristics of progressive and traditional teachers

Progressive	*Traditional*
1 Integrated subject matter	1 Separate subject matter
2 Teacher as guide to educational experiences	2 Teacher as distributor of knowledge
3 Active pupil role	3 Passive pupil role
4 Pupils participate in curriculum planning	4 Pupils have no say in curriculum planning
5 Learning predominantly by discovery techniques	5 Accent on memory, practice and rote
6 External rewards and punishments not necessary, i.e. intrinsic motivation	6 External rewards used, e.g. grades, i.e. extrinsic motivation
7 Not too concerned with conventional academic standards	7 Concerned with academic standards
8 Little testing	8 Regular testing
9 Accent on cooperative group work	9 Accent on competition
10 Teaching not confined to classroom base	10 Teaching confined to classroom base
11 Accent on creative expression	11 Little emphasis on creative expression

Two pilot studies were carried out to make possible the reduction and modification of ambiguous items. The final form of the questionnaire contained twenty-eight items although a number were in multiple form. Question 28 for example required a break-down of the time spent on every aspect of the syllabus in the last full week prior to completing the questionnaire. Similarly question 16 required the teachers to indicate the time spent on five basic pedagogical approaches. The questionnaire in its final form was included as a separate section of a larger questionnaire which also contained sections on the teacher, class and classroom and on teacher opinions about educational issues. . . . (See Appendix A, [pages 131–40].)

Questionnaire survey approaches are rare in the literature of teaching styles, and it is instructive to consider the content and format of the questionnaire developed for this study in relation to other published sources. Only three other studies have been located, one British (Simon, 1972) and two American (Adams, 1970; Walberg and Thomas, 1971). This number is likely to increase, however. The Walberg and Thomas study is an investigation into 'open education', which, for the purpose of this discussion, is taken to be synonymous with 'progressive education' as defined in Plowden.

The Simon study is not directly comparable since it concentrated in greater depth on a narrower range of content. Nevertheless, although the questionnaires were developed concurrently, and in isolation, there is considerable overlap between them in certain areas such as classroom arrangement.

The Adams questionnaire was developed for a comparative survey of perceived teaching styles in the United Kingdom, Australia, New Zealand

and the United States. The author isolated seven 'variable classes' from a review of traditional educational thinking which, he claimed, represent areas of generally widespread concern to teachers. They were: content orientation; cognitive emphasis; interaction mode; organisational differentiation; control source; control mode; and motivational mode. Each is described briefly below:

1 *Content orientation:* whether teaching emphasis is placed primarily on subject matter, on interpersonal relationships, or on discipline and control: in other words, whether the teaching is traditional, progressive or authoritarian
2 *Cognitive emphasis:* the kind of learning being promoted – the acquisition of skill, fact or understanding
3 *Interaction mode:* the communication pattern in the classroom; this encompasses three basic patterns – teacher dominated (lecture); teacher–pupil communication where teacher retains a measure of control; and free communication with no necessary teacher domination
4 *Organisational differentiation:* the way in which tasks are allocated and organised – whether all pupils are working on the same task collectively; differentiated groups working on the same task; or differentiated groups working on different tasks
5 *Control source:* whether classroom rules are determined by the teacher alone, by the teacher in collaboration with pupils or by pupils alone
6 *Control mode:* whether these rules are prescriptive, proscriptive or permissive
7 *Motivational mode:* whether intrinsic or extrinsic motivational procedures are manifest

These variable classes were operationalised by building items around the three categories in each. The twenty-one items were provided with five response categories relating to the degree of emphasis given in classroom teaching. The results of the survey are of little interest in the present context since the analysis simply compared teachers in the four countries on each variable class.

Walberg and Thomas (1971) were concerned that the concept 'open' had not been analysed into its component parts. They too carried out a review of traditional educational literature, and, in addition, of the analytic writings of Barth (1972), Bussis and Chittenden (1970) and Rathbone (1971). They finally isolated eight themes and built a fifty-item teacher questionnaire and rating scale around them. The eight themes and item representation are:

1 *Provisioning for learning:* range of materials supplied; freedom of pupil movement and talk; ability grouping; pupil choice of seating (twenty-five items)
2 *Humaneness:* materials developed by children; pupil abilities reflected in classroom environment; teacher care when dealing with conflicts (four items)

3   *Diagnosis of learning events:* regrouping of pupils on basis of test results; tests and assessment (four items)
4   *Instruction:* whether based on individual child; subject centred *v.* integration; lectures (five items)
5   *Evaluation of diagnostic information:* recording of cognitive and emotional development of pupils; teacher uses tests for comparative progress; evaluation as guide to instruction (five items)
6   *Seeking opportunities for professional growth:* teacher uses assistance of someone in supportive capacity; has helpful colleagues (two items)
7   *Self perception of teacher:* teacher tries to keep all her pupils in sight (one item)
8   *Assumptions about children and learning process:* Warm emotional climate; clear guidelines given to class; children involved in what they are doing; emphasis on achievement (four items)

This questionnaire does not seem to be particularly satisfactory. The number of items representing each theme varies from twenty-five to one, with classroom management and organisation heavily overweighted. In addition to the problem of the validity of its content, there is the problem that the themes must differ greatly in reliability. Neither do the themes appear to be independent.

However, it is conceptual rather than constructional considerations which are of greater interest, and here the degree of overlap with this study in the content of the Adams and the Walberg and Thomas scale is very high, although they have been given different titles.

Sampling

Sampling considerations are paramount in an attempt to create valid typologies. Cluster techniques group people together who share common characteristics. If the sample is unrepresentative in terms of these characteristics the resultant typology will not be generalisable, and will consequently be of little utility.

A random sample of teachers taken on a national basis would have been the ideal sampling model, but the ideal is rarely possible given the limited resources of time, cost and staffing. Such was the case in this study. Instead it was decided to attempt a census of all third- and fourth-year primary teachers teaching in a given geographical area. For convenience this comprised the administrative counties of Lancashire and Cumbria.

Within this region can be found a wide range of school and environmental contexts, from schools whose intake areas cover the centres of industrial cities to those serving moorland villages, schools ranging in size of intake from four children to four forms, old schools and new schools, church schools and state schools – in all, an area rich in educational diversity.

The questionnaires were despatched to each headmaster in the 871 primary schools which serve the region. Included within the package were sufficient questionnaires for each relevant member of staff together with separate envelopes so that the class teacher could seal the completed questionnaire before returning it to the head teacher for despatch. This was designed to ensure complete confidentiality. A separate questionnaire was also included for the head teacher concerning school particulars and policy. Finally a stamped addressed envelope was provided for the return of all the questionnaires.

The packages were distributed to schools in late November and early December, despite the dictates of methodological folklore. Nevertheless 65 per cent of the schools had returned their questionnaires before the Christmas holidays, and by the end of January, after two follow-up letters, 88 per cent had responded, and a further 3 per cent had written explaining why they could not take part. This is an exceptionally high response rate for a postal survey and enables a high degree of confidence to be placed in the accuracy of the sample.

General teaching pattern

In order to assess whether age of class taught had any effect on the teaching style adopted, item response levels were computed separately for three levels – third year, third and fourth year mixed, and fourth year. The most striking feature of the result is the similarity of response pattern on most items, which suggests that in general teaching styles do not vary by age of pupils taught. The three groups were therefore combined to give the following general picture of primary school practice in upper primary schools.

Most teachers sit their pupils separately or in pairs rather than in larger groups, and most pupils remain in the same seats for most activities. Approximately one third of teachers use some form of internal streaming device by placing or grouping pupils on the basis of ability, whereas a similar proportion allow complete freedom in the choice of seating.

A high degree of permissiveness does not appear to be the norm in primary classrooms despite assertions to the contrary. Teacher control of physical movement and talk is generally high. Two thirds of teachers restrict these, a similar proportion expect their pupils to be quiet most of the time, and most require that pupils request permission to leave the room.

Responses to items concerning curriculum organisation also reflect a structured approach. In item 16 teachers were asked to indicate the emphasis placed on teacher talking to class as a whole, individual versus group work, and teacher-given versus pupil-chosen work. The results, in terms of the percentage of time devoted to each type of activity, are as follows:

Teacher talking to whole class	19%
Pupils working in groups on teacher tasks	21%
Pupils working in groups on tasks of own choice	10%
Pupils working individually on teacher tasks	37%
Pupils working individually on tasks of own choice	13%

These figures indicate that in general pupil work is teacher directed 77 per cent of the time and pupil directed 23 per cent of the time. Group work also seems to be much less favoured than individual work.

Other indications of structure include the fact that eight out of ten teachers require their pupils to know their multiplication tables off by heart, and one in three teachers give their pupils homework, although it should be noted that this is not so prevalent at third-year level, which possibly reflects the effect of the eleven-plus selection procedures at the later stage.

In addition a subject centred curriculum would seem to predominate. The teachers were asked to estimate the amount of time spent on all aspects of the curriculum in the last full week prior to completing the questionnaire. The average number of hours available for actual teaching each week has been found by Duthie (1970) to be twenty-five, and this was adopted as a standard. Three groupings were made of these data:

1 *'Academic' subjects taught separately:* included number work, English, reading, history, geography, French, science and scripture
2 *'Aesthetic' subjects:* included P.E. and games, music, art and craft, music and movement and drama
3 *'Integrated' subjects:* included environmental studies, social studies, project and topic work, free choice periods and other integrated work

Of the twenty-five hours, fifteen and a quarter were devoted to academic subjects, five to aesthetic subjects, and four and three quarters to all forms of integrated subjects.

Despite the subject centred approach there does seem to be a move towards emphasising fluency and originality in written work, even if this is achieved at the expense of grammatical accuracy. Nevertheless spelling and grammatical errors are usually corrected even if few teachers assign an actual grade to pupils' work. Assessment of work in the shape of tests of arithmetic and spelling take place each week, and over half the teachers set end-of-term tests.

Discipline does not appear to be a problem at the primary level. Less than one in ten teachers claim to have many pupils who create discipline problems, and over 95 per cent find that verbal reproof is normally sufficient to deal with such problems. Nevertheless, for persistent disruptive behaviour a number of other measures are used, the most common being withdrawal of privileges, extra work and smacking. It was somewhat surprising to find that over half the teachers admitted to smacking when it appears to be frowned on at the official level.

This general picture, although of interest, does not provide information about the range of teaching approaches adopted by teachers. In order to isolate the variety of these styles a cluster analysis was undertaken. This is a useful technique since it allows people to be grouped together who have similar characteristics, in this instance teachers who had a similar profile of responses to all the questionnaire items. These groupings are often denoted 'types', which McQuitty (1967) defines as categories of persons such that every person in the category is more like every other person in the category than he is like any other person in any other category. The cluster analysis is based on the 468 fourth year teachers, and is described further by Bennett (1975) and Bennett and Jordan (1975).

Twelve teacher types or styles were extracted from the cluster analysis, and can be described as follows:

Type 1
These teachers favour integration of subject matter, and, unlike most other groups, allow pupil choice of work, whether undertaken individually or in groups. Most allow pupils choice of seating. Less than half curb movement and talk. Assessment in all its forms – tests, grading, and homework – appears to be discouraged. Intrinsic motivation is favoured.

Type 2
These teachers also prefer integration of subject matter. Teacher control appears to be low, but the teachers offer less pupil choice of work. However, most allow pupils choice of seating, and only one third curb movement and talk. Few test or grade work.

Type 3
The main teaching mode of this group is class teaching and group work. Integration of subject matter is preferred and is associated with taking their pupils out of school. These teachers appear to be strict, most curbing movement and talk, and offenders are smacked. The amount of testing is average, but the amount of grading and homework below average.

Type 4
These teachers prefer separate subject teaching but a high proportion allow pupil choice of work both in group and individual work. None seat their pupils by ability. They test and grade more than average.

Type 5
A mixture of separate subject and integrated subject teaching is characteristic of this group. The main teaching mode is pupils working in groups of their own choice on tasks set by the teacher. Teacher talk is lower than average. Control is high with regard to movement but not to talk. Most give tests every week and many give homework regularly. Stars are rarely used, and pupils are taken out of school regularly.

Type 6
These teachers prefer to teach subjects separately with emphasis on groups working on teacher-specified tasks. The amount of individual work is small. These teachers appear to be fairly low on control, and in the use of extrinsic motivation.

Type 7
This group are separate subject orientated, with a high level of class teaching together with individual work. Teacher control appears to be tight, few teachers allow movement or choice of seating, and offenders are smacked. Assessment, however, is low.

Type 8
This group of teachers has very similar characteristics to those of type 3, the difference being that these prefer to organise the work on an individual rather than a group basis. Freedom of movement is restricted, and most expect pupils to be quiet.

Type 9
These teachers favour separate subject teaching, the predominant teaching mode being individuals working on tasks set by the teacher. Teacher control appears to be high; most curb movement and talk, and seat by ability. Pupil choice is minimal, regular spelling tests are given, but few mark or grade work, or use stars.

Type 10
All these teachers favour separate subject teaching. The teaching mode favoured is teacher talk to whole class, and pupils working in groups determined by the teacher, on tasks set by the teacher. Most curb movement and talk, and over two thirds smack for disruptive behaviour. There is regular testing and most give stars for good work.

Type 11
All members of this group stress separate subject teaching by way of class teaching and individual work. Pupil choice of work is minimal, although most teachers allow choice in seating. Movement and talk are curbed, and offenders smacked.

Type 12
This is an extreme group in a number of respects. None favours an integrated approach. Subjects are taught separately by class teaching and individual work. None allows pupils choice of seating, and every teacher curbs movement and talk. These teachers are above average on all assessment procedures, and extrinsic motivation predominates.

The types have been subjectively ordered, for descriptive purposes, in order of distance from the most 'informal' cluster (type 1). This suggests that they can be represented by points on a continuum of 'informal–formal', but this would be an over-simplification. The extreme types could be adequately described in these terms, but the remaining types all contain both informal and formal elements.

Validation

This analysis provides an indication that the ubiquitous use of dichotomous descriptions of teaching styles fails to take into account the multiplicity of elements involved. When construed unidimensionally on the progressive–traditional range, only a minority of styles are adequately described. The majority of teachers appear to adopt a mixed or intermediate style for which the progressive–traditional dimension provides inadequate description.

However, the claim that the above typology provides a more adequate description of classroom reality is of little value unless it can be established that the classification is valid. Evidence of validity has therefore been sought from three sources: ratings by research staff; ratings by local authority advisers; and descriptions of the school day by the pupils.

Thirty-seven teachers whose responses most closely matched the central profiles of seven of the twelve clusters (see Bennett, 1976, chapter 5) agreed to participate in the second stage of the project, and it is from these teachers that evidence concerning validity has been derived. Research staff spent two days in each of the classrooms during the course of data collection, and on their return were asked to write a description of each classroom based on the items in the questionnaire and cluster analysis. Although they were unaware of the cluster membership of the teachers, their reports related closely to the cluster descriptions.

The second source of evidence was gained from the L.E.A. advisers. All the primary school advisers from all of the participating authorities attended a meeting at which the questionnaire, the analysis, and the cluster descriptions were discussed. Although the thirty-seven teachers were already known to them, the advisers agreed to visit each teacher in their authority again and report their observations in terms of the questionnaire items and cluster descriptions. Again, the cluster membership of each teacher was unknown to them. An analysis of these reports indicated an 80 per cent agreement between their ratings and the cluster description.

Of interest was the fact that the research staff and the advisers isolated the same two instances where the way in which the teacher said he taught did not correspond too closely with how he was actually teaching. Fortunately these were isolated cases, and other indications are that response bias did not operate widely. The fact that the analysis delineated so few progressive teachers when there appears to be pressure to teach in this manner, and that so many teachers admitted to smacking when this is discouraged both by the L.E.A.s and the N.U.T., are indications of this.

The third, and perhaps most interesting, source of evidence is that gained from content analyses of an essay written by all the pupils in the thirty-seven classes entitled 'What I did at school yesterday'. In this the pupils were asked to record as accurately as possible all that had happened at school the previous day. Nine classrooms have been analysed. Initially two assistants were given the essays from the same class and were asked to provide independent descriptions of the classroom. The two descriptions were virtually identical, indicating a very high inter-judge agreement. Brief descriptions of two classrooms are reported to indicate the type of data gained from this approach.

Class A (class teacher: Mrs B.)

Mrs B. allows her children freedom of choice and of movement before school officially begins and before she enters the room, and this freedom is mirrored elsewhere in the school day. Most of the children begin the day with verbal reasoning, though a few work in books titled *Objective English* and *Word Perfect*. When they have completed verbal reasoning, the first choice point in the day occurs. As Andrew E. explains it, 'we did verble resoning. After working a bit we could finish our paintings. But I did clay modeling with Paul C. And he made an awful mess . . .' While some children were building models and painting, others were working on projects such as fossils and water, while still others worked on *Objective English* or *Word Perfect*. The choice which children have here seems a real choice, without teacher 'management'; most of the children have finished their work before assembly and have time for a second activity.

After assembly and playtime, children who have not already done so are expected to finish off the verbal reasoning. Then they may select an activity, again with no apparent management from Mrs B. The thirty-nine pupils split into ten activities including *Word Perfect, Objective English*, projects, modelling (apparently from oddments), a play (involving three girls), sewing soft toys, making collages for an exhibition, drawing, clay work, and maths. The children take an especially active interest in the work during this period; both evaluative and descriptive comments were prevalent:

Then after maths I started to do a drawing about a war. The drawing had a main aircraft which had rockets on it. (Andrew G.)
After playtime I started on the ship with David H. I made some brilliant steps for it. The ship was called the Graf Spee. (Christopher H.)
Then Stephen and I did some clay modelling. I did a waterfall, but I didn't turn out right so I demolished it. (Jonathan S.)
Then I did a play with Mary and Debbie, Debbie got Mandy and went away so Mary and I did it by ourself. We didn't do it all so we are going to finish it off tomorrow. (Louise B.)

Louise's comment indicates a firm expectation that tomorrow will once again include periods for pupil choice.

The choice period ends and the pupils move to one of the three reading groups taken by Mr A., Mr K. and Mrs B. The children know which group to join, but it is not clear on what basis the groups are formed. This continues until lunch.

After lunch a short time is spent going over homework. A quiz follows which had been requested by Stephen L. during the morning. This indicates that the pupils as well as the teacher are able to influence curriculum activity. The whole class are involved and it develops into a competition of boys versus girls.

During the last period most of the children are involved in a rehearsal for a Christmas play. The pupils who are not in the play can apparently choose what they would like to do in the classroom.

The degree of pupil choice in this classroom appears particularly high. All children had at least one choice period, during the morning between playtime and reading. Most of the children had a second choice period just before morning assembly, and a few had a third choice time at the end of the day when the others were practising the Christmas play. Also all of the children had the opportunity for choice before school began, when at least seven different activities were available without teacher supervision.

Class A was delineated as type 1 by the cluster analysis, but this class was deliberately chosen for detailed report here for another reason: it highlights the effect of external factors or pressures on the teaching decisions taken. It may seem incongruous to some that a progressive teacher begins the day with verbal reasoning practice, and sets homework. However, this is explained by the fact that the school is in an area which has retained the eleven-plus selection procedure. Separate analyses have been carried out relating factors such as the presence of selective examinations, size of school, church affiliation and type of intake area, to teaching style adopted. (See Bennett, 1976, chapter 4.)

Class B (class teacher: Mr M.)

Before school a few of the boys play football in the playground, while one child goes into the building to open windows. After assembly their teacher Mr M. 'gave us some of our marks from the test we had just took' (Pauline F.) until Mrs P. arrived to teach the class English.

After playtime, the class has French with Mrs H. 'who is the school only french teacher' (Ian C.). According to Andrew F. they 'learnt how to wright the numbers in French'.

After French Mr M. returned to take part of the class swimming while 'the rest stay behind with Mrs P. doing Topic work' (Beverley H.). The topics were apparently determined by the individual students; Suzanne M.'s topic book 'is on Ballet'. She later comments: 'when playtime finished I left school because I went to my Ballet Exam at 3.00. Most of my friends hoped that I would do well.'

After dinnertime Mr M. 'gave out the names of the people who came in the Top Ten' (Suzanne M.). Several of the children reported positioning, and the exam results took up two periods in the day. Andrew F. reports: 'then at 2.10 we went down to the hall and had P.E. We played a game called dogge ball . . . Red's won every game, and I am in the Reds.' After P.E. and playtime, the class wrote the composition 'Invisible for a day' (this was for the project).

When we came in Mr. M. told us to get just our pencils out and I thought oh here we go another test. It was not a test it was a composition we had to write just like this one. (Nichola W.)

We went in and wrote a composition about an Invisible day I made my story as funny as I could snipping strings of balloons making bottle of washing up liquid dance and frightening people I had fun writing it and pretending to be Sylvia (Julie T.)

In contrast to class A no choice period is offered to pupils in this class. Choice within a session is only offered once, i.e. for topic work, but this almost

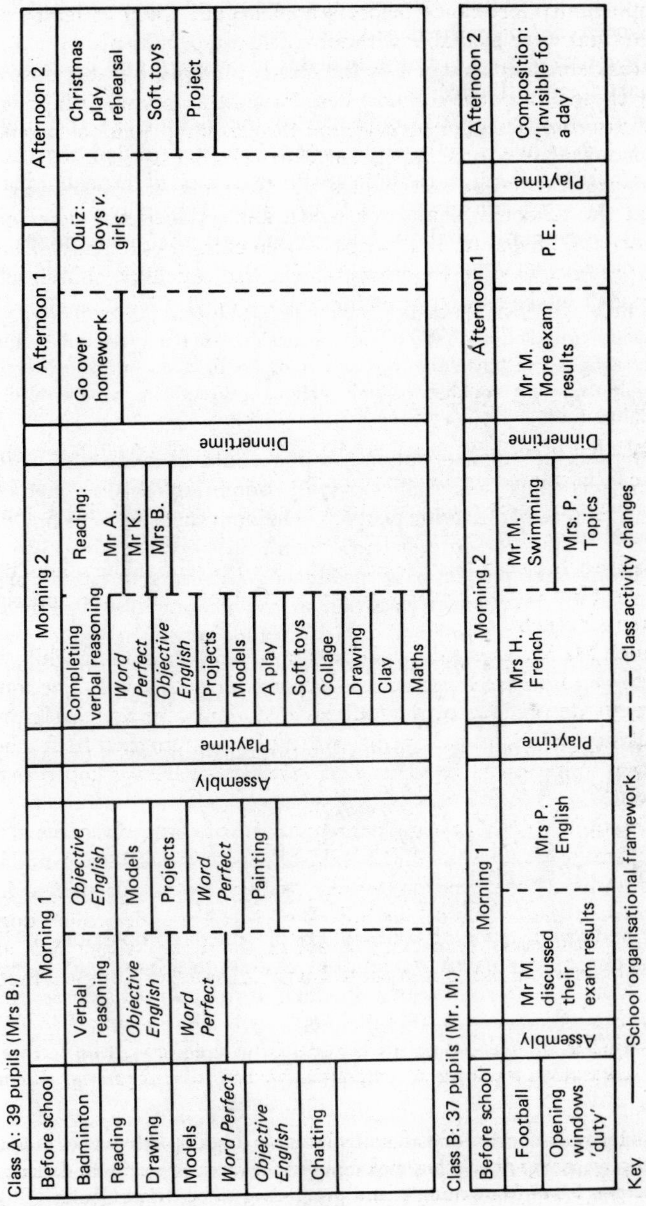

Class A: 39 pupils (Mrs B.)

Before school	Morning 1				Assembly	Playtime	Morning 2			Dinnertime	Afternoon 1		Afternoon 2	
Badminton	Verbal reasoning	*Objective English*					Completing verbal reasoning	Reading: Mr A.			Go over homework	Quiz: boys v. girls	Christmas play rehearsal	
Reading		*Objective English*	Models						Mr K.					
Drawing				Projects			*Word Perfect*		Mrs B.				Soft toys	
Models	*Word Perfect*			*Word Perfect*			*Objective English*						Project	
Word Perfect							Projects							
Objective English				Painting			Models							
Chatting							A play							
							Soft toys							
							Collage							
							Drawing							
							Clay							
							Maths							

Class B: 37 pupils (Mr. M.)

Before school	Assembly	Morning 1		Playtime	Morning 2		Dinnertime	Afternoon 1		Playtime	Afternoon 2
Football		Mr M. discussed their exam results	Mrs P. English		Mrs H. French	Mr M. Swimming		Mr M. More exam results	P.E.		Composition: 'Invisible for a day'
Opening windows 'duty'						Mrs P. Topics					

Key   ——— School organisational framework   ----- Class activity changes

Figure 1   Content and sequence of the school day for class A and class B.

seemed to be a 'filler' while the remainder of the class went swimming. Except for this period the class was taught as a whole throughout the day. There is an obvious emphasis on testing, extrinsic motivation and competition. Class B was delineated type 12 by the cluster analysis.

The content and sequence of the school day in classes A and B is presented in a summary form in Figure 1.

These brief outlines fail to do justice to the richness of the original descriptions. Nevertheless, sufficient has been reported to demonstrate the type of information gained, and to indicate the usefulness of the technique as a complement to other approaches. For example, Hargreaves (1972) has argued that interaction analysis fails to explore the assumptions and perspectives of teachers and pupils.

We discover little of the overall teacher–pupil relationship as it is experienced by the teacher or by individual pupils. Yet it is this relationship which may not only influence the meaning assigned to particular verbal statements or acts, but also exercise a pervasive influence which is not immediately obvious or directly open to measurement by traditional methods.

Content analysis of relevant pupil output could provide this sort of information. According to Kerlinger (1973), content analysis is a method of observation. 'Instead of observing people's behaviour directly, or asking them to respond to scales, or interviewing them, the investigator takes the communications that people have produced, and asks questions of the communicator.' In this instance classroom action has been observed through the eyes of the pupils, a method which would appear to have certain advantages. It can, for example, be considered a low inference procedure: an activity occurs, the children involved report it, the investigator tallies it and incorporates it in the description. Since often some thirty children are describing the same event the resulting description would seem to have high reliability and validity.

Postscript to Plowden

The cluster analysis of teaching styles makes possible a comparison between current practice, and current conceptions of that practice. The Plowden Report described a pattern of teaching which, it maintained, represented a general and quickening trend. (See Bennett, 1976, chapter 1.)

Later writers have attempted to quantify this 'general trend'. Blackie (1967) maintained that a third of primary schools were working along these lines, and Silberman (1970), drawing upon the work of Rogers (1970) felt safe in saying that 25 per cent of English primary schools fitted the Plowden model, and that another third were moving towards it. Simon's study did not substantiate this trend however, and neither do the findings reported here. Only type 1 corresponds closely to the Plowden definition, containing just 9 per cent of the population studied. A separate analysis of third year teachers isolated similar types, and the corresponding group at this level contained only 8 per cent of the population. It could of course be argued that the sample studied is not representative of primary teachers as a whole. This may be true, but the H.M.I. study of teaching practices, contained in the Plowden Report, found little regional variation. These findings together with those provided by Simon indicate that progressive teaching is less prevalent than has hitherto been supposed.

Appendix A

Teacher questionnaire

UNIVERSITY OF LANCASTER

DEPARTMENT OF EDUCATIONAL RESEARCH

SSRC PRIMARY SCHOOL PROJECT

The way in which teachers arrange their classrooms, and methods of teaching adopted, naturally reflect factors such as the conditions under which the school operates, and the characteristics of the pupils. At present all too little is known about the way in which teachers adapt their methods to circumstances, and hence little advice can be passed on to students training to be teachers. In an attempt to obtain information which may be useful in this and other ways, this questionnaire has been devised. It is in three parts, reflecting the attempt to relate circumstances to teaching methods. Thus, part one asks for background information about the teacher, class and school, part two is designed to cover various aspects of classroom and curriculum organisation, and part three asks for teachers' opinions on various educational topics. Additional space is provided at the end of the questionnaire should you wish to elaborate on any of your answers.

For our work to be of any value, we must obtain responses from a wide cross-section of teachers. I hope you will feel that this project is sufficiently worthwhile to merit your support. It generally takes about half an hour to complete the questionnaire, and of course, replies are confidential. It is important in part two that you try to record as objectively as you can what actually happens in your classroom, since student teachers often appear to receive misleading impressions in their training, which later experiences contradict.

Most of the items in this questionnaire ask you to choose one answer from a number of alternatives, by circling the appropriate CODE NUMBER. We realise that this procedure may occasionally involve oversimplification. Other items require a more specific response and you are asked to enter the appropriate figure in the box provided. It is important to answer all questions.

Part 1 Teacher, Class and Classroom		For Computer Use

Personal Details

1. Name   1–5
   Name and address of school ....   Code
   .... Number

2. Sex.	Male	0	6
	Female	1	
3. Age.	Under 30 yrs.	0	
	30–39 yrs.	1	
	40–49 yrs.	2	7
	50–59 yrs.	3	
	Over 60 yrs.	4	

4. Training.
   (i) Higher education spent mainly at University .   0
       College   1   8
   (ii) Qualification   Graduate   0
       Non-graduate   1   9
   (iii) Formal teacher training
       None   0
       Primary oriented   1   10
       Secondary oriented   2

5. Teaching experience (in years)
   Total ....   [ ]   11–12
   In primary schools ....   [ ]   13–14
   In secondary schools ......   [ ]   15–16

Class and Classroom

6. Number of pupils in class.
   Boys ....   [ ]   17–18
   Girls ....   [ ]   19–20
   Total ....   [ ]   21–22

7. Year group you are teaching.
   3rd year Juniors   0
   4th year Juniors.   1
   2nd/3rd year mixed   2   23
   3rd/4th year mixed   3

8. If the pupils are streamed by ability, which stream do you teach?
   No streaming   0
   Stream A   1
   Stream B   2   24

	Code Number	For Computer Use
Stream C	3	
Remedial	4	

9. Approximate area of classroom (in square yards) . . ▢   25–27

10. What type of desk is used in the class?

Single with seat attached . . .	0	
Single with separate seat. . . .	1	
Double with seat attached. . .	2	28
Double with separate seat . . .	3	
Table style seating 3 or more	4	
Other (please specify)	5	
. . . .		

11. Is there a small library or store of books in the classroom?

No	0	
Yes	1	29

12. Are there storage facilities in the class room?

No	0	
Yes	1	30

13. Is the heating adequate in the classroom?

No	0	
Yes	1	31

14. Is the lighting adequate in the classroom?

No	0	
Yes	1	32

15. What is the level of ability of your pupils?

Mostly bright	0	
Bright/Average	1	
Average	2	
Average/dull	3	33
Mostly dull	4	
Full ability range	5	

Part 2 Teaching Methods Adopted	Card II

Seating Arrangements ▢	1–5

1. Do your pupils decide for themselves where they sit in the classroom?

No	0	6
Yes	1	

2. Are the seats usually arranged so that pupils sit

separately or in pairs?	0	
in groups of 3 or more?	1	7

	Code Number	For Computer Use

3. Are pupils allocated to places or groups on the basis of their ability?

	Code Number	For Computer Use
No..........	0	
Yes	1	8

4. Do pupils stay in the same seats or groups for most of the day?

	Code Number	For Computer Use
No..........	0	
Yes	1	9

Classroom Organisation

5. Do you usually allow your pupils to move around the classroom

	Code Number	For Computer Use
generally whenever they wish?	0	
only during certain kinds of curricular activity?........	1	10

6. Do you usually allow your pupils to talk to one another

	Code Number	For Computer Use
usually whenever they wish?	0	
only during certain kinds of curricular activity?........	1	11

7. Do you expect your pupils to ask you permission before leaving the room?

	Code Number	For Computer Use
No..........	0	
Yes	1	12

8. Do you expect your pupils to be quiet most of the time?

	Code Number	For Computer Use
No..........	0	
Yes	1	13

9. Do you appoint monitors with responsibility for certain jobs?

	Code Number	For Computer Use
No..........	0	
Yes	1	14

Organising the Curriculum

10. Do you regularly take pupils out of school as part of your normal teaching activities?

	Code Number	For Computer Use
No..........	0	
Yes	1	15

11. Do you use a timetable for organising the week's work?

	Code Number	For Computer Use
No..........	0	
Yes	1	16

		Code Number	For Computer Use

12. For basic subjects do you more often use
    text books? . . . .　　0
    specially prepared materials? .　　1　　17

13. Do you require that your pupils know their multipli-
    cation tables off by heart?
    No . . . .　　0
    Yes . . . .　　1　　18

14. Teaching sometimes requires reference materials. Do
    you normally
    supply most of this material for
    your pupils? . . . .　　0
    ask the pupils to find their
    own? . . . .　　1　　19

15. Do you regularly give your pupils homework?
    No . . . .　　0
    Yes . . . .　　1　　20

16. In organising the work of your class, roughly what
    emphasis do you give to each of these five different
    approaches? Indicate approximately what percen-
    tage of time is spent on each approach. Your total
    should come to 100 %, although this is not intended to
    imply that all the work necessarily fits into these five
    categories.　　　　　　　　　　　　Percent

    1. Teacher talking to the class as a whole. . . . . . .　21
    2. Pupils working together co-operatively in groups,
       on work given by the teacher . . . .　22
    3. Pupils working together co-operatively in groups,
       on work of their own choice. . . . .　23
    4. Pupils working individually, at their own pace, on
       work given by the teacher. . . . .　24
    5. Pupils working individually at their own pace, on
       work of their own choice . . . .　25

    　　　　　　　　　　　　　　　Total　100%　26–28

17. On which aspect of number work do you place *more*
    emphasis?
    (i) Developing computational skills through graded
       exercises? . . . .　0
    (ii) Exploring concepts with materials or apparatus?　1　29

18. Do you encourage fluency and originality in written
    English, even if for many children this may be at the
    expense of grammatical accuracy?
    No . . . .　0
    Yes . . . .　1　30

	Code Number	For Computer Use

Testing and Marking

19. Do you put an actual mark or grade on pupils' work?

No....................	0	
Yes	1	31

20. Do you correct most spelling and grammatical errors?

No....................	0	
Yes	1	32

21. Are stars, or their equivalent given to pupils who produce the best work?

No....................	0	
Yes	1	33

22. Do you give your pupils an arithmetic (mental or written) test at least once a week?

No....................	0	
Yes	1	34

23. Do you give your pupils a spelling test at least once a week?

No....................	0	
Yes	1	35

24. Do you have 'end of term' tests?

No....................	0	
Yes	1	36

Discipline

25. Do you have many pupils who create discipline problems?

No....................	0	
Yes	1	37

26. Do you find verbal reproof and/or reasoning normally sufficient?

No....................	0	
Yes	1	38

27. For persistent disruptive behaviour, where verbal reproof fails to gain the pupils' co-operation, do you use any of the following disciplinary measures?

(i) extra work	No....................	0	
	Yes	1	39
(ii) smack	No....................	0	
	Yes	1	40
(iii) withdrawal of privileges			
	No....................	0	
	Yes	1	41

	Code Number	For Computer Use

(iv) send to head teacher

        No.................. 0

        Yes 1   42

(v) sent out of room

        No.................. 0

        Yes 1   43

Allocation of Teaching Time

28. When time has been deducted for registration and assembly, the number of hours per week left for teachers is 25. Estimate as accurately as possible how this is distributed among subjects and activities in the table below, by putting the appropriate number of hours in the boxes provided. Please use last week as your reference unless this was in some way unusual. (for example, Open day)

	Number of Hours	For Computer Use
Number work		
English (including creative writing) ...		
Reading		44
History.......................		
Geography		
French		
Science (including nature study)		
Scripture		
P.E........................		
Music		
Art and Craft		45
Music and Movement		
Drama		
Environmental Studies		
Social Studies		
Project work		
Free choice activity		
Integrated studies		
Total 25 (approx.)		46

	Code Number	For Computer Use

Card III

In this section we ask you to give your opinions about a number of educational topics. We are anxious to record the frank opinions of professional teachers and there is no suggestion that there are right or wrong answers. It is important to answer every question. If you would like to elaborate on any item please make use of the space provided at the end of the questionnaire.

1–5

Teaching Aims

The following are probably all worthwhile teaching aims, but their relative importance may be influenced by the situation in which the teacher works. Please rate each aim on the five-point scale to indicate its importance in relation to your class, by circling the appropriate code number.

	Not important	Fairly important	Important	Very important	Essential	
A. Preparation for academic work in secondary school	1	2	3	4	5	6
B. An understanding of the world in which pupils live	1	2	3	4	5	7
C. The acquisition of basic skills in reading and number work ...	1	2	3	4	5	8
D. The development of pupils' creative abilities............	1	2	3	4	5	9
E. The encouragement of self-expression.................	1	2	3	4	5	10
F. Helping pupils to co-operate with each other	1	2	3	4	5	11
G. The acceptance of normal standards of behaviour..........	1	2	3	4	5	12
H. The enjoyment of school	1	2	3	4	5	13
I. The promotion of a high level of academic attainment	1	2	3	4	5	14

Opinions about Education Issues

Please indicate the strength of your agreement or disagreement with the following statements by circling the appropriate code.

	Strongly disagree	Disagree	No opinion	Agree	Strongly agree	Code Number For Computer Use
A. Most pupils in upper junior school have sufficient maturity to choose a topic to study, and carry it through	1	2	3	4	5	15
B. Most pupils in upper junior school feel more secure if told what to do and how to do it . .	1	2	3	4	5	16
C. 'Creativity' is an educational fad, which could soon die out .	1	2	3	4	5	17
D. Firm discipline by the teacher leads to good self-discipline on the part of the pupils	1	2	3	4	5	18
E. Streaming by ability is undesirable in junior school	1	2	3	4	5	19
F. The teacher should be well liked by the class	1	2	3	4	5	20
G. Children working in groups waste a lot of time arguing and 'messing about'	1	2	3	4	5	21
H. Pupils work better when motivated by marks or stars	1	2	3	4	5	22
I. Too little emphasis is placed on keeping order in the classroom nowadays	1	2	3	4	5	23
J. Teachers need to know the home background and personal circumstances of their pupils . .	1	2	3	4	5	24

Opinions about Teaching Methods

To what extent would you agree or disagree with the following statements when they are applied to (a) FORMAL teaching methods, and (b) INFORMAL teaching methods?

	a) FORMAL METHODS					b) INFORMAL METHODS					
	Strongly disagree	Disagree	No opinion	Agree	Strongly agree	Strongly disagree	Disagree	No opinion	Agree	Strongly agree	
(i) Could create discipline problems	1	2	3	4	5	1	2	3	4	5	25–26
(ii) Fail to bring the best out of bright pupils	1	2	3	4	5	1	2	3	4	5	27–28
(iii) Make heavy demands on the teacher	1	2	3	4	5	1	2	3	4	5	29–30
(iv) Encourage responsibility and self-discipline	1	2	3	4	5	1	2	3	4	5	31–32
(v) Teach basic skills and concepts effectively ...	1	2	3	4	5	1	2	3	4	5	33–34
(vi) Encourage time wasting or day-dreaming	1	2	3	4	5	1	2	3	4	5	35–36
(vii) Leave many pupils unsure of what to do ..	1	2	3	4	5	1	2	3	4	5	37–38
(viii) Provide the right balance between teaching and individual work ..	1	2	3	4	5	1	2	3	4	5	39–40
(ix) Allow each child to develop his full potential .	1	2	3	4	5	1	2	3	4	5	41–42
(x) Teach pupils to think for themselves	1	2	3	4	5	1	2	3	4	5	43–44

THANK YOU FOR COMPLETING THIS QUESTIONNAIRE

If you would like to make additional comments, or elaborate on answers to our questions, or to suggest aspects of the classroom we have overlooked, please make use of the space below. We should be grateful for your comments.

References

ADAMS, R. S. (1970) 'Perceived teaching styles.' *Comparative Education Review*, February 1970, pp. 50–9.

AUSUBEL, D. P. (1963) *The Psychology of Meaningful Verbal Learning*. New York: Grune and Stratton.

BARTH, R. S. (1972) *Open Education and the American School*. New York: Agathon Press.

BENNETT, S. N. (1975) 'Cluster analysis in educational research.' *Research Intelligence*, I, pp. 64–70.

BENNETT, (S.) N. (1976) *Teaching Styles and Pupil Progress*. London: Open Books.

BENNETT, S. N. and JORDAN, J. (1975) 'A typology of teaching styles in primary schools.' *British Journal of Educational Psychology*, 45, pp. 20–8.

BLACKIE, J. (1967) *Inside the Primary School*. London: H.M.S.O.

BRUNER, J. S. (1961) 'The act of discovery.' *Harvard Educational Review*, 31, pp. 21–32.

BUSSIS, A. M. and CHITTENDEN, E. A. (1970) 'Analysis of an approach to open education.' Report to Princeton N. J. Education Testing Service.

DUTHIE, J. H. (1970) *Primary School Survey*. Edinburgh: H.M.S.O.

HADOW REPORT (1931) *Report of the Consultative Committee on the Primary School*. London: H.M.S.O.

HARGREAVES, D. (1972) *Interpersonal Relations and Education*. London: Routledge and Kegan Paul.

KERLINGER, F. N. (1973) *Foundations of Behavioral Research*. New York: Holt, Rinehart and Winston.

MCQUITTY, L. L. (1967) 'A mutual development of some typological theories and pattern analysis methods.' *Educational and Psychological Measurement*, 26, pp. 253–65.

PLOWDEN REPORT (1967) *Children and their Primary Schools*. Report of the Central Advisory Council for Education (England). London: H.M.S.O.

RATHBONE, C. H. (1971) *Open Education – The Informal Classroom*. New York: Citation Press.

ROGERS, V. R. (1970) *Teaching in the British Primary Schools*. New York: Macmillan.

SHERMAN, V. S. (1970) *Two Contrasting Educational Models: Applications and policy implications*. Menlo Park, Calif.: Stanford Research Institute.

SILBERMAN, C. E. (1970) *Crisis in the Classroom*. New York: Random House.

SIMON, B. (1972) 'The nature of classroom learning in primary schools.' S.S.R.C. Report HR 291.

WALBERG, H. J. and THOMAS, S. C. (1971) 'Characteristics of open education: towards an operational definition.' Report to U.S. Office of Education No. OEC–1–7–062805–3936.

2.4 The types of behavioural objectives

Hilda Taba

An organized statement of objectives should be more than a mere grouping of individual objectives. It should also convey the fundamental rationale on which the very conception of objectives is based. This rationale should indicate what is important in education and where the subsidiary values lie. Such a statement should be useful in establishing priorities in the grand design of the curriculum, as well as in the smaller decisions such as those about sampling content for a particular unit or whether to spend time on analyzing historic documents. It should yield some criteria for the scope of the educational effort and set some limits for the specificity or depth desired. In this sense an organized statement of objectives expresses the philosophy of education of a particular school system or of a particular school.

The two-dimensional model of stating and classifying objectives by a description of behaviour and of the content to which this behaviour applies illustrates both the advantage of greater clarity and the difficulty of living up to it. It conveys the idea that the fundamental point in education is to change behaviour. It also creates some difficulty in producing a clear-cut classification. Either one or the other could be used as a basis for classification. If the types of behaviour are used for a basis, the kinds of content to which the behaviour is addressed is bound to be less clearly represented and less systematically sampled. If the content of behaviour is used for a basis, the types of behaviour involved tend to be obscured, as do the areas of life to which these behaviours are related. Recently, however, classification by types of behaviour has been favoured because it seems more functional as a basis for curriculum development and for evaluation than classification by content.

Knowledge: facts, ideas and concepts

In the simplest behavioural definition this area of objectives is that of remembering, of recalling facts, ideas, or phenomena in the form in which they were experienced or learned. The broader definition involves the idea of 'understanding' or 'insight', implying that knowledge which cannot be reorganized and used in new situations, which does not also involve seeing relationships and making judgments, is of little value. There is therefore some obscurity as to where possession of knowledge leaves off and the behaviour called thinking starts.

On the surface, the objective of acquiring knowledge should require no discussion. Acquisition of knowledge is the dominant objective today as it has been for centuries. For many educators the change in the amount and the

Source: TABA, H. (1962) *Curriculum Development: Theory and Practice*. New York: Harcourt Brace and World, pp. 211–31.

kind of knowledge is the primary or even the sole objective of education. Even the so-called progressives, who revolted against the tyranny of packaged knowledge, wanted more, not less, knowledge.

It is assumed that knowledge of any sort is an index of one's acquaintance with reality. As an individual increases his knowledge he also increases his understanding of the world around him. Knowledge is also regarded as a prerequisite to the development of intellectual powers. Often the maturity and the intelligence of an individual is judged by the amount of knowledge he possesses. In addition, teachers often prize information for its own sake simply because it is more easily taught and learned than any other educational outcome. For these reasons such objectives as 'factual information about currents events', 'knowledge of the physical and chemical properties of common elements and compounds', or 'familiarity with important historic events' figure heavily among the statements of objectives. There is some emphasis on knowledge of the ways and means by which to deal with specific facts, such as 'knowledge of the standard representational devices used in maps and charts', and knowledge of the various classifications and categories, such as 'familiarity with the types of literature', or 'the ways of classifying plants and animals'.

Because knowledge is vast and of different levels of relevance, one problem in organizing an adequate statement of the objectives of knowledge is to achieve both a proper scope and a proper differentiation of priorities of significance. The levels of knowledge . . . differentiating the specific facts, basic ideas, concepts, and thought systems (Taba, 1962b, chapter 12) in effect represent such a sequence of priorities among the objectives of knowledge.

Specific facts have only a temporary utility as means of acquiring ideas. Therefore, their acquisition and retention probably should have the lowest priority. Factual information is too vast, is increasing at too great a rate, is too much subject to obsolescence, and is too difficult to retain even if it were useful. Research has shown that about 80% of disconnected facts are forgotten in two years or so. Thus, to learn isolated facts is inefficient, even if their possession were important. A careful differentiation is needed between those facts which are important *per se* and those which are used as instruments for attaining some other objectives, and hence need not be regarded as a permanent equipment to be retained and recollected over a long period of time.

Much of the curriculum today operates on an assumption almost the reverse of the above. It stresses largely knowledge of the first level, the accumulation of specific, often isolated facts. Proceeding on the assumption that one has to have facts before one can generalize or think, the educators have also fallen into the trap of assuming that a great deal of knowledge needs to be piled up before thinking can begin. No doubt a defective concept of how intelligence develops and functions has contributed to the prevalence of this assumption (ibid., chapter 8, pp. 100–5, 107–12).

Undifferentiated concentration on specific facts has created several phantoms that have tended to reduce the level of productive learning. One is the phantom of 'covering the ground'. When mastering facts alone is the measure of knowledge, 'coverage' can become onerous, absorbing so much time that there is little room to learn anything else. The other phantom is that young people cannot deal adequately with complex concepts, that they lack the intellectual resources for handling abstract thought processes. This phantom has reduced the level at which the higher mental processes are challenged. There is a measure of truth in the assumption that when neither the organization of the curriculum nor the methods of teaching supports an organized development of concepts and abstractions, only a few bright souls catch on. Evidence is accumulating, however, that abstract concepts can be developed much earlier and at a higher level, provided that the curriculum is organized to focus on ideas and that teaching is guided by adequate knowledge of how concepts are learned (ibid., chapter 8, pp. 118–20). The explorations of the author in curriculum development have indicated, for example, that third graders can learn concepts such as those of comparative culture and comparative geography, provided the curriculum and teaching are organized to this end. (Contra Costa County Schools, 1959. See also Taba, 1962b, chapter 20 on developing a unit.)

The second level of knowledge, the knowledge of principles and basic ideas, is represented in objectives such as 'understanding the principle of gravitation or the biological laws of heredity and reproduction', the basic ideas of the 'ways in which cultures differ and are similar to each other', or the generalizations about 'the effect of frontier in shaping the way of life in the United States'. These basic ideas naturally vary tremendously in their degree of abstractness and complexity. They range from a simple idea, such as that 'community services change to meet community needs', which is appropriate for the second-grade study of community workers, to ideas that describe the control of the economy by the government or the nature and the behaviour of the atom.

Knowledge on this second level is more useful than that on the first, mainly because it is more general and therefore more widely applicable. This type of knowledge is also productive in a sense that it can create new knowledge. General ideas are transferable: they can be applied to understanding things and events not learned directly. For example, the idea developed in connection with the study of one desert that deserts form a belt around the earth and that they occur only in certain latitudes under certain climatic and topographical conditions, provides a more transferable knowledge than would all the available details about all deserts.

Basic ideas are the fundamentals of content. But even here a choice is indicated, because the number of basic ideas that can be mastered is also limited. A variety of criteria can be used to select the basic ideas: they must have scientific validity; they must be learnable at the age level at which they are offered; they must have utility in our current culture. Historically, each of these criteria has been stressed separately and in turn. Our earlier curriculum committees, largely composed of specialists who had more insight into the requirements of becoming a specialist than into processes of learning or cultural needs, were most concerned with scientific validity of the content and produced a curriculum centred on concepts with a highly academic orientation. An increasing awareness of the difference in the knowledge required for the general education of youth from that required to become a specialist and an emphasis on producing alert and intelligent citizens led to applying the test of utility and learnability to the ideas to be included in the curriculum. This emphasis produced a curriculum strong in 'learnability' but weak in scientific validity. It is possible that the current method of cooperative curriculum projects, in which curriculum workers and teachers work with content specialists, might prevent this one-sidedness and produce curricula which have a valid content but are also oriented to produce intelligent laymen, and have content which is learnable and has social importance in the culture of today.

The third level of knowledge – the concepts which relate bodies of generalizations and principles – is represented by objectives such as the understanding of the concepts of evolution, of number, of measurement, or of personality. This type of knowledge is seldom acquired in a brief treatment; it is usually a product of many experiences over a long period of time and in many different contexts. This is especially true of concepts such as justice, which have no concrete sense referents and denote abstract qualities of behaviour. These last two categories of knowledge involve more than memorization and recollection; such knowledge must be developed by abstracting from many experiences of differentiating and synthesizing.

The problem of how to master facts, ideas, and concepts has been debated for a long time in education. The earliest model for learning concepts was derived from learning arbitrary facts which had no special logic. As Brownell and Hendrickson show, there is no special logic in calling a certain river 'Euphrates'. Learning such facts is a matter of arbitrary association (1950, p. 95). A different problem altogether is involved in acquiring abstract ideas and concepts, for they must be invested with meaning by the learner if they are understood at all. Learning them involves what Dewey called transactional experience (1933), and what more recently has been called the discovery method (Bruner, 1961; Taba, 1962a). Both these terms imply active learning. They also involve the question of whether learning concepts and ideas is purely verbal or whether there is such a thing as intuitive perception of the relationships which constitute the concept or the principle (Ausubel, 1961; Hendrix, 1961). A recent study is postulating further that discovery of concepts and general principles comes through using the inquiry method (Suchman, July 1961).

Precision stands out as one criterion for such knowledge, especially with reference to scientific knowledge. A vague concept of 'vacuum' (e.g. as identified with emptiness or suction) makes the concept useless for either prediction or explanation. Perhaps for concepts which have no concrete referents, such as justice or democracy, operational differentiation of their meaning in various contexts takes the place of the kind of precision that these concepts cannot achieve by verbal definition.

Reflective thinking

One scarcely needs to emphasize the importance of critical thinking as a desirable ingredient in human beings in a democratic society. No matter what views people hold of the chief function of education, they at least agree that people need to learn to think. In a society in which changes come fast, individuals cannot depend on routinized behaviour or tradition in making decisions, whether on practical everyday or professional matters, moral values, or political issues. In such a society there is a natural concern that individuals be capable of intelligent and independent thought.

But this concern does not ensure that the meaning of critical thinking is clearly understood or that there is an adequate analysis of the behaviours that compose it. The status of this objective is similar to that of other 'intangible' objectives: the behaviour called thinking has many meanings and is called by many names. All intellectual skills and abilities from concept formation to problem solving are likely to be identified with thinking.

The psychologists are even debating about the distinctions between thinking and concept formation. The term 'understanding' is often used to encompass processes of investing verbal symbols with meaning and of making inferences. A fairly recent yearbook on measurement of understanding found it difficult to define understanding. It seemed easier to say what it was *not* than to describe what it was (National Society for the Study of Education, 1946, p. 2). It is no surprise, then, to find that the development of thinking is an objective to which we pay lip service, but which we do not practise.

Critical thinking involves many different processes, each of which must be distinguished fairly clearly if this objective is to serve as a guide either to curriculum development or evaluation.

Interpretation of data

One cluster of behaviours is related to the ability to interpret data of various sorts and to generalize from them: to distil meaning from a literary passage, to 'read' a cartoon, a statistical table, or a series of mathematical formulas. Essentially the process of interpretation involves singling out important facts or ideas from a context, relating them to each other, and deriving generalizations from them.

Specifically, interpretation may consist of a simple reading of points or of trends, of comparing these points or trends, and of inferring causes or consequences. Evaluating the dependability of data and recognizing their limits is involved also. These processes naturally include the ability to read the meaning of symbols of all sorts and the capacity to analyze or to break down complex sets of data into their components. Logically this process is described as inductive thinking.[1]

The operations necessary to make legitimate and valid interpretations also differ according to the character of the data, such as whether their content is scientific or literary, quantitative or verbal, highly abstract or concrete. For example, in interpreting quantitative graphic data about the relationship of the changes in the price of cars to the wages paid to automobile workers over a period of years, precision and accuracy are important and the generalizations that can be drawn are limited to what is given in the data. The interpreter must refrain from extrapolating possible causes of these changes, their effects or purposes, unless data on these are included. Different processes and criteria are involved in reading a pamphlet about problems of delinquency, studying the statistics on slum conditions, or reading a play like *Dead End,* even though each deals with the same subject. To learn what these materials have to offer, a student should be able to ferret out the relevant facts and ideas in each and draw appropriate inferences by using appropriate processes. But ferreting pertinent facts from statistics on slum conditions involves a more exacting process than does reading a pamphlet on delinquency. The play offers less precise data on delinquency but more adequate information on the psychological dynamics of becoming or being one. The interpretation of a play, therefore, has more latitude; while 'going beyond the data' is a fault in reading a chart, 'reading between the lines' is a necessity in interpreting a play (Taba, 1940).

Application of facts and principles

Applying facts and principles to the solution of new problems and to the prediction and explanation of new phenomena is another aspect of thinking. To predict the consequences of an increased sales tax on cigarettes, one may apply what is known about the effect of the sales tax on various groups in society and the general principles of taxation, including the principles of democracy. When a car is skidding toward a ditch on a wet pavement, the principles of friction could be applied to predict what the driver needs to do to bring it out of the skid.

This process involves first a sufficient grasp of the principle. It involves discrimination of the principles that have relevance to the particular problem from those that do not. It involves also a sufficient understanding of the new problem or phenomenon to see the relationship between it and what one knows. And it always involves restructuring and reorganization of knowledge to make it appropriate to new problems and situations.

As in interpreting, the process of applying principles involves using criteria to determine the quality of the process and of the product. The process of application may be limited or productive, may involve precise reasoning or reasoning by analogy, or even misconceptions. The inferences may represent convergent thinking in the sense of being limited to the most obvious and immediate or be divergent in the sense of introducing innovation and subtlety (E. R. Smith and Tyler, 1942, pp. 77–84; Bloom, 1954, pp. 110–15).

As in interpreting data, the processes used in application vary depending on the content with which one deals. Generalizations, principles, and facts, for example, vary in the degree of universality which can be assumed. Some generalizations or principles, especially those of the physical sciences, are relatively universal and dependable. For example, the law of gravity is universal and dependable: a stone will fall in the U.S. *and* in Russia. Other generalizations are both less dependable and less universal, such as generalizations regarding causes of revolutions. (At different times and in different places different circumstances lead to revolutions.) Many social-science generalizations lack universality and dependability: some are little more than hypotheses, others involve value judgments and beliefs. These types of generalizations must be applied and used in a different manner from those of physical science, and their application needs to be surrounded with different sets of qualifying conditions.

Most social and human phenomena are also subject to multiple causation. One can assume no one-to-one connections between *a* principle and *a* solution, *a* prediction or *an* explanation. Usually a constellation of qualifying facts and generalizations must be considered, and the conclusions are at best much more tentative than is the case with applying the principles of science.

Value judgments and feelings also enter in interpretations. Thus in explaining why delinquency exists or predicting how it will change if certain measures are employed, it is necessary to consider not only the ways in which human behaviour is caused but also what one believes about equality, justice, and other democratic values and how one feels about the worth of all human beings, about deviate behaviour, or about adolescents. These feelings may interfere with the clarity of thinking; they may block rational thought processes, and touch off subjectivity, irrationality, bias, and wishful thinking. We know, for example, that correct facts and valid principles about such matters as the role of racial minorities in American society, even if known, are either distorted or not applied because they contradict feelings or emotional dispositions. Some recent research has demonstrated that emotionalized and autistic thinking prevails over rational processes in many 'closed' areas, among which are the problems of minority groups and race relations (Adorno *et al.*, 1950, pp. 145–50).

Because of these difficulties, learning to apply principles of science or some other 'neutral' material is no assurance that the same processes will be used in fields that present various obstacles to clear thinking. Learning to reason logically about abstract and emotionally neutral problems is no guarantee of logical reasoning on more complex issues or on issues which involve feelings and values (Taba, April 1944, p. 394).

The fact that the effectiveness of school learning depends on the extent to which students can apply to new situations what they have learned makes the transfer of learning an extremely important objective. And the greater the leap of transfer, the more profitable the learning. Yet, . . . this ability is by and large not well provided for in our curriculum (Taba, 1962b, chapter 8, p. 115). Students in high schools and colleges are not especially adept either at analyzing and attacking problems or in using what they know to solve them.

Logical reasoning

The ability to reason logically and critically and to analyze ideas for the same qualities is another aspect of thinking. Conflicting statements on the same issue may appear in different sources. Many conclusions are based on a mistaken or hidden assumption. Convincing arguments are supported insufficiently or with unacceptable evidence. Advertising and propaganda often try to impress us with the desirability of buying a certain soap to make us beautiful or of supporting a political platform which guarantees the best government by using distorted logic and emotional appeal.

Since all such reasoning is carried on with reference to assumptions, defensible or not, hidden or open, the ability to detect faulty assumptions and to formulate adequate ones is important. The individual in modern society needs to judge assumptions and to weigh evidence discriminatingly if he is not to be at the mercy of salesmanship of all sorts. He needs to judge where facts end and opinions begin and to recognize conclusions based on faulty assumptions of faulty logic. For example, when reading a plea for economy in government or hearing a discussion of the causes of war, students should be able to ask themselves what the author takes for granted, whether he has considered all the important factors, and how relevant his facts and arguments are to his conclusions. In many contexts, such as reading novels, it is especially important to examine intelligently the assumptions being made about human motivation.

It is also necessary to recognize fallacious devices, such as attacking a person to discredit an idea, deliberate shifting of definition, or the use of emotionally charged words. In many cases the use of the principles of logical inference, such as the 'if-then' principle, is a necessary part of criticizing arguments. Or one may need to be aware of the crucial words and phrases and their definitions and to recognize that changed definitions may produce changed conclusions.

The ability to judge critically other people's arguments does not automatically improve one's own logic, and awareness of the specious qualities in other people's reasoning does not assure avoidance of the same qualities in one's own reasoning. Sound argumentation involves the capacity to follow a logical chain of reasoning from assumptions or premises to conclusions, and to construct a logical structure of argument, and not, as Salinger points out, 'trying to make a very convenient generalization stay still and docile long enough to support a wild, specific premise' (1959, p. 65). (For further descriptions of these aspects of thinking, see Taba, 1950; E. R. Smith and Tyler, 1942, chapters 2 and 3.)

It is clear that thinking is not a simple thing to be learned in a few easy lessons, in a single subject, or in one unit. Its development requires continued practice in many different contexts. While it is possible that certain subjects provide special opportunities for special forms of thinking, such as pursuing proof in geometry, an effective skill develops only by practising thinking in a variety of contexts.

Furthermore, thinking is something that can be learned only by doing. Whichever of its elements one considers – deciding what is important to think about, analyzing facts, generalizing, pursuing the steps of logical inference, or comparing and contrasting different sets of facts – all require consistent practice for mastery.

Neither can the ability to think critically be taught all at once, no matter how thorough the emphasis. Serious provisions for thinking require some continuity. A course in logic, which has been proposed as a means for lifting the level of thinking, will not solve the problem. Thinking as a behaviour has a developmental sequence, and therefore a developmental plan is needed to learn it effectively. Unfortunately, . . . too little is yet known about the nature of the developmental sequence in thinking: which skills and processes can be mastered at which age level, which aspects must precede which others, what type of generalizations and what level of abstraction young children can master in contrast to high school students.

There are several ways to strengthen the implementation of this objective. One is the more careful planning of sequences in the development of thought, such as providing for accumulative sequence in the development of abstract ideas, in the rigour used in applying generalizations, or in the development of the facility to follow a logical sequence of thought. A sequential development is possible only if there is a clear enough understanding of both the specific behaviours that compose thinking and of the necessary steps in their development. In such a sequence concrete experiences with pertinent examples must precede the development of perception of abstractions. To become capable of being logical or insightful about the 'democratic freedoms' requires a preceding exploration of both democracy and freedom in a concrete context which is sufficient to give meaning to these abstractions.

Second, the organization of curriculum might take greater account of the fact that the basic process of thinking is the common factor among the various subjects. A form of integration in pooling forces for this development is therefore possible, no matter how diverse the content of these subjects. Discriminating thinking, like discriminating taste, is best developed by comparison. If thinking were stressed in the various subjects and the differences in the processes of interpretation and application according to context were made conscious, comparative training in thinking would become a matter of course. Students would experience variations in the rigour and the precision of thinking and would learn discrimination in the use of data, generalizations, and principles according to the degrees of their universality. A comparison of the process of proof in geometry and in an article on politics would add greatly to the understanding of what logical proof is all about.

Third, it is quite evident that the usual separation of curriculum planning from the planning of teaching strategies adds up to insufficient provision for the development of thinking. Effective and consistent training is possible only if the whole gamut of decisions, ranging from the selection and organization of content to the choice of materials and the method of asking questions or of making examinations, are focused continuously on this objective. Too often the organization of content constitutes a veritable 'obstacle course' to thinking at all, let alone to thinking critically, so that unusual methods, such as special training in inquiry or courses in logic, must be resorted to in order to encourage thinking. Or again, when the treatment of content is persistently addressed to seeking *the* right answer, or *the* only cause, special occasions must be created for creative and divergent thinking.

Values and attitudes

This is an area of objectives of the greatest concern to those who are oriented to social analysis and the study of cultural needs of today. . . . The mainsprings of culture and of human motivation and action lie in the realm of values and feelings (Taba, 1962b, chapters 3 and 4). There seems to be consensus that the technological culture of the twentieth century is increasingly in danger of submerging its social and human values to things and techniques, whether in nuclear weapons, skyscrapers, or urban renewal, and that education could or should be a countervailing force to this danger.

Many who judge the problem of values to be the most compelling find it at the same time the most perplexing one. There are criticisms to the effect that the school curriculum stresses fact finding to the exclusion of the study and the development of values, that this emphasis has produced a dangerous pseudo-neutrality toward moral issues, and that in many areas, such as morality, religion, minority relations, nationalism and patriotism, decisions are governed by blind emotional reactions, prejudices, and taboos (ibid., chapter 3, pp. 35–9; chapter 4, pp. 57–64).

The statements of objectives in this area do not reflect this urgency. There is perhaps even less clarity in the area of values and attitudes than in the area of thinking, and this lack of clarity extends to all important aspects of formulating objectives: the identification of important values, attitudes, and areas of sensitivity, the differentiation among various types of values and attitudes, and the analysis of specific behaviours which would be part of 'valuing' or 'having an attitude'.

The consequences of this confusion and vagueness of definition were well illustrated in the attempts a few years ago to develop a sharper emphasis on moral and spiritual values. Most symposia and conferences held on the subject and the pamphlets that followed ended in relegating this task either to religious education or to education for democracy, because, defined vaguely, these values seemed to have something to do with either religion or democracy. It seemed impossible to secure a fresh analysis of what was meant by moral and spiritual values and to specify the behaviour involved. This lack of clear specification characterizes statements of objectives pertaining to values and attitudes in other areas also. Statements regarding respect for the individual, the democratic way of life, and responsible citizenship abound among curricular objectives, but behavioural analysis of these objectives is hard to come by.

A great deal more analysis is needed to produce more functional objectives in this area. It may be important to distinguish the different kinds of values in order to gain clarity about how values can be acquired. Getzels, for example, distinguishes two different kinds: those representing the democratic creed in American society, which he calls the 'sacred values', and those he calls the 'secular values', which guide daily conduct in our culture and which shape the American character (1958, p. 149). Among the 'sacred values' are the traditional democratic tenets, the values which everyone cherishes and presumably wants his children to cherish. These include faith in democracy, the idea that the welfare of the many is more important than the welfare of the few, that those who are affected by consequences of decisions need to be involved in making them, and that the people are the best judges of their needs. They involve also the tenets on freedoms, such as the freedom to hold a wrong opinion, to speak out, to assemble, and to organize.

Another facet of the democratic creed is that the individual is a source of initiative and responsibility and has a right to self-development. The political and economic implications of individualism involve the right to free enterprise, to government by the citizenry, and such privileges as living one's own life in one's own way and choosing one's own religion.

From the principle of individualism flows the principle that all individuals, whatever their personal capacities, must have equal opportunity to develop themselves and equal rights before law and justice. Part and parcel of the democratic creed is the belief in human perfectibility, an optimism about improving people as well as the human condition.

[Among] the secular values . . . dealing with character development in American society (Taba, 1962b, chapter 4) are the values referred to as the work success ethic: acceptance of the value of competitive achievement, the ideal of individual success, and respect for the value of work and work responsibility. Still other 'secular' values flow from the democratic ideals and the Christian ethic: tolerance, cooperation, regard for the welfare of others, and respect for individuals. From the basic orientation toward the future – another characteristic of the American character – emerge such values and attitudes as the importance of planning for the future, of sacrificing current needs for future ones, of thrift, and of using time economically and wisely.

The conflicts inherent in these values are also reflected in the objectives dealing with values and attitudes. There is, for example, a cleavage between the objectives which stress independence and individuality and those which emphasize the importance of obedience to rules, getting along with others, and adjustment (according to certain interpretations of it). This cleavage of values produces a certain hesitancy in specifying the content of these objectives and also, therefore, a difficulty in analyzing clearly the behaviour involved. As a consequence, there is little to guide a teacher or a curriculum maker in deciding exactly what behaviours to seek or how these behaviours could be learned. It is no wonder, then, that the statements of objectives of social values largely cling to generalized clichés about democracy and the worth of the individual personality. Only in the area of personal living can one find more concrete statements of values and attitudes to be achieved, such as willingness to undertake and to carry through a job to a completion (responsibility), and willingness to help others and to work with others for desirable group goals.

These difficulties naturally affect the quality of the curriculum and teaching. The teaching of values is largely of three types: teaching about them, moralizing, and hoping that they will emerge as a by-product of other things in the program. It is no wonder, then, that school programs have less of an effect on the development of values than might be expected, and offer meagre experiences for the internalization of important values.

Sensitivities and feelings

Sensitivity is the term used by those who are concerned with the experiencing of feelings and values instead of descriptive learning about them. Sensitivity can be defined as a capacity to respond to the social and cultural environment and as a personal and unique quality in perception, meaning, and response. Involved in this capacity is the empathic ability, or the capacity to 'take the role of the other', and to respond empathically to social and human situations (Cottrell, 1950, pp. 706–8).

In some programs concerned with human and intergroup relations the development of a cosmopolitan social sensitivity, the capacity to respond empathically across the barriers of cultural differences, has been regarded as a cornerstone for democratic human relations. The rationale for this emphasis is based upon the analysis of social needs in today's world. . . . Living in today's world demands an understanding and acceptance of a vast scope of cultural and human differences (Taba, 1962b, chapter 3). We are required to meet and to understand ways of life, attitudes, values, and feelings of a diversity of people undreamed of in earlier days. We cannot afford not to learn to 'see' other people as they see themselves and to communicate across the personal as well as cultural barriers. The normal socializing process does not prepare individuals for this demand, because in any society the process of socialization tends to be parochial. . . . An individual is socialized in a sense in a cultural shell (ibid., chapter 4): in a family with a particular style of life, according to its social status, religious orientation, and cultural or national background. This 'cultural location' circumscribes the values and standards which are internalized and become the criteria for conduct and expectation. Eventually these standards and valuations are universalized and applied as criteria in judging all behaviour. Socialization also trains the individuals to accent certain behaviours and to reject others as unfitting. The more successful this unconscious socialization is, the greater the danger of prejudice, of rejection of differences in values and behaviour and of ethnocentricity in feelings, valuations, and standards. This unconscious socialization seldom prepares an individual for either a sympathetic under-standing of differing values and feelings or objectivity in assessing their role in his own conduct or in that of the others.

Attempts to analyze social sensitivity as an objective in education and to measure growth toward it began as early as 1935. Early definition was largely concerned with the cognitive aspects of sensitivity and included such behaviours as 'concern about social problems, events and issues', the capacity to evaluate problems and action in terms of values, consequences and purposes, and loyalty to democratic values and principles as a personal point of view (Taba, 1936; 1942, pp. 160–1).

The studies in intergroup education extended the definition to include empathy and feelings. Chief among the behaviours of social sensitivity stressed in these programs were the following: 'Capacity to identify oneself with the feeling, values, and aspirations of others . . . the ability to project oneself into the lives, problems, and dilemmas of other people and the capacity to understand them in their own terms rather than interpreting them ethnocentrically.' Some emphasis also was put on the capacity to com-municate across the barriers of differences, the ability to accept differences, and the capacity to use cosmopolitan value criteria in interpreting and assessing human situations (Taba, Brady, and Robinson, 1952, p. 41).

Extension of feelings is an important aspect of sensitivity, whether social, moral, or aesthetic. Feelings figure in most human situations. It is difficult to understand people without understanding their feelings. Feelings are also at the bottom of many forms of distorted reasoning: hostile stereotyping, an uncritical use of ethnocentric assumptions, and so on. In conflict situations, persons with no understanding of how feelings function tend to counter feelings with feelings. Only one who is literate in the ways of feelings, who can read and interpret them, can use them as factual material from which to fashion solutions to conflicts.

But besides understanding feelings, there is also the problem of generating feelings and extending the capacity to identify, to empathize, and to make 'a really personal contact and entry' (Niblett, 1955, pp. 36–7).

Feelings, values and sensitivities are matters that need to be discovered rather than taught. Neither democratic values nor feelings of tolerance can be developed solely by teaching about them. This means that the provisions for these objectives must include opportunities for direct experiencing of some sort and materials which affect feelings. A much more conscious use is needed of the experience of students, of literature, and of other materials which reproduce life in its full emotional meaning and which express and affect feelings and values.

This makes the modification of attitudes and feelings one of the most difficult of educational tasks. Many question whether it is a proper task for education, or one that is attainable by means available to schools (Taba, 1962b, chapter 2, pp. 18–21). However, experiments in many schools have demonstrated the feasibility of extending by educational means the capacity to 'feel with', to accept and understand, and to modify the standards and values learned in one's own immediate culture. Using literature systematically for extending the capacity to feel and to respond and to identify values has been among the chief ways.

Because feelings are learned by imitation, the extension of feelings and sensitivities also requires a living laboratory. Therefore, assembling groups with heterogeneities of backgrounds and providing for open interaction among these heterogeneities has been another method. The incongruity of teaching democratic principles and ideals but allowing the classroom climate and the life in school to instill the antithesis has long been recognized.

Finally, it is well to remember that to change sensitivities and feelings requires indirection and a lot of freedom on the part of the individual to do his own examining and changing.[2]

Skills

There are skills to be learned in connection with any area of competency. The objectives pertaining to skills, therefore, range from the basic academic skills, such as reading, writing, and arithmetic, to skills in democratic citizenship and group living. Usually the objectives pertaining to skills are concentrated on the 'three Rs', which constitute the basis for academic study. In the minds of some persons these constitute the essentials, at least on the elementary level.

The skills necessary for independent and creative intellectual work – the ability to locate and evaluate information from sources other than textbooks and the processes of solving problems and analyzing data – have received some emphasis. These skills are especially important in programs that have made a transition from 'following the textbook' to assignments which require the use of multiple sources.[3]

Emphasis on problem solving suggests a need for additional skills, such as the ability to define problems of investigation, to plan a method of inquiry, to assess discriminatingly the appropriateness and limitations of the sources for particular purposes and the ability to master simple research skills, such as tabulating and classifying information and experimenting with different ways of organizing and interpreting.

An especially neglected area of skills is the complex pertaining to the management of interpersonal relations and the conduct of groups. These are usually referred to as social or group skills. The emphasis on these skills has not always been very broad in scope, nor pertinent. Often training is confined to the routines of polite etiquette and to mastering parliamentary procedure. In some primary schools with acculturation problems the training in the common routines of social communication, such as saying 'hello', expressing appreciation or regret, may be pertinent. But it must be recognized that even in such schools many children are not prepared for group living in school. There are children whose homes have not given them much training in the ordinary social disciplines, whose communication skills are at a minimum, and who have only a minimal mastery of such common routines as group listening, controlling the impulses of anger, or following rules of conduct. For these children acquiring a 'common culture' in the sense of developing a modicum of common social skills becomes a necessity. For the students from minority groups or from homes on lower economic levels, the problem is even more serious. The deficiency in the needed social skills leads to an almost inevitable failure in social situations and to a defensive 'chip-on-the-shoulder' attitude, hostility, or withdrawal.

Because the problems of interpersonal relations, especially those of handling interpersonal conflicts, rebuff, misunderstanding, or criticism, are with us everywhere, the skills in managing interpersonal relations have acquired some importance. There is scarcely a child or adolescent who does not face such conflicts with peers, family, or adults and who would not benefit from some emphasis on the skills needed to deal constructively with interpersonal conflict, or for the development of constructive human relations. The deficiency of these skills showed clearly in responses to a survey on the question, 'What makes me mad and what I do about it,' conducted by the Intergroup Education Project (unpublished material). The results showed that the range of skills brought to solving conflicts were as meagre as they were ineffective. Both children and adolescents resorted with equal frequency to retaliation in one form or another as the major device. Withdrawing from a situation or taking it out on someone else or something else followed in frequency. Few thought of talking it through. A special feature of these replies was the tendency to 'blame' someone. Practically no one looked at the situation to discover what factors provoked the conflict, because he did not have even the idea of a situational causation of behaviour, much less the skills for conducting such an analysis.

To manage conflict situations it is also necessary to gauge the feelings of the opposite party, to assess objectively the reactions of people to one's own behaviour, and to discover the situational rather than the personal causes of difficulty. Many difficulties in interpersonal relations occur because individuals are unaware of the discrepancy between their own motives and their actual conduct. They don't realize how what they do looks from the 'outside'. Understanding and applying certain simple principles of behavioural causation, such as that anger begets anger, that hurting stimulates further hurting, or that a smile produces a smile, helps to extend perception of what goes on in human interaction and with it the rational control over conduct even for the misbegotten and maladjusted.

Still another needed skill is that of managing authority democratically. In school as well as out of school there are many occasions to exercise authority. The usual practice on such occasions is to resort to authoritarian controls, including using the power to mete out 'punishments according to crime'. Many a monitor or traffic boy will tend to enforce his authority by authoritarian methods, not so much because he admires these procedures as because he knows no alternatives. This practice not only causes much conflict but also teaches undesirable methods of control; both dangers could be avoided by a development of skills in democratic use of authority.

Training in the ways of using authority democratically would greatly reduce the cleavages on which schools spend such a large amount of time. For example, sociodramatic training in resolution of conflicts provides opportunities for learning the more difficult democratic procedures for control (Taba *et al.*, 1949, pp. 109–17).

The growth in sophistication about group relations and group processes has opened up still another area of skills, those related to participation in and the conduct of groups. Group activity is becoming increasingly important in modern life, so much so that many students of society insist that the fundamental relations of men are now with groups rather than with individuals as such. As a consequence the development of vastly improved techniques of group deliberation and of making group decisions is considered one of the major tasks of society today – and, therefore, of the schools today. Furthermore, most of the work of the schools is carried on in groups, and much of it wastefully, at worst, and less productively than it might be, at best. In surveying the status of group skills, the staff of the Intergroup Education Project pointed out that one serious deficiency was a lack of skills in the effective functioning of groups: thinking, planning, making group decisions, participation. While the schools recognized the importance of these skills, scarcely any analysis was available of what the skills entailed, much less any tangible methods for learning them (Taba, Brady, and Robinson, 1952, pp. 47–52).

Productivity in group situations requires a variety of skills: doing orderly thinking, planning group goals, focusing on the central task, controlling egocentric drives, managing conflicting ideas, progressing from dissension to consensus. A series of skills are involved also in making group work productive – focusing, clarifying, involving, initiating ideas, harmonizing feelings, and a host of others (Cunningham *et al.*, 1951; Benne and Sheats, 1951, pp. 98–104; D. Hall, 1957, chapter 12).

Many a committee or a work group, adult or child, founders because individuals in it are energized by their own personal needs and are insufficiently sensitive to the need for focusing on the group task, do not know how to help the group effort, cannot discover the group goals, or fail to identify with them. Giving social space to a variety of viewpoints and feelings is as much a matter of skill as it is a matter of inclination. Group discussions can be more than either a rambling conversation or a strait jacket in which there is no room for all to participate constructively. It is possible to learn ways of moving from dissension to consensus. In other words, besides good will and democratic intent, many specific skills go into making groups productive and effective. These skills can be learned and, if learned, make group work vastly more effective (Taba *et al.*, 1950, chapters 5 and 6).

Learning appropriate leadership roles is another factor in group productivity. The conventional concept of leadership, derived largely from the operation of the official leadership positions, assumes that a few persons are the leaders and the rest the followers. Recent experiments and studies in group procedures have disclosed a wide range of possible leadership roles, all of which can be performed by a large number of group participants. A wide distribution of these roles is both needed and possible.

Training in carrying on a variety of these roles is important both for immediate effectiveness and productiveness and for ultimate maturity in group participation in adult life. Distribution of leadership is further useful for opening up leadership opportunities to those who most need it: students whose home backgrounds have left them short in adequate group skills and, hence, incapable of assuming a part in the school's program or activities. This reversal of emphasis is needed if we are to correct the current practice of throwing into leadership roles persons who already show capacity and who, because of their home environment or cultural advantages, already have developed the qualities and skills necessary for assuming such roles (Taba, 1955, p. 115).

Notes

1 For a fuller description of the processes involved in various aspects of interpretation, see Bloom (1954, pp. 74–81) and E. R. Smith and Tyler (1942, pp. 38–47).
2 For examples of programs addressed to this objective see Taba and Elkins, 1950; Taba *et al.*, 1950; Heaton, 1952; Heaton and Lewis, 1955.
3 See Taba and Elkins, 1950, pp. 157–64, for the problems encountered and the skills needed in such a transition.

References

ADORNO, T. W. *et al.* (1950) *Authoritarian Personality*. New York: Harper.

AUSUBEL, D. P. (1961) 'In defense of verbal learning.' *Educational Theory*, 11, January 1961.

BENNE, K. D. and SHEATS, P. (1951) 'Functional roles of group members', in BENNE, K. D. and MUNTYAN, B. (1951) *Human Relations in Curriculum Change*. New York: Dryden Press; Holt, Rinehart and Winston, pp. 98–104.

BLOOM, B. S. (ed.) (1954) *The Taxonomy of Educational Objectives*. London: Longmans Green.

BROWNELL, W. A. and HENDRICKSON, G. (1950) 'How children learn information, concepts and generalizations', in NATIONAL SOCIETY FOR THE STUDY OF EDUCATION (1950) *Learning and Instruction*. Forty-ninth Yearbook, Part 1. Chicago, Ill.: University of Chicago Press, Chapter 4.

BRUNER, J. S. (1961) 'The act of discovery.' *Harvard Educational Review*, 31, Winter 1961, pp. 21–32.

CONTRA COSTA COUNTY SCHOOLS (1959) *Social Studies, Grades 1–6*. Pleasant Hill, Calif.

COTTRELL, L. S. (1950) 'Some neglected problems in social psychology.' *American Sociological Review*, 15, December 1950.

CUNNINGHAM, R. *et al.* (1951) *Understanding Group Behaviour of Boys and Girls*. The Horace Mann-Lincoln Institute of School Experimentation, Teachers College, Columbia University, New York.

DEWEY, J. (1933) *How We Think* (revised edition). Lexington, Mass.: Heath.

GETZELS, J. W. (1958) 'The acquisition of values in school and society', in CHASE, F. S. and ANDERSON, H. A. (eds) (1958) *The High School in the New Era*. Chicago, Ill.; University of Chicago Press.

HALL, D. M. (1957) *Dynamics of Group Action*. Danville, Ill.: Interstate Printers and Publishers.

HEATON, M. (1952) *Feelings are Facts*. National Conference of Christians and Jews.

HEATON, M. and LEWIS, H. (1955) *Reading Ladders for Human Relations* (revised and enlarged edition). Washington, D. C.: American Council on Education.

HENDRIX, G. (1961) 'Learning by discovery.' *Mathematics Teacher*, 54, pp. 290–9.

NATIONAL SOCIETY FOR THE STUDY OF EDUCATION (1946) *The Measurement of Understanding*. Forty-fifth Yearbook, Part 1. Chicago, Ill.: University of Chicago Press.

NIBLETT, W. R. (1955) *Education – The Lost Dimension*. Wm. Sloane Associates.

OPPENHEIMER, R. (1958) 'An inward look.' *Foreign Affairs*, 36 (January 1958), pp. 209–20.

SALINGER, J. D. (1959) 'Seymour: An Introduction.' *The New Yorker*, 6 June 1959, p. 42.

SMITH, E. R. and TYLER, R. W. (eds) (1942) *Appraising and Recording Student Progress*. New York: Harper.

SUCHMAN, J. R. (1961) 'Inquiry training: building skills for autonomous discovery.' *Merrill-Palmer Quarterly*, July 1961.

TABA, H. (1936) *Social Sensitivity*. Progressive Education Association (mimeograph).

TABA, H. (1940) 'Significant aspects of growth in learning situations', in GRAY, W. S. (ed.) (1940) *Reading and Pupil Development*. Supplementary Educational Monograph No. 51 (October 1940). Chicago, Ill.: University of Chicago Press, pp. 11–19.

TABA, H. (1942) 'Evaluation of social sensitivity', in SMITH, E. R. and TYLER, R. W. (eds) (1942) *Appraising and Recording Student Progress*. New York: Harper.

TABA, H. (1944) 'What is proof?' *Educational Leadership*, 1 (April 1944).

TABA, H. (1950) 'The problems in developing critical thinking.' *Progressive Education*, 28 (November 1950).

TABA, H. (1955) *School Culture*. Washington, D.C.: American Council on Education.

TABA, H. (1962a) 'Learning by discovery.' Talk at the Symposium of the American Educational Research Association Convention, Atlantic City (20 February 1962).

TABA, H. (1962b) *Curriculum Development: Theory and Practice*. New York: Harcourt Brace and World.

TABA, H., BRADY, E. and ROBINSON, J. (1952) *Intergroup Education in Public Schools*. Washington, D.C.: American Council on Education.

TABA, H. and ELKINS, D. (1950) *With Focus on Human Relations*. Washington, D.C.: American Council on Education.

TABA, H. et al. (1949) *Curriculum in Intergroup Relation: Secondary School*. Washington, D.C.: American Council on Education.

TABA, H. et al. (1950) *Elementary Curriculum in Intergroup Relations*. Washington, D.C.: American Council on Education.

2.5 The form of objectives

Ralph W. Tyler

Objectives are sometimes stated as things which the instructor is to do; as for example, to present the theory of evolution, to demonstrate the nature of inductive proof, to present the Romantic poets, to introduce four-part harmony. These statements may indicate what the instructor plans to do; but they are not really statements of educational ends. Since the real purpose of education is not to have the instructor perform certain activities but to bring about significant changes in the students' patterns of behaviour, it becomes important to recognize that any statement of the objectives of the school should be a statement of changes to take place in students. Given such a statement, it is then possible to infer the kinds of activities which the instructor might carry on in an effort to attain the objectives – that is, in an effort to bring about the desired changes in the student. The difficulty of an objective stated in the form of activities to be carried on by the teacher lies in the fact that there is no way of judging whether these activities should really be carried on. They are not the ultimate purposes of the educational program and are not, therefore, really the objectives. Hence, although objectives are often stated in terms of activities to be carried on by the instructor, this formal statement operates as a kind of circular reasoning which does not provide a satisfactory guide to the further steps of selecting materials and devising teaching procedures for the curriculum.

A second form in which objectives are often stated is in listing topics, concepts, generalizations, or other elements of content that are to be dealt with in the course or courses.
[. . .]
Objectives stated in the form of topics or generalizations or other content elements do indicate the areas of content to be dealt with by the students but they are not satisfactory objectives since they do not specify what the students are expected to do with these elements. . . .

A third way in which objectives are sometimes stated is in the form of generalized patterns of behaviour which fail to indicate more specifically the area of life or the content to which the behaviour applies. For example, one may find objectives stated as 'To Develop Critical Thinking', 'To Develop Appreciation', 'To Develop Social Attitudes', 'To Develop Broad Interests'. Objectives stated in this form do indicate that education is expected to bring about some changes in the students and they also indicate in general the kinds of changes with which the educational program is expected to deal. However, from what we know about transfer of training it is very unlikely that efforts to aim at objectives so highly generalized as this will be fruitful. It is necessary to

Source: TYLER, R. W. (1949) *Basic Principles of Curriculum and Instruction*. Chicago, Ill.: University of Chicago Press, pp. 44–125 (in part).

specify more definitely the content to which this behaviour applies, or the area in life in which such behaviour is to be used. It is not adequate to talk simply about developing critical thinking without reference to the content or the kinds of problems in which the thinking is to be done. It is not a clear enough formulation of an objective to state that the aim is to develop wide interests without specifying the areas in which the interests are to be aroused and stimulated. It is not satisfactory to indicate that the objective is to develop social attitudes without indicating more clearly what the objects of the attitudes are that are sought. Hence, the formulation of objectives in terms of behaviour types alone is not likely to prove a satisfactory way of stating objectives if they are to be used as direct guides to the further development of curriculum and instruction.

The most useful form for stating objectives is to express them in terms which identify both the kind of behaviour to be developed in the student and the content or area of life in which this behaviour is to operate. If you consider a number of statements of objectives that seem to be clear and to provide guidance in the development of instructional programs, you will note that each of these statements really includes both the behaviour and the content aspects of the objective.

[. . .]

Since a clearly formulated objective has the two dimensions of the behavioural aspect and the content aspect, it is often useful to employ a graphic two-dimensional chart to express objectives concisely and clearly. An illustration of such a chart is presented [below]. This is an illustration of the use of a two-dimensional chart in stating objectives for a high school course in biological science. It is not assumed that this course is an ideal course nor that these are ideal objectives. The purpose of the chart is to show how the chart can more compactly indicate the objectives that are being sought and how each objective is defined more clearly by the chart in terms both of the behavioural aspect and the content aspect.

[. . .]

When objectives are formulated on a two-dimensional chart of this sort it becomes a concise set of specifications to guide the further development of the course. For example, in the case of the illustrative chart, the instructor by looking at the several columns can see more clearly the kind of learning experiences that will have to be set up. It should be clear that the kind of experience the student needs to have in order to get understanding of important facts and principles is more than that required to memorize these things; it will involve analysis, interpretation, application to various illustrations to see the meaning; that is, it will involve the kind of mental operations that lead to a clearer interpretation and understanding. In similar fashion, the fact that the second column states familiarity with dependable sources of information provides a second specification. It is not enough that the student shall understand important facts and principles and remember them. He must also learn where to go to get dependable information as he needs it. This implies experience in consulting various sources of information,

Illustration of the use of a two-dimensional chart in stating objectives for a high school course in biological science

Content Aspect of the Objectives	Behavioural Aspect of the Objectives						
	1 Understanding of important facts and principles	2 Familiarity with dependable sources of information	3 Ability to interpret data	4 Ability to apply principles	5 Ability to study and report results of study	6 Broad and mature interests	7 Social attitudes
A Functions of Human Organisms							
1 Nutrition	X	X	X	X	X	X	X
2 Digestion	X		X	X	X	X	
3 Circulation	X		X	X	X	X	
4 Respiration	X		X	X	X	X	
5 Reproduction	X	X	X	X	X	X	X
B Use of Plant and Animal Resources							
1 Energy relationships	X		X	X	X	X	X
2 Environmental factors conditioning plant and animal growth	X	X	X	X	X	X	X
3 Heredity and genetics	X	X	X	X	X	X	X
4 Land utilization	X	X	X	X	X	X	X
C Evolution and Development	X	X	X		X	X	X

some practice in analyzing these sources to see where they are adequate and where they are unsatisfactory, the development of certain criteria by which to judge the dependability of a particular source of information. In brief, the development of the kind of objective implied by the second column requires somewhat different learning experiences than those implied by the first column. [. . .]

Turning to the content aspects of the objectives, we can also see how they serve to specify more clearly the steps to be taken for the further development of the curriculum. The rows of the chart indicate the content headings to which the behavioural aspects apply; but they also indicate in connection with the behavioural aspects, the specifics to be developed under each heading. Thus, under nutrition, important facts and principles are to be identified, dependable sources of information are to be worked with, new nutrition data are to be presented to students for interpretation, problems involving the application of the important facts and principles are to be provided, interesting materials in nutrition are to be found, and the social implications of nutrition work are to be sought out. In similar fashion, each column indicates the kind of content analysis required. Hence, by putting these two aspects of objectives together, we get a clear enough specification to indicate on the one hand the kinds of behaviour changes that are aimed at, and on the other hand to specify the particular materials, the particular ideas, the particular kinds of situations to be used in connection with each of these behavioural objectives. This provides a much more adequate specification of the educational objectives for a particular course or for a whole school than is normally available in the formulations to be found in courses of study and other curriculum reports. [. . .]

The attaining of objectives

Thus far we have been considering the ends to be attained by the educational program. These ends or objectives have been defined in terms of the kind of behaviour involved and the content with which the behaviour deals. We next are to consider the question of how these ends can be attained. Essentially, learning takes place through the experiences which the learner has; that is, through the reactions he makes to the environment in which he is placed. Hence, the means of education are educational experiences that are had by the learner. In planning an educational program to attain given objectives we face the question of deciding on the particular educational experiences to be provided, since it is through these experiences that learning will take place and educational objectives will be attained. [. . .]

Although the particular learning experiences appropriate for attaining objectives will vary with the kind of objectives aimed at, there are certain general principles that apply to the selection of learning experiences, whatever the objectives may be. The first of these is that for a given objective to be attained, a student must have experiences that give him an opportunity to practise the kind of behaviour implied by the objective. That is to say, if one of the objectives is to develop skill in problem solving, this cannot be attained unless the learning experiences give the student ample opportunity to solve problems. [. . .]

A second general principle is that the learning experiences must be such that the student obtains satisfactions from carrying on the kind of behaviour implied by the objectives. For example, in the case of learning experiences to develop skill in solving health problems, it is important that the experiences not only give the student an opportunity to solve health problems, but also that effective solutions to these problems shall be satisfying to him. [. . .]

A third general principle with regard to learning experiences is that the reactions desired in the experience are within the range of possibility for the students involved. That is to say, the experiences should be appropriate to the student's present attainments, his predispositions, and the like. This is another way of stating the old adage that 'the teacher must begin where the student is'. If the learning experience involves the kind of behaviour which the student is not yet able to make, then it fails in its purpose. [. . .]

A fourth general principle is that there are many particular experiences that can be used to attain the same educational objectives. As long as the educational experiences meet the various criteria for effective learning, they are useful in attaining the desired objectives. [. . .]

A fifth principle is that the same learning experience will usually bring about several outcomes. Thus, for example, while the student is solving problems about health, he is also acquiring certain information in the health field. He is also likely to be developing certain attitudes toward the importance of public health procedures. He may be developing an interest or a dislike for work in the field of health. Every experience is likely to bring about more than one learning objective. On the positive side this is a decided advantage because it permits economy of time. A well-planned set of learning experiences will be made up of experiences that at the same time are useful in attaining several objectives. Negatively, it means that the teacher must always be on the lookout for undesirable outcomes that may develop from a learning experience planned for some other purpose. Thus, the effort of the teacher to develop skill in interpreting Shakespeare's plays may be pushed to a point that at the same time the student is developing a strong dislike for Shakespeare. [. . .]

We have been considering the kinds of learning experiences useful for attaining various types of objectives. These learning experiences have been considered in terms of their characteristics but not in terms of their organization. Since learning experiences must be put together to form some kind of coherent program, it is necessary for us now to consider the procedures for organizing learning experiences into units, courses, and programs. [. . .]

There are three major criteria to be met in building an effectively organized group of learning experiences. These are: continuity, sequence, and integration. Continuity refers to the vertical reiteration of major curriculum elements. For example, if in the social studies the development of skills in reading social studies material is an important objective, it is necessary to see that there is recurring and continuing opportunity for these skills to be practised and developed. This means that over time the same kinds of skills will be brought into continuing operation. In similar fashion, if an objective in science is to develop a meaningful concept of energy, it is important that this concept be dealt with again and again in various parts of the science course. Continuity is thus seen to be a major factor in effective vertical organization.

Sequence is related to continuity but goes beyond it. It is possible for a major curriculum element to recur again and again but merely at the same level so that there is no progressive development of understanding or skill or attitude or some other factor. Sequence as a criterion emphasizes the importance of having each successive experience build upon the preceding one but to go more broadly and deeply into the matters involved. . . .

[. . .]

Integration refers to the horizontal relationship of curriculum experiences. The organization of these experiences should be such that they help the student increasingly to get a unified view and to unify his behaviour in relation to the elements dealt with. For example, in developing skill in handling quantitative problems in arithmetic, it is also important to consider the ways in which these skills can be effectively utilized in social studies, in science, in shop and other fields so that they are not developed simply as isolated behaviours to be used in a single course but are increasingly part of the total capacities of the student to use in the varied situations of his daily life. Correspondingly, in developing concepts in the social studies it is important to see how these ideas can be related to work going on in other subject fields so that increasingly there is unity in the student's outlooks, skills, attitudes and the like.

[. . .]

In identifying important organizing principles, it is necessary to note that the criteria, continuity, sequence, and integration apply to the experiences of the learner and not to the way in which these matters may be viewed by someone already in command of the elements to be learned. Thus, continuity involves the recurring emphasis in the learner's experience upon these particular elements; sequence refers to the increasing breadth and depth of the learner's development, and integration refers to the learner's increased unity of behaviour in relating to the elements involved. This means that the organizing principles need to be considered in terms of their psychological significance to the learner.

Over the years there has been a general recognition of the distinction between logical and psychological organization. When such a distinction is made, it is an effort to point out the difference between the relationship of curriculum elements as viewed by an expert in the field and the relationship as it may appear to the learner. No doubt there are many cases in which a logical organization, that is, a relationship which has meaning and significance to an expert in the field, is also an appropriate psychological organization, that is, it can be a scheme of development in relations meaningful to the learner himself. On the other hand, there are times when sharp differentiation can be made between the connections seen by the expert in the field and the developments which are meaningful to the learner himself.

[. . .]

Since we have considered the operations involved in choosing and formulating educational objectives and in selecting and organizing learning experiences, it may appear that we have completed our analysis of curriculum development. Although the steps previously discussed provide the plans for the day by day work of the school, they do not complete the planning cycle. Evaluation is also an important operation in curriculum development.

[. . .]

Evaluation

The process of evaluation begins with the objectives of the educational program. Since the purpose is to see how far these objectives are actually being realized, it is necessary to have evaluation procedures that will give evidence about each of the kinds of behaviour implied by each of the major educational objectives.

[. . .]

This means that the two-dimensional analysis which served as a basis for planning the learning experiences also serves as the basis for planning the evaluation procedures. The two-dimensional analysis of objectives thus serves as a set of specifications for evaluation.

[. . .]

It is, of course, assumed that these 'behavioural objectives' have been clearly defined by the curriculum worker. They should have been defined clearly so as to provide a concrete guide in the selection and planning of learning experiences. If they have not yet been clearly defined, it is absolutely essential that they be defined in order to make an evaluation since unless there is some clear conception of the sort of behaviour implied by the objectives, one has no way of telling what kind of behaviour to look for in the students in order to see to what degree these objectives are being realized. This means that the process of evaluation may force persons who have not previously clarified their objectives to a further process of clarification. Definition of objectives, then, is an important step in evaluation.

The next step in evaluation procedure is to identify the situations which will give the student the chance to express the behaviour that is implied by the educational objectives. The only way that we can tell whether students have acquired given types of behaviour is to give them an opportunity to show this behaviour. This means that we must find situations which not only permit the

expression of the behaviour but actually encourage or evoke this behaviour.
[. . .]

Although the principle is simple, there are still many problems involved in finding situations that are sufficiently under control and permit the teacher or other evaluator to have access to them in order to see the types of behaviours the students are developing. In case some situations are difficult to handle, then one of the tasks of the specialist in evaluation is to try to find other simpler situations that will have a high correlation with the result obtained when the situation is used which directly evokes the kind of behaviour to be appraised.

It is only after the objectives have been identified, clearly defined, and situations listed which give opportunity for the expression of the behaviour desired that it is possible to examine available evaluation instruments to see how far they may serve the evaluation purposes desired. It is not really possible to look at a particular test and to decide whether it would do for appraising a certain educational program until the objectives of the program have been identified and defined and until the kinds of situations that would give an opportunity for this behaviour to be expressed have also been identified. After these steps have been taken, one can then examine particular tests and see how far they sample the types of objectives that are to be appraised and how far the tests either use situations which directly evoke the kind of behaviour to be appraised or else use situations which have been correlated with the situations that directly evoke the type of behaviour.
[. . .]

When available evaluation instruments are checked in this way, it is quite probable that the curriculum constructor will find that there are available instruments that will be quite satisfactory for certain of the educational objectives, that there are other available instruments which can be modified somewhat and made appropriate for certain other educational objectives, and finally, that there are some educational objectives for which no available evaluation instruments can properly be used. For these last, it may be necessary to construct or devise methods for getting evidence about the student's attainment of these objectives. The construction of evaluation instruments can be a very difficult task if the purpose is to get a highly refined instrument, but a great deal can be done of a less refined sort by collecting evidence in rather simple ways relating to these various educational objectives. We shall discuss illustrations of these a little later.

If it is necessary to construct an evaluation instrument for a particular objective, the next step is actually to try out some of the situations suggested as situations that give the student a chance to express the behaviour desired. This try-out provides an opportunity to see whether these situations will serve as convenient ways of getting evidence. Thus, it may appear that the type of situation likely to give students a chance to show their ability to analyze problems is a situation in which a number of problems are presented in written form and the students are asked to analyze them. Situations of this sort can actually be tried out with students to see how far the responses obtained provide an adequate basis for checking the student's ability to analyze problems. Or, a situation that is likely to give students a chance to indicate their interests is to present a questionnaire in which a variety of activities are listed and the students are asked to check those in which they are interested and also to mark those in which they have no interest. If this appears to be a situation likely to give students an opportunity to show interests, then it should be used in trial form to see how satisfactorily it works. This step is a useful step in developing possible evaluation devices into forms where they can be satisfactorily used.

After deciding on certain situations used to get evidence about the behaviour of students, it is then necessary to devise a means of getting a record of the student's behaviour in this test situation. In the case of a written examination the student makes his own record in his writing. Hence, the problem of getting a record of his behaviour is not a serious one. On the other hand, a situation that gives nursery school children a chance to play and work together may be a good situation to provide evidence of personal-social adjustment but it is necessary to get some record of the children's reaction in this situation if there is to be opportunity to appraise this reaction after it has been made. This may involve making a detailed description of reaction by an observer, it may suggest the use of a motion picture or sound recording, it may suggest the use of an observer's check list by which he checks off particular types of behaviour that commonly appear or it may involve some other means of getting a satisfactory record of the children's reaction. This is a step that must be considered in connection with each test situation to be sure that the situation not only evokes the desired behaviour but that a record can be obtained which can be appraised later.

The next step in developing an evaluation instrument is to decide upon the terms or units that will be used to summarize or to appraise the record of behaviour obtained. This method of appraising the behaviour should, of course, parallel the implications of the objective itself. For example, if reading interests as an educational objective are to be defined as the development of increasingly broad and mature interests, it then becomes necessary to decide upon units by which a record of children's reading can be summarized to indicate breadth and to indicate maturity. Breadth may be indicated by a number which measures the different categories of reading material included in the youngster's reading for the year. Thus, a child who reads only Wild West stories and detectives stories would have his reading list classified under two categories only and the figure 2 would represent a measure of breadth. This would be in contrast to a boy whose reading record could be classified under four categories such as adventure, romance, psychological, sociological. The fact that the second boy reads materials classified under a wider number of categories would be represented by the number 4 in contrast to the number 2. Correspondingly, if different reading levels can be classified under different levels of maturity, it becomes possible to summarize a reading record in terms of its average level of maturity and thus to provide a measure of that aspect of reading interest. This illustration has been chosen because it is very different from the problem as it is usually viewed by the person who reads and scores the test; and, yet, essentially all evaluation involves this problem, that is, the decision upon the characteristics that are to be appraised in the behaviour and the unit to be used in the measurement or summarization of these characteristics. In the case of reading interests, the characteristics used were range and maturity so that the methods of summarization provided a rating for range and maturity.

The problem is a similar one in summarizing a typical objective type test. Suppose it is a measure of knowledge. The question then to be faced is: Will knowledge be summarized in terms of the number of different items in the sample which the student was able to remember properly, or is it better indicated by some classification of the items so as to indicate which topics he remembers best and which less well, or is there some other way by which the objective of knowledge can be most satisfactorily summarized or appraised in order to serve the purpose of evaluation? Every kind of human behaviour which is appraised for its part as an educational objective must be summarized or measured in some terms and the decision about these terms is an important problem in the development and use of evaluation instruments.

It should be clear that for most purposes the appraisal of human behaviour should be an analytic one rather than a single score summary. Simply to know that John Smith made a score of 97 and Mary Jones made a score of 64 on some evaluation instrument used is not an adequate kind of summary likely to be most helpful for improving the curriculum. It is much more useful to have summaries which indicate the kinds of strengths and weaknesses, summaries at least in terms of each objective; and in many cases it may be desirable to have several scores or summaries for each objective so as to describe more adequately the achievement of this particular sort of objective. Thus, it is useful to know whether the students are making progress in developing a range of reading interests even though they may be making less progress in developing maturity of reading interests. It is helpful to know that students are making progress in their skill of interpretation in reading although their reading interests may not be as satisfactory as hoped. This kind of analytic summary which indicates particular strengths and weaknesses is, of course, invaluable in using the results to improve the curriculum. It means that the plan for appraisal must be developed before scoring and rating is actually made. Decisions about these points are necessary decisions in developing an evaluation program.

The next step in the construction of an evaluation instrument is to determine how far these rating or summarizing methods are objective, that is, to what degree two different persons, presumably competent, would be able to reach similar scores or summaries when they had an opportunity to score or summarize the same records of behaviour. If the scores or summaries vary markedly, depending upon who does the scoring or summarizing, it is clearly a subjective kind of appraisal and requires improvement in its objectivity in order to be a more satisfactory means of appraising a human behaviour. Sometimes improvement can be made through clarifying the specifications for scoring, sometimes through getting a more refined record of behaviour itself. It is beyond the scope of the present discussion to outline the various techniques for refining and improving the objectivity of the instruments. It is necessary, however, to recognize this problem and to attempt to get a more objective procedure when necessary. When these possible evaluation instruments have been tried out, one cannot only check on the objectivity of the scoring or summary but also check upon the adequacy of the sample of behaviour included in the instrument. In general, the size of the sample of behaviour to be obtained depends upon how variable that behaviour is. If one wishes to get evidence about the social attitudes of students and these attitudes are highly consistent in each individual, it takes only a few samples to get a rather dependable indication of the attitude of each student. On the other hand, if there is wide variability in each student's attitudes, for example, if he is highly selfish at some points and highly social at others, it takes a much larger sample of his behaviour in order to infer reliably about the degree of his social or selfish attitudes. Hence, it is not possible to be sure in advance how large a sample of behaviour must be collected regarding a given objective in order to have a dependable sample from which to draw conclusions about the individual's status. It is possible after trying out an instrument to find out what the variation among the items in the instrument is and thus to estimate how reliable the sample is and whether a larger or smaller sample would do satisfactorily. This is the problem of reliability of a test or other evaluation device; and, although it is beyond the scope of this discussion to describe methods of estimating reliability, it is important to recognize what reliability means and to realize that if a given test is too short to provide an adequate sample or if a given set of observations does not cover a large enough span of time to get an adequate sample of the student's behaviour, it will be necessary to extend the sample before dependable conclusions can be drawn.

Since we have used the two terms for two of the important criteria for an evaluation instrument, namely, objectivity and reliability, it is necessary to emphasize the third and most important criteria of an evaluation instrument, namely, validity. Validity applies to the method and indicates the degree to which an evaluation device actually provides evidence of the behaviour desired. Validity can be assured in one of two ways. One way is by getting directly a sample of the kind of behaviour to be measured, as when one observes directly the food children are selecting as the basis for inferring food habits, or one obtains an actual record of reading done as an indication of reading habits, or one presents problems for children to analyze to get evidence of their ability to analyze problems. This is known as 'face validity' – the evaluation instrument is valid on the face of it because it directly samples the kind of behaviour which it is desired to appraise. The other way of assuring validity is through correlating a particular evaluation device with the result obtained by a directly valid measure. If it can be shown that the results of a certain reading questionnaire correlate very highly with the results obtained from an actual record of reading, then the reading questionnaire might be used as a valid indication of what children read. It would be valid because the results are shown by experimental methods to correlate highly with the direct evidence. In some cases, persons developing tests find that it is expensive or difficult or otherwise impracticable to get evidence by the direct method and they try out various possible ways for getting evidence which are simpler and easier to handle. None of these should be used, however, as a valid instrument until it has been shown to correlate highly with the evidence obtained directly, that is, from an instrument which has face validity.

These steps indicate the procedures followed in making an evaluation and in developing an instrument for an evaluation. In case the instrument is found to have too little objectivity or reliability, it is necessary to improve it. It is also necessary to make any other revisions indicated by the preliminary tryout, such as eliminating ambiguities in directions, dropping out parts of the instrument which got no significant reactions from students. In general then, the result is a continually improved instrument for getting evidence about the degree to which students are attaining given educational objectives.

These instruments are used in order to obtain summarized or appraised results. These results may be in the form of scores, or descriptions, or both, depending upon the form which can be most satisfactorily used to summarize the behaviour in terms that are appropriate for the objectives desired.

Using the results of evaluation

Since every educational program involves several objectives and since for almost every objective there will be several scores or descriptive terms used to summarize the behaviour of students in relation to this objective, it follows that the results obtained from evaluation instruments will not be a single score or a single descriptive term but an analyzed profile or a comprehensive set of descriptive terms indicating the present student achievement. These scores or descriptive terms should, of course, be comparable to those used at a preceding date so that it is possible to indicate change taking place and one can then see whether or not educational progress is actually happening. If it is found, for example, that the range of students' interests in reading is no greater at the end of the tenth grade than it was at the end of the ninth grade, it is clear that no appreciable change is taking place in reading interest. Correspondingly, if it is shown that the ability to interpret reading passages critically is no higher at the end of the tenth grade than at the end of the ninth grade, again, no educational change is taking place. It is, therefore, essential to compare the results obtained from the several evaluation instruments before and after given periods in order to estimate the amount of change taking place. The fact that these are complex comparisons, that they involve a number of points and not a single score, may complicate the process, but it is necessary for the kind of identification of strengths and weaknesses that will help to indicate where the curriculum may need improvement. For example, in connection with one curriculum program which involved the development of a core focused upon contemporary social problems, it was found that at the end of the first year, the students had acquired a great deal more information about these contemporary problems, that they had shifted their social attitudes slightly in the direction of greater social and less selfish attitudes, but that their attitudes were much more confused and inconsistent than before, that they had not gained any skill in analyzing social problems, and that their ability to interpret social data was worse because the students were drawing more unwarranted conclusions than before. Putting all of these things together gave the teachers the chance to see the kinds of strengths, which were largely covering more material and more ideas, and the kinds of weaknesses, which had to do with their greater inconsistencies, less ability to analyze critically and the like. This is more helpful in getting at the seat of the difficulty in this particular core curriculum than if there had been a single score which indicated a small amount of improvement but did not analyze this improvement into a number of different categories.

It is not only desirable to analyze the results of an evaluation to indicate the various strengths and weaknesses, but it is also necessary to examine these data to suggest possible explanations or hypotheses about the reason for this particular pattern of strengths and weaknesses. In the case just cited, after examining all the data available, it is suggested that this implied that a great deal more ground was covered and that not enough time was being spent in careful critical analysis. This was checked against the actual amount of reading provided which turned out to be more than 6,000 pages and the number of social problems dealt with, which turned out to be twenty-one, both of which in the light of these data seemed to be excessive and suggested that a possible explanation for these weaknesses was that too much material was being covered and not enough time devoted to critical analysis, interpretation, and application.

When hypotheses have been suggested that might possibly explain the evaluation data, the next step is to check those hypotheses against the present available data, that is, against additional data that may be available, and to see whether the hypotheses are consistent with all the data then available. If they appear to be consistent with the available data, the next step is to modify the curriculum in the direction implied by the hypotheses and then to teach the material to see whether there is any actual improvement in student achievement when these modifications are made. If there is, then it would suggest that the hypotheses are likely explanations and the basis for improving the curriculum has been identified. In the case just cited it was possible to reorganize the course for the coming year and to reduce the number of major problems from twenty-one to seven and to reduce the quantity of reading material by more than half so as to utilize more time in interpreting, applying, analyzing, and otherwise treating the material dealt with. At the end of the second year, it was found that, although the students had not gained quite so much in the range of information acquired, they had gained greater consistency in social attitudes, had gained greater skill in analyzing social problems, and had become able to draw better generalizations from the data presented to them. This would indicate that the hypothesis that what was wrong with the course was that it covered too much ground seemed to be a sound one. This is a typical procedure that can be followed in using evaluation results so as to modify and improve the curriculum and instructional program.

What is implied in all of this is that curriculum planning is a continuous process and that as materials and procedures are developed, they are tried out, their results appraised, their inadequacies identified, suggested improvements indicated; there is replanning, redevelopment and then reappraisal; and in this kind of continuing cycle, it is possible for the curriculum and instructional program to be continuously improved over the years. In this way we may hope to have an increasingly more effective educational program rather than depending so much upon hit and miss judgment as a basis for curriculum development.

Other values and uses of evaluation procedures

In the foregoing discussion of evaluation, we have concentrated primarily upon the use of evaluation procedures in identifying the strengths and weaknesses of the curriculum program. This is its main function in curriculum work. It also serves other purposes. The very fact that it is not possible to make an evaluation until objectives are clearly enough defined so that one can recognize the behaviour to be sought means that evaluation is a powerful device for clarifying educational objectives if they have not already been clarified in the curriculum planning process.

Evaluation also has a powerful influence upon learning. It has been shown in the New York Regents' Inquiry that the Regents' examinations which are the evaluation instruments of the state have more effect upon what is taught in New York State than course of study outlines as such. Students are influenced in their study by the kind of evaluation to be made and even teachers are influenced in their emphasis by the sort of evaluation which they expect to be made. This means that unless the evaluation procedure closely parallels the educational objectives of the curriculum the evaluation procedure may become the focus of the students' attention and even of the teachers' attention rather than the curriculum objectives set up. Hence, evaluation and curriculum must be closely integrated so that the effect will not be for the curriculum planning to be ignored in order for diverse objectives appraised by evaluation to be given major attention.

Evaluation procedures also have great importance in the individual guidance of pupils. It is not only valuable to know about students' background but also to know about their achievement of various kinds of objectives in order to have a better notion of both their needs and their capabilities. Any comprehensive evaluation program provides information about individual students that can be of great value.

Evaluation can also be used continuously during the year as a basis for identifying particular points needing further attention with particular groups of students and as a basis for giving individual help or planning individual programs for students in the light of their particular progress in the educational program.

Finally, evaluation becomes one of the important ways of providing information about the success of the school to the school's clientele. Ultimately, schools need to be appraised in terms of their effectiveness in attaining important objectives. This means that ultimately evaluation results need to be translated in terms that will be understandable to parents and the public generally. Only as we can describe more accurately the results we are attaining from the curriculum are we in a position to get the most intelligent support for the educational program of the school. Neither parents nor the public can be satisfied long with reports about the number of children enrolled and the number of new buildings built and things of that sort. Eventually, parents have a right to know what kind of changes are being brought about in their children. Now, most of the reports of this sort that they get are from appraisals that are not fairly made. We hear about the number of persons rejected because of lack of reading ability or lack of physical health in connection with Selective Service, but we have no means of tracing those cases back to particular schools. Increasingly, we must expect to use evaluation procedures to determine what changes are actually taking place in students and where we are achieving our curriculum objectives and where we must make still further modifications in order to get an effective educational program.

2.6 The teaching of literary appreciation

F. R. Leavis

Even as a specialist business literary scholarship is apt to defeat even its own limited purpose through having neglected to provide itself with a minimum gleam of critical intelligence; and the English 'Honours' man who, dealing with Shakespeare, cannot show more competence as a reader of English poetry than is commonly evidenced by footnotes in (say) his *Arden* edition has certainly defeated the true purpose of the School responsible for his training. Literary history, as a matter of 'facts about' and accepted critical (or quasi-critical) description and commentary, is a worthless acquisition; worthless for the student who cannot as a critic – that is, as an intelligent and discerning reader – make a personal approach to the essential data of the literary historian, the works of literature (an approach is personal or it is nothing: you cannot take over the appreciation of a poem, and unappreciated, the poem isn't 'there'). The only acquisition of literary history having any educational value is that made in the exercise of critical intelligence to the ends of the literary critic. Does this need arguing? Yet I have known the 'outlines of literary history' proposed as part of a test that, taken early in the 'Honours' course, should determine whether or not the student should be allowed to proceed – proposed, that is, as a subject of preparatory study.

It is plain that in the work of a properly ordered English School (and here we have the positive corollary of the negative proposition thrown out above) the training of reading capacity has first place. By training of reading capacity I mean the training of perception, judgment and analytic skill commonly referred to as 'practical criticism' – or, rather, the training that 'practical criticism' ought to be. Sureness of judgment, of course, implies width of experience, and there is an unending problem of adjusting, in the student's work, the relations of intensive to extensive. Nevertheless, 'practical criticism' has a certain obvious priority; otherwise the acquisition of experience will be (as it so often is) an illusory matter. With the gain in experience will go more advanced and extended applications of critical method that develop out of the limited initial work – more difficult and sustained exercises in the essential discipline.

Practical criticism, training of perception and judgment, analysis – what are these, or what can they be, to justify this stress laid on them, the key-function here assigned them, as discipline? That the question will be asked by some of those to whom my 'sketch' must be thought of as being addressed has now to be recognized, though there is no way of giving a convincing answer here to the most sceptical kind of asker. The only conceivably effective answer would be some fairly prolonged exemplification of relevant work as it would

Source: LEAVIS, F. R. (1943) *Education and the University: A sketch for an 'English School'*. London: Chatto and Windus, pp. 68–74.[1]

be carried on in routine practice. It is obviously impossible to produce in this note the substance of a manual of analytic method – and the book to send the reader to doesn't exist. That the problem of demonstration should arise as such brings home how little, in the way of performance of their function, is commonly expected, or to be expected, either of literary critics or of English Schools.

For surely, as one might say to one's beginning students, it should be possible, by cultivating attentive reading, to acquire a higher skill than the untrained reader has: a skill that will enable the trained reader to do more with a poem than ejaculate approval or disapproval, or dismiss it with vaguely reported general impressions, qualified with the modest recognition that (in Arnold Bennett's words) 'taste after all is relative.' Analysis, one would go on, is the process by which we seek to attain a complete reading of the poem – a reading that approaches as nearly as possible to the perfect reading. There is about it nothing in the nature of 'murdering to dissect', and suggestions that it can be anything in the nature of laboratory-method misrepresent it entirely. We can have the poem only by an inner kind of possession; it is 'there' for analysis only in so far as we are responding appropriately to the words on the page. In pointing to them (and there is nothing else to point to) what we are doing is to bring into sharp focus, in turn, this, that and the other detail, juncture or relation in our total response; or (since 'sharp focus' may be a misleading account of the kind of attention sometimes required), what we are doing is to dwell with a deliberate, considering responsiveness on this, that or the other node or focal point in the complete organization that the poem is, in so far as we have it. Analysis is not a dissection of something that is already and passively there. What we call analysis is, of course, a constructive or creative process. It is a more deliberate following-through of that process of creation in response to the poet's words which reading is. It is a re-creation in which, by a considering attentiveness, we ensure a more than ordinary faithfulness and completeness.

As addressed to other readers it is an appeal for corroboration; 'the poem builds up in this way, doesn't it? this bears such-and-such a relation to that, don't you agree?' In the work of an English School this aspect of mutual check – positively, of collaboration 'in the common pursuit of true judgment' – would assert itself as a matter of course.

To insist on this critical work as discipline is not to contemplate the elaboration of technical apparatus and drill. The training is to be one in the sensitive and scrupulous use of intelligence; to that end, such help as can be given the student will not be in the nature of initiations into technical procedures, and there is no apparatus to be handed over – a show of such in analytic work will most likely turn out to be a substitute for the use of intelligence upon the text. Where help can and should be got, of course, is in examples of good practice, wherever these can be found. 'Instruction' will take the form of varied and developing demonstration, offered to the actively critical student (i.e. in discussion-work conditions) as exemplifying a suitable use of intelligence. [. . .]

If the dubious reader has by now some notion of what at any rate the literary critical discipline is not, that is something gained. To go very far in a positive account is not possible here, and by some readers (by most, perhaps, of those I shall actually have) will not be thought necessary. It will be gathered that demonstration and guidance even at the outset will take as little as possible the form, 'this is the correct method.' In the early stages, of course, there must be some pretty positive initiation. This would be done in terms of type-cases so elementary and obvious that the use they are put to could hardly be questioned by anyone of literary experience. [. . .]

In criticism, of course (one would emphasize), nothing can be proved; there can, in the nature of the case, be no laboratory-demonstration or anything like it. Nevertheless, it is nearly always possible to go further than merely asserting a judgment or inviting agreement with a general account. Commonly one can call attention to this, that or the other detail by way of making the nature and force of one's judgment plain.

Note

1 F. R. Leavis' book has been reprinted in a second revised edition by Cambridge University Press, 1979.

2.7   The importance of structure

Jerome S. Bruner

In order for a person to be able to recognize the applicability or inapplicability of an idea to a new situation and to broaden his learning thereby, he must have clearly in mind the general nature of the phenomenon with which he is dealing. The more fundamental or basic is the idea he has learned, almost by definition, the greater will be its breadth of applicability to new problems. Indeed, this is almost a tautology, for what is meant by 'fundamental' in this sense is precisely that an idea has wide as well as powerful applicability. It is simple enough to proclaim, of course, that school curricula and methods of teaching should be geared to the teaching of fundamental ideas in whatever subject is being taught. But as soon as one makes such a statement a host of problems arise, many of which can be solved only with the aid of considerably more research. We turn to some of these now.

The first and most obvious problem is how to construct curricula that can be taught by ordinary teachers to ordinary students and that at the same time reflect clearly the basic underlying principles of various fields of inquiry. The problem is twofold: first, how to have the basic subjects rewritten and their teaching materials revamped in such a way that the pervading and powerful ideas and attitudes relating to them are given a central role; second, how to match the levels of these materials to the capacities of students of different abilities at different grades in school.

The experience of the past several years has taught at least one important lesson about the design of a curriculum that is true to the underlying structure of its subject matter. It is that the best minds in any particular discipline must be put to work on the task. The decision as to what should be taught in American history to elementary school children or what should be taught in arithmetic is a decision that can best be reached with the aid of those with a high degree of vision and competence in each of these fields. [. . .]

There is at least one major matter that is left unsettled even by a large-scale revision of curricula in the direction indicated. Mastery of the fundamental ideas of a field involves not only the grasping of general principles, but also the development of an attitude toward learning and inquiry, toward guessing and hunches, toward the possibility of solving problems on one's own. Just as a physicist has certain attitudes about the ultimate orderliness of nature and a conviction that order can be discovered, so a young physics student needs some working version of these attitudes if he is to organize his learning in such a way as to make what he learns usable and meaningful in his thinking. To instill such attitudes by teaching requires something more than the mere

Source: BRUNER, J. S. (1960) *The Process of Education*. Cambridge, Mass.: Harvard University Press, extracted from pp. 18–31.

presentation of fundamental ideas. Just what it takes to bring off such teaching is something on which a great deal of research is needed, but it would seem that an important ingredient is a sense of excitement about discovery – discovery of regularities of previously unrecognized relations and similarities between ideas, with a resulting sense of self-confidence in one's abilities. Various people who have worked on curricula in science and mathematics have urged that it is possible to present the fundamental structure of a discipline in such a way as to preserve some of the exciting sequences that lead a student to discover for himself. [. . .]

It is the consensus of virtually all the men and women who have been working on curriculum projects that making material interesting is in no way incompatible with presenting it soundly; indeed, a correct general explanation is often the most interesting of all. Inherent in the preceding discussions are at least four general claims that can be made for teaching the fundamental structure of a subject, claims in need of detailed study.

The first is that understanding fundamentals makes a subject more comprehensible. This is true not only in physics and mathematics, where we have principally illustrated the point, but equally in the social studies and literature. Once one has grasped the fundamental idea that a nation must trade in order to live, then such a presumably special phenomenon as the Triangular Trade of the American colonies becomes altogether simpler to understand as something more than commerce in molasses, sugar cane, rum, and slaves in an atmosphere of violation of British trade regulations. The high school student reading *Moby Dick* can only understand more deeply if he can be led to understand that Melville's novel is, among other things, a study of the theme of evil and the plight of those pursuing this 'killing whale'. And if the student is led further to understand that there are a relatively limited number of human plights about which novels are written, he understands literature the better for it.

The second point relates to human memory. Perhaps the most basic thing that can be said about human memory, after a century of intensive research, is that unless detail is placed into a structured pattern, it is rapidly forgotten. Detailed material is conserved in memory by the use of simplified ways of representing it [. . .]. We remember a formula, a vivid detail that carries the meaning of an event, an average that stands for a range of events, a caricature or picture that preserves an essence – all of them techniques of condensation and representation. What learning general or fundamental principles does is to ensure that memory loss will not mean total loss, that what remains will permit us to reconstruct the details when needed. A good theory is the vehicle not only for understanding a phenomenon now but also for remembering it tomorrow.

Third, an understanding of fundamental principles and ideas, as noted earlier, appears to be the main road to adequate 'transfer of training'. To understand something as a specific instance of a more general case – which is what understanding a more fundamental principle or structure means – is to have learned not only a specific thing but also a model for understanding other things like it that one may encounter. If a student could grasp in its most human sense the weariness of Europe at the close of the Hundred Years' War and how it created the conditions for a workable but not ideologically absolute Treaty of Westphalia, he might be better able to think about the ideological struggle of East and West – though the parallel is anything but exact. A carefully wrought understanding should also permit him to recognize the limits of the generalization as well. The idea of 'principles' and 'concepts' as a basis for transfer is hardly new. It is much in need of more research of a specific kind that would provide detailed knowledge of how best to proceed in the teaching of different subjects in different grades.

The fourth claim for emphasis on structure and principles in teaching is that by constantly reexamining material taught in elementary and secondary schools for its fundamental character, one is able to narrow the gap between 'advanced' knowledge and 'elementary' knowledge. Part of the difficulty now found in the progression from primary school through high school to college is that material learned earlier is either out of date or misleading by virtue of its lagging too far behind developments in a field. This gap can be reduced by the kind of emphasis set forth in the preceding discussion. [. . .]

Perhaps the chief arguments put forward in opposition to the idea of such efforts at teaching general principles and general attitudes are, first, that it is better to approach the general through the specific and, second, that working attitudes should be kept implicit rather than being made explicit. For example, one of the principal organizing concepts in biology is the persistent question, 'What function does this thing serve?' – a question premised on the assumption that everything one finds in an organism serves some function or it probably would not have survived. Other general ideas are related to this question. The student who makes progress in biology learns to ask the questions more and more subtly, to relate more and more things to it. At the next step he asks what function a particular structure or process serves in the light of what is required in the total functioning of an organism. Measuring and categorizing are carried out in the service of the general idea of function. Then beyond that he may organize his knowledge in terms of a still more comprehensive notion of function, turning to cellular structure or to phylogenetic comparison. It may well be that the style of thought of a particular discipline is necessary as a background for learning the working meaning of general concepts, in which case a general introduction to the meaning of 'function' might be less effective than teaching it in the context of biology.

As for 'attitude' teaching or even the teaching of heuristic in mathematics, the argument runs that if the learner becomes too aware of his own attitudes or approach, he may become mechanical or trick-oriented in his work. No evidence exists on the point, and research is needed before any effort is made to teach in this way. Work is now going on at Illinois on training children to be more effective in asking questions about physical phenomena, but much more information is needed before the issue is clear. [. . .]

A word is needed, finally, on examinations. It is obvious that an examination can be bad in the sense of emphasizing trivial aspects of a subject. Such examinations can encourage teaching in a disconnected fashion and learning by rote. What is often overlooked, however, is that examinations can also be allies in the battle to improve curricula and teaching. Whether an examination is of the 'objective' type involving multiple choices or of the essay type, it can be devised so as to emphasize an understanding of the broad principles of a subject. Indeed, even when one examines on detailed knowledge, it can be done in such a way as to require an understanding by the student of the connectedness between specific facts. There is a concerted effort now under way among national testing organizations like the Educational Testing Service to construct examinations that will emphasize an understanding of fundamental principles. Such efforts can be of great help. Additional help might be given to local school systems by making available to them manuals that describe the variety of ways in which examinations can be constructed. The searching examination is not easy to make, and a thoughtful manual on the subject would be welcome.

2.8 A process model

Lawrence Stenhouse

Within knowledge and arts areas, it is possible to select content for a curriculum unit without reference to student behaviours or indeed to ends of any kind other than that of representing the form of knowledge in the curriculum. This is because a form of knowledge has structure, and it involves procedures, concepts and criteria. Content can be selected to exemplify the most important procedures, the key concepts and the areas and situations in which the criteria hold.

Now it might be thought that this is to designate procedures, concepts and criteria as objectives to be learned by the students. This strategy could, of course, be followed, but it would, I believe, distort the curriculum. For the key procedures, concepts and criteria in any subject – *cause*, *form*, *experiment*, *tragedy* – are, and are important precisely because they are, problematic within the subject. They are the focus of speculation, not the object of mastery. Educationally, they are also important because they invite understanding at a variety of levels. The infant class considering the origins of a playground fight and the historian considering the origins of the First World War are essentially engaged in the same sort of task. They are attempting to understand by using the concepts of causation; and they are attempting to understand both the event and the concept by which they seek to explicate it.

It is the building of curriculum on such structures as procedures, concepts and criteria, which cannot adequately be translated into the performance levels of objectives, that makes possible Bruner's 'courteous translation' of knowledge and allows of learning which challenges all abilities and interests in a diverse group. (See Stenhouse, 1975, Raths' point 5, page 87)

The translation of the deep structures of knowledge into behavioural objectives is one of the principal causes of the distortion of knowledge in schools noted by Young (1971), Bernstein (1971) and Esland (1971). The filtering of knowledge through an analysis of objectives gives the school an authority and power over its students by setting arbitrary limits to speculation and by defining arbitrary solutions to unresolved problems of knowledge. This translates the teacher from the role of the student of a complex field of knowledge to the role of the master of the school's agreed version of that field.

What is the nature of historical causation? Can the concept of causation be used successfully to understand complex situations? How might one attack the origins of the First World War by using the concept, and how successfully? These are the kinds of question raised by adopting *cause* as a key concept in

Source: STENHOUSE, L. (1975) *An Introduction to Curriculum Research and Development*. London: Heinemann, pp. 85–96.

history. There is no generally acceptable and pre-specifiable answer to them. The use of the objectives model has led to the provision of arbitrary answers in the form of specifications of the causes of the First World War which can be tested and marked and this necessarily distorts the knowledge included in the curriculum.

It is quite possible to evolve principles for the selection of content in the curriculum in terms of criteria which are not dependent on the existence of a specification of objectives, and which are sufficiently specific to give real guidance and to expose the principles to criticism.

[. . .]

In arguing for the use of behavioural objectives in curriculum design, Tyler (1949) mentioned and dismissed two other possibilities. I now want to take those up.

The first was that we might specify what the teacher is to do. And you will remember that he argues (see Stenhouse, 1975, page 53) that if an objective is stated in the form of activities to be carried on by the teacher, there is no way of judging whether these activities are justifiable, since they are not the ultimate purpose of education. These ultimate purposes are, he avers, changes in the students. And they need to be prespecified, spelled out in advance. We have noted the shortcomings of an ends–means model in education, and looked towards the specification of principles of procedure which refer to teacher activity.

The second possibility which Tyler dismissed was that one might specify the content to be dealt with. This too he regards as unsatisfactory as it does not tell us what the students are to do with the content. I have argued that where a form of knowledge exists, a specification of content does imply how it is to be handled.

I now want to consider by reference to practical cases whether we can reasonably set about curriculum design by attempting to define the classroom process in terms of what the teacher is to do at the level of principles and what the content is. In such a case our statement about a curriculum would be an answer to the question: how is the teacher to handle what? I shall of course have to consider this approach in relation to changes in the students.

I propose to examine two curricula, *Man: A Course of Study* and the Humanities Curriculum Project, both of which are designed on a basis other than that of behavioural objectives.

Man: A Course of Study is an American social science curriculum mainly for the 10–12 year-old age range. It is film-based and is rich in materials. It was directed by Peter Dow with Jerome Bruner as chief consulting scholar, and the force of Bruner's ideas was powerful throughout the process of development.

A brief specification of the content of the course does not reach the heart of it. It consists of a rather detailed study of the Pacific salmon, the herring gull, the baboon and the Netsilik eskimo with a running comparison with the students' own society and experience. The method is comparative, and the curriculum is based in the behavioural sciences and anthropology.

Bruner writes:

The content of the course is man: his nature as a species, the forces that shaped and continue to shape his humanity. Three questions recur throughout:
    What is human about human beings?
    How did they get that way?
    How can they be made more so?

(Bruner 1966, 74)

The ambiguities in these questions and the shift to a value implication in the last one (where strictly speaking 'humane' might be more appropriate than 'human') are intended. They invite teacher and students to speculate about humanness in the broadest sense as they study the materials of the course.

A good deal more than this could be said about content, but that is enough for the present purpose. The content is speculation about humanness through a study of behavioural science in a context of value questions. The teacher then is asked to be, for the purpose of the course, a speculative behavioural and social scientist alive to the value issues raised by his work.

Bruner notes the problem which immediately hits the teacher when he is confronted with such a demand:

The first and most obvious problem is how to construct curricula that can be taught by ordinary teachers to ordinary students and that at the same time reflect clearly the basic or underlying principles of various fields of inquiry.

He notes the need for powerful and intelligent materials and for adjustment to students of different abilities. He discusses in detail the demands on the teacher implicit in the position he takes.

Either the teacher must be an expert or he must be a learner along with his students. In most cases, the teacher cannot in the nature of the case be an expert. It follows that he must cast himself in the role of a learner. Pedagogically this may in fact be a preferable role to that of the expert. It implies teaching by discovery or inquiry methods rather than by instruction.

The teacher is not free to cast himself in the role of the learner without regard to the learning of his students for which he must accept responsibility. What is required of him to make him a senior learner capable of offering something of worth to the junior learners with whom he works? Skills in finding things out, of course. But more than that: some hold on, and a continual refinement of, a philosophical understanding of the subject he is teaching and learning, of its deep structures and their rationale. The teacher needs to take on to his agenda a desire to understand the nature of social science, the value problems it raises and its relation to the questions at the centre of the course. Only when he has gone some way towards structuring his own understanding of these issues can he adopt the pedagogy of the course.

The principles behind this pedagogy have been expressed as pedagogical aims:

1   To initiate and develop in youngsters a process of question-posing (the inquiry method);

2　To teach a research methodology where children can look for information to answer questions they have raised and use the framework developed in the course (e.g. the concept of the life cycle) and apply it to new areas;

3　To help youngsters develop the ability to use a variety of first-hand sources as evidence from which to develop hypotheses and draw conclusions;

4　To conduct classroom discussions in which youngsters learn to listen to others as well as to express their own views;

5　To legitimize the search; that is, to give sanction and support to open-ended discussions where definitive answers to many questions are not found;

6　To encourage children to reflect on their own experiences;

7　To create a new role for the teacher, in which he becomes a resource rather than an authority.

(Hanley, Whitla, Moo, Walter 1970, 5)

And the authors comment: 'It is clear that these goals centre around the process of learning, rather than around the product.' They are in fact principles of procedure, and they are spelled out more fully in the course materials, and particularly in the teachers' handbook on *Evaluation Strategies*.

Let us take stock. *Man: A Course of Study* is a curriculum designed on a specification of content – objects of study and some master concepts and the point of view of social science – and a specification of what the teacher is to do expressed in terms of principles of procedure. It is not designed on a pre-specification of behavioural objectives. Of course there are changes in students as a result of the course, but many of the most valued are not to be anticipated in detail. The power and the possibilities of the curriculum cannot be contained within objectives because it is founded on the idea that knowledge must be speculative and thus indeterminate as to student outcomes if it is to be worthwhile. And it is a practical and orderly course in use in a large number of schools.

Man: A Course of Study sustains coherence within a process model partly at least because of its reliance on the structures of knowledge. It is often argued that education should be founded on the disciplines of knowledge because they provide a framework of criteria and principles of procedure and a means of justifying these. I believe that if the advantages of this framework are to be gained, a process model should be used rather than an objectives model.

Does this mean that the process model implies the disciplines of knowledge as a framework? Are they the only source of process criteria?

In its experimental design the Humanities Project is an attempt to explore this problem. The content selected, controversial human issues, has in common with knowledge in the disciplines a necessary indeterminacy of student outcomes, but there is no disciplinary structure.

The argument runs thus. Controversial issues are defined empirically as issues which do *in fact* divide people in our society. Given divergence among students, parents and teachers, democratic principles are evoked to suggest that teachers may wish to ensure that they do not use their position of authority in the classroom to advance their own opinions or perspectives, and that the teaching process does not determine the outcome opinions and perspectives of the students. It is important that there is no epistemological base to this argument. The position is that, given a dispute in society about the truth of a matter, the teacher in a compulsory state school might wish to teach the dispute rather than the truth as he knows it. A similar position could be taken on different grounds in almost any area of knowledge.

However, without the support of a discipline of knowledge as a base – though disciplined knowledge is an ingredient – it proved possible to operate a design on the process model.

The Humanities Curriculum Project (1970; Stenhouse, 1971) concentrated its research on the technical problems of operating a discussion-based form of teaching in which the group critically examined evidence as it discussed issues under the chairmanship of a teacher who submitted his work to the criterion of neutrality.

The pedagogical (as opposed to the research) aim of the Project is to develop an understanding of social situations and human acts and of the controversial value issues which they raise. (Retrospectively, I think it would have been better to delete 'value', since as it stands the aim may appear to imply that the only controversial issues are value issues or even that value issues are necessarily controversial.)

Two implications of this aim are worth pointing out. First, it is implied that both students and teachers develop understanding, that is, the teacher is cast in the role of a learner. Second, understanding is chosen as an aim because it cannot be achieved. Understanding can always be deepened. Moreover, there must always be dispute as to what constitutes a valid understanding. The teacher and the group have to accept as part of their task an exploration of the nature of understanding.

The hypotheses and suggestions offered to teachers by the Project were largely based on the observation of classrooms and had two principal logics. One logic was that of group dynamics. For example, the arrangement of chairs may be important for encouraging discussion across the group, and slow-paced discussions may broaden participation. Such hypotheses are virtually independent of content. Other hypotheses about procedure, however, are content-linked. For example, understanding of controversy is better achieved by listening to a range of views carefully and using questions to elicit amplification rather than by arguing against opponents and attempting to resolve divergence.

In the Humanities Project we were hammering out in collaboration with teachers a procedural discipline like that of 'procedure at meetings' or parliamentary procedure with the important distinction that we were concerned not with a decision-making group, but with a learning group aiming to develop understanding. And the very existence of such forms as procedures at meetings, the mediaeval disputation and indeed the epic or the novel, should indicate that such procedures can have logical structures which are not dependent on epistemological structures. Controversiality is a particularly interesting theme in this respect, since it contains a paradox. Since the controversy involves (for all but the relativist) competing claims to truth, it implies the notion of some non-controversial standard of truth to which appeal is being made.

The process model of curriculum development raises problems for the assessment of student work. They may be difficult in practice, but they are not difficult to understand. The objectives model is closely related to the American movement towards examination reform. Discontent was felt at the subjectivity of marking and there was a pressure towards objective tests, the criteria for which were supplied by statements of objectives.

Now, of course, compromises could be made between the objectives and the process models in practice, but in its logically pure form I think that the process model implies that in assessment or appraisal the teacher ought to be a critic, not a marker. The worthwhile activity in which teacher and students are engaged has standards and criteria immanent in it and the task of appraisal is that of improving students' capacity to work to such criteria by critical reaction to work done. In this sense assessment is about the teaching of self-assessment.

Such assessment is not purely subjective since it appeals to public criteria, but it is concerned with difficult judgments and hence performance will vary from teacher to teacher. Critical assessment of work is an activity which exposes the strengths and weaknesses of teachers very clearly. This presents problems. If I as a student trust my teacher's judgment, I want criticism rather than marking. If I do not trust his judgment, I want marking rather than criticism. In the classroom there is no way of compensating me for the loss I suffer in working with a teacher whose judgment I do not trust. But I do want to be protected when it comes to public examination.

There is a conflict of demand between appraisal as teaching and appraisal as grading. In appraisal as teaching, the differing abilities and strengths of teachers are acceptable. That is why a singer may choose to be taught by several teachers in succession. The capacity of the limited teacher to limit us is the price we pay for the capacity of the profound teacher to extend us. But since grading counts for so much, we want to be assured that the limitations of our teachers do not seriously penalize us in examinations. The more objective an examination, the more it fails to reveal the quality of good teaching and good learning. By objective tests Michelangelo and Russell Flint both get distinctions, yet it is the difference of quality between them that is of fundamental importance in art.

The process model is essentially a critical model, not a marking model. It can never be *directed* towards an examination *as an objective* without loss of quality, since the standards of the examination then override the standards immanent in the subject. This does not mean that students taught on the process model cannot be examined, but it does mean that the examination must be taken in their stride as they pursue other aspirations. And if the examination is a by-product there is an implication that the quality the student shows in it must be an under-estimate of his real quality. It is hence rather difficult to get the weak student through an examination using a process model. Crammers cannot use it, since it depends upon commitment to educational aims.

Unfortunately, examinations are so important in our society that most teachers, faced as they often are with choosing between education and opportunity for a substantial proportion of their pupils, opt for the latter. Their aim is to get their pupils through examinations they do not deserve to pass. And it is quite possible to get O or A level passes in chemistry or history or literature (not to mention a respectable degree) without really understanding the subject in the sense of grasping its deep structures and the concerns of scholars in it. The process-based curriculum pursues understanding rather than grades when the two conflict, and since grades are attainable without understanding, this penalizes the limited student in terms of opportunity even though it is educationally advantageous to him.

References

BERNSTEIN, B. (1971) *Class, Codes and Control, Vol I: Theoretical Studies towards a Sociology of Language*. London: Routledge and Kegan Paul.

BRUNER, J. (1966) *Towards a Theory of Instruction*. Cambridge, Mass.: Harvard University Press.

ESLAND, G. (1971) 'Teaching and learning as the organization of knowledge', in YOUNG, M. (ed.) 1971 *Knowledge and Control*. London: Collier-Macmillan.

HANLEY, JANET, P. *et al.* (1970) *Curiosity, Competence, Community: Man; a course of study, An Evaluation*. Cambridge, Mass.: Educational Development Center.

HUMANITIES CURRICULUM PROJECT (1970) *The Humanities Project: an introduction*. London: Heinemann.

STENHOUSE, L. (1971) 'The Humanities Curriculum Project: the rationale.' *Theory into Practice*, Vol. 10, pp. 154–62.

STENHOUSE, L. (1975) *An Introduction to Curriculum Research and Development*. London: Heinemann.

TYLER, R. W. (1949) *Basic Principles of Curriculum and Instruction*. Chicago, Ill.: University of Chicago Press.

YOUNG, M. (ed.) (1971) *Knowledge and Control*. London: Collier-Macmillan.

2.9 Implications of classroom research for professional development

John Elliott

Process-product studies

The 'triple-play'

To date, the dominant approach to classroom research has been that of the process-product study; these studies have been reviewed by Berliner and Rosenshine (1977) and Dunkin and Biddle (1974). Studies of this type attempt to describe observable regularities in teaching performance, and then to discover whether any causal relationships exist between such performances and learning outcomes as measured by achievement tests. In discovering these relationships, process-product researchers would claim to have identified certain elements of effective teaching, which can be formulated as technical rules to be applied in teacher education. Fenstermacher (1978) suggests that the motive to furnish 'imperatives for teacher training' is so strong that process-product researchers tend to engage in a kind of 'triple-play'. He argues that research findings are usually based on statistical correlations which answer the general question 'What relationships obtain, if any, between teacher performances $P_1, P_2, P_3 \ldots P_n$ and success at learning tasks $K_1, K_2, K_3 \ldots K_n$ by students assigned to complete these tasks?' Having isolated a positive correlation, say 'P_1 and P_2 are significantly correlated with success at task K_1 by students assigned this task', researchers tend to conclude that teachers should do P_1 and P_2 in answer to the question 'What should teachers do in order to be effective in getting students to succeed at K_1 and tasks like it?'

Now Fenstermacher claims that this leap from correlational findings to prescriptions for teacher training begs two important questions; first, the causal question 'Do teacher performances P_1 and P_2 *result* in success at task K_1 by students assigned this task?' A correlational relationship does not necessarily imply a causal one. From the fact that a correlation exists between P_1-P_2 and K_1, one cannot logically infer that a causal relationship exists between them. It could be that the causal relationship exists between both these correlated variables and a third. In order to establish where the cause lies, a researcher would have to embark on a series of experimental studies. Fenstermacher argues that the standard procedure in process-product research is to assume that the correlational question answers the causal question, 'Why do P_1 and P_2 result in student success at K_1?' Thus process-product research rarely provides us with a theoretical explanation as to why

Source: HOYLE, E., MEGARRY, J. and ATKIN, M. (eds) (1980) *World Year Book of Education: The Professional Development of Teachers*. London: Kogan Page, pp. 308–24 (in part).

the correlations or causal relationships it discovers obtain in the context of the study. Having ignored this question, the third and final move is to translate the assumed cause-effect relationships between teaching and learning into rules for teacher training.

I have dealt extensively with Fenstermacher's account of how process-product classroom researchers reason from theory to practice, because it enables me to spell out the implications of some key assumptions which underlie their approach.

The assumption of teachers' causality

The first key assumption is that teaching *causes* learning. On the basis of this assumption the process-product researcher tends to focus on the performances of the teacher rather than those of students in the classroom, and to interpret correlations between these performances and learning outcomes as evidence that the former caused the latter.

This assumption also has implications for educational accountability. It suggests that teachers alone can be held accountable for student learning, rather than, say, the students themselves or educational managers and administrators. In the absence of the assumption of teacher causality the discovery of correlations between classroom events and learning outcomes might be a stimulus for entertaining the possibility that, rather than being causally linked with each other, these variables are caused by factors originating beyond the classroom in its institutional and administrative context. The assumption of teacher causality is bureaucratically and politically convenient since it suggests that deficiencies in educational provision can only be rectified by doing something about the way teachers perform in classrooms rather than by doing something about the way schools as institutions are organized, or the provision of educational resources administered.

The causal knowledge generated by process-product researchers can easily be formulated as sets of technical means-ends rules intended to govern teacher performance. One might argue that the researcher's knowledge is based on the view that teaching is a technology or form of instrumental action (see Habermas, 1972). Such action involves the agent (teacher) administering certain treatments (teaching methods) to passive objects (students) in order to produce preconceived outputs (objectives). In the field of social relations, instrumental action influences people's behaviour by securing compliance, and this involves the employment of power expressed in the use of positive and negative sanctions (rewards and punishments). Thus teaching conceived as instrumental action is power-coercive and its object, learning, is power-dependent.

When teaching is conceived as instrumental action, learning is conceived as passive behaviour directed by the teacher rather than self-directed by students. Presupposed in the process-product approach is a bias against the ideas of 'self-directed', 'discovery', 'inquiry' learning. If effective teaching is a set of causally efficacious performances then by definition it cannot result in learning conceived in these ways. It should hardly be surprising, then, that process-product correlations fail to demonstrate 'the effectiveness' of informal teaching methods when employed by teachers who construe learning in the terms cited above. Yet the failure to establish causal relationships here is interpreted by the researchers as an outcome of their research, rather than being an inevitable implication of their research design. There is no way in which progressive methods of teaching can 'look good' from the perspective of process-product research.

Finally, the assumption of teacher causality implies a division of labour between researchers who produce causal knowledge and teachers who apply it in practice. The causal statements produced by process-product researchers refer to publicly observable acts rather than the subjective states of teachers. They can be tested independently of any reference to the beliefs, intentions, and meanings teachers express in their actions. Thus the production of knowledge about teaching does not have to be validated against teachers' understanding of their own actions, and does not require their participation: their role is to apply the knowledge researchers produce. The process of professional development involves the application of research knowledge but not its production.

Generalizability

Let me now turn to the second key assumption underlying process-product research. Power (1976) sums it up neatly when he argues that for this kind of research, 'situations and events are not regarded as unique. This means actions can be repeated and probability statements linking situations and actions made . . . Generalizations across classrooms about classroom phenomena, their antecedents and consequences are believed to be both possible and useful'. This is the assumption of *formal generalizability*, that there are general laws governing the relationship between classroom events to be discovered. This assumption explains the process-product researcher's apparent failure to explain why the causal relationships he infers from his correlations obtain. Such an explanation would be given only if the researcher thought that it might not be possible to generalize across all classroom contexts.

It is my view that process-product generalizations are applicable only to some learning contexts. Doyle (1979) argues that process-product research has tended to assume a homogeneity in the quality of learning tasks given to students, leading to the use of a single criterion for assessing outcomes. The result is a general focus on the quantifiable aspects of teaching and learning. Thus *how much* is learned becomes more significant than the type of learning involved, and in an attempt to discover correlations, quantifiable aspects of teaching, such as pacing of content and the amount covered, have priority over qualitative aspects.

Three types of learning task

Doyle distinguishes three types of learning tasks. First, there are 'understanding' tasks, requiring students to apply cognitive operations, such as classification, inference, deduction and analysis, to instances not previously encountered, or to comprehend information by reproducing it in transformed or paraphrased form. Secondly, there are 'memory' tasks, requiring recognition or recall of facts, principles, or solutions the student has previously been acquainted with. Thirdly, there are 'routine problem-solving' tasks, such as dividing fractions or squaring numbers, which require students to learn a standard and reliable formula or principle. Doyle goes on to argue that different types of learning tasks can be compared in the light of the degrees of ambiguity and risk inherent in them. Ambiguity inheres in a learning task, not because of the teacher's lack of clarity, but because it does not tell the student the exact performance that will be required and how to produce it. Risk refers to the likelihood of students being able to cope with the demands of a task. According to Doyle 'understanding' tasks score high on both ambiguity and risk. 'Memory' and 'routine problem-solving' tasks on the other hand are low on ambiguity and when the amount of content to be covered is small or the routines to be mastered simple, low on risk.

In the light of these qualitative differences between learning tasks, Doyle suggests that one can expect greater variance in learning outcomes, and therefore lower mean achievement, on 'understanding' tasks than on 'memory' or 'routine problem-solving' ones. This implies that it is easier for teachers to control mean achievement when the learning tasks are of the latter rather than the former kind. It follows that one is more likely to discover general rules for maximizing learning outcomes when the learning tasks are of the 'memory' or 'routine problem-solving' kind than of the 'understanding' kind. If this is correct, then we have a possible explanation for the causal generalizations established by process-product research. It is that they only apply to classroom contexts where students are performing on 'memory' or 'routine problem-solving' tasks. The fact that the criteria employed by process-product research tend to measure outcomes of these kinds of tasks reinforces this point.

The qualities of ambiguity and risk, intrinsic to 'understanding' tasks, indicate why process-product methodology is quite inappropriate for the study of classrooms where students are performing them. Such qualities imply that learning is contingent on the personal characteristics of individual students and thereby introduce an element of unpredictability into teaching. In 'understanding' contexts one can no longer assume that the relationship between teaching performance and learning outcomes is a causal one, let alone generalizable across students and classrooms. A new paradigm of classroom research is required, but before sketching it, I want briefly to return to the implications of process-product research for teacher education.

Teacher training and teacher education

Most educational theorists would view education as a process of 'teaching for understanding'. Process-product research therefore masks and distorts education. This is why I have elsewhere described such research as 'research on education' rather than 'educational research' (Elliott, 1978b). The outcomes of education cannot be detected by its methods, and *educational* methods are bound to show up rather poorly in its research findings. If these findings are then translated into prescriptions for competency-based teacher education and implemented on a large scale, the teachers of the future will certainly not be equipped to be educators of children. Moreover, the process of teacher training will also not be an *educational* one. All process-product research can do is to furnish rules governing teaching performance in typical situations. These rules are learned by applying them uncritically in such situations. In other words the process of teacher training will involve teachers performing 'routine problem-solving' rather than 'understanding' tasks. In my view the professional development of teachers is an educational process which involves developing understanding of the particular classroom situations in which they work. The application of general rules pre-empts such understanding.

Educational action research

Curriculum development as a context for research

It is no coincidence that action research in classrooms tended to emerge in association with the curriculum development movement in the 1960s and early 1970s. Many of the projects which constituted this movement were concerned with shifting the learning context in classrooms from 'memory' and 'routine problem-solving' to 'understanding' tasks. Such innovations tended to articulate this shift in terms of ideas like 'self-directed', 'discovery', and 'inquiry' learning. As I suggested earlier these ideas embody a more active and personal conception of the learning process than the one presupposed by process-product research. Each of the above terms picks out a particular aspect of this process. 'Self-directed' implies that learning outcomes are the result of the student's own autonomous activity and not of teaching. 'Inquiry' provides a general description of the kind of activity involved, constituted by the cognitive operations cited by Doyle in his account of 'understanding' tasks. 'Discovery' refers to the quality of the intellectual experience which results from this kind of activity, indicating both its personal and impersonal aspects. In its impersonal aspect an objective reality which exists independently of the student's own thinking is disclosed. In its personal aspect this reality can only be personally appropriated by the student as he brings his own cognitive structures to bear on the problems defined by the task. These orienting ideas, employed in the curriculum development movement, simply pick out different dimensions of performance on 'understanding' tasks in terms of its agency, the operations involved, and the quality of the intellectual experience which results.

The problems teachers experienced in initiating and sustaining student performance on 'understanding' tasks generated a whole movement of classroom research conducted largely by people attached to the development teams of national projects in collaboration with participating teachers. (See Barnes, 1976; Elliott and MacDonald, 1972; Elliott and Adelman, 1976; Jenkins, 1977; Parlett and Hamilton, 1973; Smith and Schumacher, 1972; Walker and Adelman, 1972; Wild, 1973.) Interestingly, this research conceptualized the problems of teaching in a radically different way from process-product research. In place of technical problems of selecting causally effective means for bringing about certain pre-specified learning outcomes, the problems were seen as ones of achieving a certain quality of communication with students about the problems and issues posed by learning tasks. Teaching was viewed as a mode of communicative rather than instrumental action (see Habermas, 1972).

In viewing teaching in this way classroom researchers were simply adopting the same perspective as the curriculum developers. Indeed, many of them, like myself, played the dual roles of developer and researcher. The reason I have called this alternative mode of research action research is simply because it adopts the action perspective of curriculum developers (Elliott, 1978a). I will now attempt to give a more detailed account of this perspective.

The action perspective of curriculum development

Many curriculum development projects neglected to spell out the pedagogical implications of 'teaching for understanding' in the content areas they were concerned with. Perhaps naïvely it was assumed that they would be tacitly understood by teachers. Stenhouse's *Humanities Curriculum Project* (1971) and Bruner's *Man: a course of study* (1970) were notable exceptions. Both formulated pedagogic principles which specified conditions of teaching and learning to be realized in classrooms rather than learning objectives. Stenhouse called them 'principles of procedure', while Bruner used the phrase 'pedagogical aims'. Such principles or aims specified intrinsically, rather than instrumentally, valuable qualities of teaching and learning tasks. Although some curriculum development projects attempted to fit their ideas to a behavioural objectives model of curriculum design, Stenhouse (1975) claimed that such a model was inconsistent with teaching for understanding and education. He argued that the Humanities Project's aim of 'developing an understanding of controversial issues' could not be broken down into specific learning objectives without distorting its nature. This is entirely consistent with Doyle's account of 'understanding' tasks as high in ambiguity, in the sense that there are no absolute rules for producing correct answers, and therefore no ways of predicting in advance exactly what constitutes successful performance.

Stenhouse posed the 'process model' of curriculum design as an alternative to 'behavioural objectives'. He claimed that the general aim of 'understanding' could be logically analysed into principles governing the process of teaching and learning in classrooms. For example, he argued that the teacher who used his position of authority in the classroom to promote his own views would necessarily impose constraints on the development of an understanding of controversial issues. The actions involved would be logically inconsistent with such development. From this consideration Stenhouse formulated the principle of procedural neutrality, ie the obligation to refrain from taking sides on a controversial issue *qua* teacher. Similarly, he argued that students would necessarily lack opportunities to develop their understanding of issues if the teacher denied them access to some views rather than others. Thus failure to protect divergence in classroom discussion was logically inconsistent with the project's aim. Only the teacher whose actions realized the principle 'protect the expression of divergent views' would be acting consistently. Stenhouse's 'procedural principles' functioned as criteria for selecting teaching acts which were logically consistent with the development of understanding on learning tasks. Acts which realized these criteria constituted a worthwhile form of teaching regardless of their outcomes. His inspiration for the 'process model' of curriculum design came from R. S. Peters' seminal paper entitled 'Must an educator have an aim?' (1968). In this paper Peters argued that *educational* aims specify what is to count as a worthwhile educational process rather than its extrinsic outcomes.

The process model embodies a radically different set of assumptions about the relationship between teaching and learning from the behavioural objectives model and the process-product research which matches it. The aim of teaching is viewed as 'enabling', 'facilitating' or 'providing opportunities for' the development of understanding. Such aim descriptions specify conditions to be realized by the teacher rather than his students. A teacher can *enable* pupils to perform certain learning tasks successfully without them then actually doing so. The student's task performance is ultimately his or her responsibility. The teaching aim of 'enabling the development of understanding' must be distinguished from the learners' aim of 'developing an understanding'. The teaching aim is concerned with establishing conditions in the classroom which enable students to develop their own understanding of the subject matter. The process model, inasmuch as it specifies enabling conditions, embodies an active conception of learning and does not assume that it is caused by teaching.

I will now examine more closely the nature of the enabling conditions specified by the principles of educational procedure which govern 'teaching for understanding'. I have argued that understanding is developed by the student from 'within', through the exercise of his own rational capacities, and therefore cannot be caused from 'without'. However, a student could hardly be described as exercising his rational capacities if he were closed to the reasons and arguments put forward by others. Intellectual development necessarily involves being open to discussion. The fact that it is not causally effected does not imply that it cannot be effected in other ways. This kind of learning, although inconsistent with the employment of power strategies aimed at securing quasi-causal compliance from the student, can be rationally influenced by teaching which involves the student in discussion or discourse about the learning task. In discourse, the teacher seeks to influence a student's task performance by citing evidence, reasons, and arguments.

According to Habermas (1974) pure discourse constitutes 'the ideal speech situation' presupposed in all interpersonal communication. It is characterized by an absence of all constraints on people's thinking, save that of 'the force of the better argument'. For Habermas, the influence exerted through this ideal form of human communication is quite distinct from the power influence exerted in instrumental action upon another. The consensus which results between the participants in discourse is a justified or warranted one. But this raises the problem of how one distinguishes a warranted from an unwarranted consensus, a rational acceptance of another's argument from a non-rational one. Applied to 'teaching for understanding' the issue becomes one of how to distinguish the rational from the non-rational influences a teacher might exert. Habermas attempts to resolve this problem in terms of the formal properties of discourse. He argues that participants must have an equal opportunity to adopt dialogue roles, and in particular equal freedom 'to put forward, call into question, and give reasons for and against statements, explanations, interpretations and justifications'. Thus the conditions of discourse correspond with the liberal-democratic values of 'equality', 'freedom' and 'justice' and constitute the conditions which enable people to develop their understanding through communication with others. In educational contexts, where students encounter 'understanding' tasks, the provision of such discourse conditions is the *educational* responsibility of teachers.

Inasmuch as it is discourse which enables, rather than causes, the development of understanding, then teachers enable this development when they realize discourse values in their communications with students. The relationship between means and ends here is not a technical or instrumental relation. Discourse values are not extrinsic outcomes of communicative acts but intrinsic norms which ideal acts of this kind ought to satisfy. They are not so much realized *by* as *in* acts of teaching.

Stenhouse's 'principles of procedure' and Bruner's 'pedagogical aims' can both be interpreted as attempts to explain the implications of discourse values for teaching in their respective subject areas.

I described the classroom research generated by the curriculum development movement as action research because it conceptualized problems of teaching from the same action perspective as those involved in developing and implementing new curricula. This perspective defines *the educational perspective* on teaching and learning and can be summarized in terms of:

1   a focus on the quality of the teacher's discourse with students about learning tasks;

2 construing learning as a student-directed rather than teacher-directed activity;

3 construing teaching as a mode of exerting rational rather than causal influence on student learning.

It might be argued that classroom action research does not necessarily adopt an educational perspective. In some classroom research contexts the action perspectives of teachers may be very different. I would agree that classroom action perspectives may differ. However, it is not merely a contingent fact that research from an educational perspective appears to be the only mode of action research currently existing in classrooms. There are some kinds of human action which can only be described from a phenomenological perspective, ie by adopting the point of view of the agent. Other kinds of action can be described without any reference to the agent's point of view. Let us compare instrumental with communicative action in this respect. An instrumental action is one which is viewed by its agent as a means to an extrinsic end. But it can be described quite independently of the instrumental meaning ascribed to it by the agent, perhaps on the basis of observational criteria alone. A communicative action on the other hand is an action defined by rules which are logically presupposed by its occurrence. For example, an assertion is an action *in* which the agent places himself under an obligation to speak the truth. Thus one cannot describe the act independently of the agent's perspective in performing it.

It is only when the teaching acts to be described are defined by the teacher's action perspective that research needs to adopt it. Inasmuch as teaching for understanding involves communicative actions defined by the teacher's obligation to realize discourse values, research can only identify them by adopting the same perspective. But inasmuch as teaching for 'routine problem solving' or 'memory' learning is a form of instrumental action, the activities involved can be identified and described quite independently of the teacher's point of view. It is only in the discourse context of teaching for understanding that classroom research must adopt the teacher's perspective if it is to produce valid accounts of such teaching. Process-product studies, by construing teaching as a form of instrumental action, assume that it can be described quite independently of the teacher's action perspective. Such studies therefore cannot be described as educational action research.

References

BARNES, D. (1976) *From Communication to Curriculum.* Harmondsworth: Penguin Books.

BERLINER, D. C. and ROSENSHINE, B. (1977) 'The acquisition of knowledge in the classroom', in ANDERSON, R., SPIRO, R. and MONTAGUE, W. (eds) (1977) *Schooling and the Acquisition of Knowledge.* Hillsdale, N.J.: Lawrence Erlbaum.

BRUNER, J. S. (1970) 'Man: a course of study', in BRUNER, J. S. (1970) *Evaluation Strategies.* Cambridge, Mass.: Educational Development Center.

DOYLE, W. (1979) *The Tasks of Teaching and Learning*. Invited address at the Annual Meeting of the American Educational Research Association, San Francisco, April 1979.

DUNKIN, M. J. and BIDDLE, B. J. (1974) *The Study of Teaching*. New York: Holt, Rinehart and Winston.

ELLIOTT, J. (1978a) 'What is action research in schools?' *Journal of Curriculum Studies*, 10, 4, pp. 355–7.

ELLIOTT, J. (1978b) 'Classroom research: science or common sense', in MCALEESE, R. and HAMILTON, D. (eds) (1978) *Understanding Classroom Life*. Slough: National Foundation for Educational Research.

ELLIOTT, J. and ADELMAN, C. (1976) *Innovation at the Classroom Level*. Course E203, Unit 28. Milton Keynes, Bucks.: Open University Press.

ELLIOTT, J. and MACDONALD, B. (1972) *People in Classrooms*. CARE Occasional Publications No. 1. Norwich, Norfolk: University of East Anglia.

FENSTERMACHER, G. D. (1978) 'A philosophical consideration of recent research on teacher effectiveness.' *Review of Research in Education*, 6.

HABERMAS, J. (1972) 'Technology and science as "ideology"', in HABERMAS, J. (1972) *Towards a Rational Society*. London: Heinemann.

HABERMAS, J. (1974) *Introduction to Theory and Practice*. London: Heinemann.

JENKINS, D. (1977) 'Saved by the bell' and 'Saved by the army', in HAMILTON, D. *et al.* (1977) *Beyond the Numbers Game*. London: Macmillan.

PARLETT, M. and HAMILTON, D. (1973) 'Evaluation as illumination', in TAWNEY, D. (ed.) (1973) *Evaluation in Curriculum Development: Twelve Case Studies*. Schools Council Research Studies. London: Macmillan.

PETERS, R. S. (1968) 'Must an educator have an aim?', in MACMILLAN, C. J. B. and NELSON, T. W. (eds) (1968) *Concepts of Teaching*. Chicago, Ill.: Rand MacNally.

POWER, C. (1976) *A Critical Review of Science Classroom Interaction Studies*. Mimeograph. School of Education, University of Queensland, Australia.

SMITH, L. and SCHUMACHER, S. (1972) *Extended Pilot Trials of the Aesthetic Education Program: A Qualitative Description, Analysis and Evaluation*. St Ann, Mo.: CEMREL.

STENHOUSE, L. (1971) 'The Humanities Curriculum Project: the rationale.' *Theory into Practice*, 10, pp. 154–62.

STENHOUSE, L. (1975) *An Introduction to Curriculum Research and Development*. London: Heinemann.

WALKER, R. and ADELMAN, C. (1972) *Towards a Sociography of Classrooms*. Final report, Social Science Research Council (Grant HR996–1), London.

WILD, R. D. (1973) *Teacher Participation in Research*. Unpublished conference paper, SSRC and Gulbenkian Project on Problems and Effects of Teaching about Race Relations, CARE. Norwich, Norfolk: University of East Anglia.

2.10 Against dogmatism: alternative models of teaching

Bruce Joyce and Marsha Weil

[In this extract] we examine and compare a wide variety of approaches to teaching. In so doing, we suggest that there are many kinds of 'good' teaching, and that the concept 'good' when applied to teaching is better stated 'good for what?' and 'good for whom?'

A model of teaching is a plan or pattern that can be used to shape curriculums (long-term courses of studies), to design instructional materials, and to guide instruction in the classroom and other settings. As we describe models and discuss their uses, we will find that the task of selecting appropriate models is complex and that the forms of 'good' teaching are numerous, depending on our purposes.

We think of teaching as a process by which teacher and students create a shared environment including sets of values and beliefs (agreements about what is important) which in turn colour their view of reality. The 'models' of teaching that we choose have much to say about the kinds of realities admitted to the classroom and the kinds of life-views likely to be generated as teacher and learner work together. Thus, it is not surprising that people care greatly about the models they use or that educators for millennia have sought the *perfect* model – the approach to teaching that will solve *all* educational problems (help every student learn everything in every way).

We begin by challenging the idea that there *is* any such thing as a perfect model. We should not limit our methods to any single model, however attractive it may seem at first glance, because no model of teaching is designed to accomplish all types of learning or to work for all learning styles. We make the assumption that there are many kinds of learning, for the most part requiring different methods of instruction. We also assume that our students come to us with different learning styles, calling for different approaches if each one is to become a productive and effective learner.

[. . .]

The search for good teaching: 'the one right way' fallacy

As in the case of art, good teaching is something many people feel they can recognize on sight, although most of us have difficulty expressing a reasoned basis for our judgments. Hence, implicit in many discussions about teaching is the notion that one certain kind of teaching is really better than all the other

---

Source: JOYCE, B. and WEIL, M. (1980) *Models of Teaching* (2nd edn). Englewood Cliffs, New Jersey: Prentice-Hall, pp. 1–2, 7–19.

kinds. We hear of child-centred teaching, inductive methods, inquiry, teachers who really work the kids, others who really make it interesting, curriculums that are process-centred, and materials built on behaviour modification principles. . . .

The research evidence dealing with this question is remarkably ambiguous. Several hundred studies compare one general teaching method to another, and most of these studies – whether curriculums are compared, specific methods for teaching specific subjects are contrasted, or different approaches to counselling are analyzed – show that differences between approaches are for specific objectives.[1] Although the results are very difficult to interpret, the evidence to date gives little encouragement to those who would hope that we have identified a single, reliable, multipurpose teaching strategy as the *best* approach.

This conclusion annoys some people. Naturally it bothers those people who feel that they *do* know such a single broad method. They are likely to say that the reason one particular approach to teaching (*their* approach) has not yet been proven superior is that our ability to measure learning outcomes is not yet sophisticated enough to detect the true power of *their* preferred strategy.

Unquestionably, their position may be correct. The art of measuring the outcomes of learning is still in its infancy, particularly with respect to the education of the emotions, the growth of personality, intellectual development, and creativity. It seems reasonable to suppose that as our technology for studying teaching and learning improves, people will discover regularities in the teaching-learning process that have not been apparent before. A few general methods *may* emerge as superior. It is more likely, however, that a few weak models will be exposed as such, but a variety of strong ones will remain.

The problem of identifying and choosing teaching strategies becomes quite different if instead of searching for a single right way we concentrate instead on the possibilities of the rich variety of models for teaching that our heritage has given us. No presently known single approach succeeds with all students or reaches all goals. Our task is to develop an environment in which the student is taught in the variety of ways that facilitate his or her development.

The search for models of teaching: 'who focuses on what?'

We have conducted a long search for useful models of teaching. And we have found them in abundance – among them models useful for every goal, and such a range that at least a few should reach every kind of student.

They cropped up in all sorts of places. Some have been invented by classroom practitioners. Others are the work of substantial lines of research in psychology and training. A number came from therapists and a great many from philosophers. Some models are simple and easy to use while others are complex and difficult to master. A few models have very broad purposes while some are useful for particular goals only (see Joyce and Weil, 1980, chapter

28). Each one, in some way, represents a view of humankind – about what is important to learn and *how* it should be learned.

Over the years, then, a great many educational models have been developed by people engaged in distinctly different kinds of activity. Models are based on practice, empirical work, theories, hunches, and on speculation about the meanings of theories and research done by others. The purpose of this extract is to draw together a number of these models for teaching and to analyze what they are good for and how they can be adapted for different students.

The families of models

From an enormous list of models we have selected twenty-two. . . . In our view they constitute a basic educational repertoire – with them we can accomplish most goals of learning.

We have grouped them into four families that represent distinct orientations toward people and how they learn.

Information-processing models

Members of the first large family of models share an orientation toward the information-processing capability of students and ways they can improve their ability to master information (see Table 1). Information processing refers to the ways people handle stimuli from the environment, organize data, sense problems, generate concepts and solutions to problems, and employ verbal and nonverbal symbols. Some information-processing models are concerned with the ability of the learner to solve problems, and thus emphasize productive thinking; others are concerned with general intellectual ability. A large number emphasize concepts and information derived from the academic disciplines. Again, however, it must be stressed that nearly all models from this family are also concerned with social relationships and the development of an integrated, functioning self. The route chosen, however, is through intellectual functioning.

Personal models

Members of the second family share an orientation toward the individual and the development of self-hood (see Table 2). They emphasize the processes by which individuals construct and organize their unique reality. Frequently, they give much attention to emotional life. The focus on helping individuals to develop a productive relationship with their environments and to view themselves as capable persons is also expected to result in richer interpersonal relations and a more effective information-processing capability.

Table 1 Information-processing models: a selection

Model	Major Theorist	Mission or Goal
Inductive Thinking Model	Hilda Taba[a]	Designed primarily for development of inductive mental processes and academic reasoning or theory building, but these capacities are useful for personal and social goals as well.
Inquiry Training Model	Richard Suchman[b]	
Scientific Inquiry	Joseph J. Schwab[c] (also much of the Curriculum Reform movement of the 1960s)	Designed to teach the research system of a discipline, but also expected to have effects in other domains (sociological methods may be taught in order to increase social understanding and social problem-solving).
Concept Attainment	Jerome Bruner[d]	Designed primarily to develop inductive reasoning, but also for concept development and analysis.
Cognitive Growth	Jean Piaget[e] Irving Sigel[f] Edmund Sullivan[g] Lawrence Kohlberg[h]	Designed to increase general intellectual development, especially logical reasoning, but can be applied to social and moral development as well (see Kohlberg, 1976).
Advance Organizer Model	David Ausubel[i]	Designed to increase the efficiency of information-processing capacities to absorb and relate bodies of knowledge.
Memory	Harry Lorayne Jerry Lucas[j]	Designed to increase capacity to memorize.

[a] Hilda Taba, *Teaching Strategies and Cognitive Functioning in Elementary School Children*, Cooperative Research Project 2404 (San Francisco, San Francisco State College, 1966).

[b] J. Richard Suchman, *The Elementary School Training Program in Scientific Inquiry*, Report to the U.S. Office of Education, Project Title VII, Project 216 (Urbana: University of Illinois, 1962).

[c] Biological Sciences Curriculum Study, Joseph J. Schwab, supervisor, *Biology Teachers' Handbook* (New York: John Wiley & Sons, Inc., 1965).

[d] Jerome Bruner, Jacqueline J. Goodnow, and George A. Austin, *A Study of Thinking* (New York: Science Editions, Inc., 1967).

[e] Jean Piaget, *The Origins of Intelligence in Children* (New York: International University Press, 1952).

[f] Irving E. Sigel, "The Piagetian System and the World of Education," in *Studies in Cognitive Development,* eds. David Elkind and John Flavell (New York: Oxford University Press, 1969).

[g] Edmund Sullivan, "Piaget and the School Curriculum: A Critical Appraisal," Bulletin No. 2 (Toronto: Ontario Institute for Studies in Education, 1967).

[h] Lawrence Kohlberg, "The Cognitive Developmental Approach to Moral Education," in *Moral Education . . . It Comes with the Territory,* ed. David Purpel and Kevin Ryan (Berkeley, Ca.: McCutchan Publishing Corp., 1976).

[i] David Ausubel, *The Psychology of Meaningful Verbal Learning* (New York: Grune & Stratton, Inc. 1963).

[j] Harry Lorayne and Jerry Lucas, *The Memory Book* (New York: Ballantine Books, Inc., 1974).

Table 2   Personal models: a selection

Model	Major Theorist	Mission or Goals
Nondirective Teaching	Carl Rogers[a]	Emphasis on building the capacity for personal development in terms of self-awareness, understanding, autonomy, and self-concept.
Awareness Training	Fritz Perls[b] William Schutz[c]	Increasing one's capacity for self-exploration and self-awareness. Much emphasis on development of interpersonal awareness and understanding as well as body and sensory awareness.
Synectics	William Gordon[d]	Personal development of creativity and creative problem-solving.
Conceptual Systems	David Hunt[e]	Designed to increase personal complexity and flexibility.
Classroom Meeting	William Glasser[f]	Development of self-understanding and responsibility to oneself and one's social group.

[a] Carl Rogers, *Client Centered Therapy* (Boston: Houghton Mifflin Company, 1971).
[b] Frederick Perls, Ralph Hefferline, and Paul Goodman, *Gestalt Therapy* (New York: Julian Press, 1951); Frederick Perls, *Gestalt Therapy Verbatim* (Lafayette, Calif.: Real People Press, 1968).
[c] William Schutz, *FIRO: A Three-Dimensional Theory of Interpersonal Behavior* (New York: Holt, Rinehart & Winston, 1958); *Joy: Expanding Human Awareness* (New York: Grove Press, Inc., 1967).
[d] William J. J. Gordon, *Synectics* (New York: Harper & Row, Publishers, Inc., 1961).
[e] David E. Hunt, "A Conceptual Level Matching Model for Coordinating Learner Characteristics with Educational Approaches," *Interchange*, 1, no. 2 (1970), 1–31.
[f] William Glasser, *Reality Therapy* (New York: Harper & Row, Publishers, Inc., 1965).

Social interaction models

The models in this family emphasize the relationships of the individual to society or to other persons (see Table 3). They focus on the processes by which reality is socially negotiated. Consequently models from this orientation give priority to the improvement of the individual's ability to relate to others, to engage in democratic processes, and to work productively in the society. It must be stressed that the social relations orientation does not assume that these goals constitute the *only* important dimension of life. While social relations may be emphasized more than other domains, social theorists are also concerned with the development of the mind and the self, and the learning of academic subjects. (It is the rare educator who is not concerned with more than one aspect of the learner's development, or who does not use more than one aspect of the environment to influence the learner's development.)

Table 3   Social interaction models: a selection

Model	Major Theorist	Mission or Goals
Group Investigation	Herbert Thelen[a] John Dewey[b]	Development of skills for participation in democratic social process through combined emphasis on interpersonal (group) skills and academic inquiry skills. Aspects of personal development are important outgrowths of this model.
Social Inquiry	Byron Massialas Benjamin Cox[c]	Social problem solving, primarily through academic inquiry and logical reasoning.
Laboratory Method	National Training Laboratory (NTL) Bethel, Maine[d]	Development of interpersonal and group skills and, through this, personal awareness and flexibility.
Jurisprudential	Donald Oliver James P. Shaver[e]	Designed primarily to teach the jurisprudential frame of reference as a way of thinking about and resolving social issues.
Role Playing	Fannie Shaftel George Shaftel[f]	Designed to induce students to inquire into personal and social values, with their own behaviour and values becoming the source of their inquiry.
Social Simulation	Sarane Boocock[g] Harold Guetzkow[h]	Designed to help students experience various social processes and realities and to examine their own reactions to them, also to acquire concepts and decision-making skills.

[a] Herbert Thelen, *Education and the Human Quest* (New York: Harper & Row, Publishers, Inc., 1960).

[b] John Dewey, *Democracy and Education* (New York: Macmillan, Inc., 1916).

[c] Byron Massialas and Benjamin Cox, *Inquiry in Social Studies* (New York: McGraw-Hill, 1966).

[d] Leland P. Bradford, Jack R. Gibb, and Kenneth D. Benne, eds., *T-Group Theory and Laboratory Method* (New York: John Wiley & Sons, Inc., 1964).

[e] Donald Oliver and James P. Shaver, *Teaching Public Issues in the High School* (Boston: Houghton Mifflin Company, 1966).

[f] Fannie Shaftel and George Shaftel, *Role Playing for Social Values: Decision Making in the Social Studies* (Englewood Cliffs, N.J.: Prentice-Hall, Inc., 1967).

[g] Sarane Boocock and E. O. Schild, *Simulation Games in Learning* (Beverly Hills, Calif.: Sage Publications, Inc., 1968).

[h] Harold Guetzkow and others, *Simulation in International Relations* (Englewood Cliffs, N.J.: Prentice-Hall, Inc., 1963).

Behavioural models

All the models in this family share a common theoretical base, a body of knowledge we refer to as behaviour theory (see Table 4). Other terms such as learning theory, social learning theory, behaviour modification, and behaviour therapy are frequently used. The common thrust is an emphasis on changing the visible behaviour of the learner rather than the underlying psychological structure and the unobservable behaviour. Behavioural models have wide applicability, addressing a variety of goals in education, training, interpersonal behaviour, and therapy. Based on principles of stimulus control and reinforcement, behavioural models have been successfully employed in interactive conditions and mediated conditions, on an individual basis and on a group basis. Perhaps more than any other family, behavioural techniques have been well researched and their effectiveness documented. In this text we describe six models, all based on behaviour theory. They include models for teaching facts, concepts, and skills as well as models for the reduction of anxiety and for relaxation.

Table 4   Behavioural models: a selection

Model	Major Theorist	Mission or Goals
Contingency Management	B. F. Skinner[a]	Facts, concepts, skills
Self-Control	B. F. Skinner	Social behaviour/skills
Relaxation	Rimm & Masters,[b] Wolpe[c]	Personal goals (reduction of stress, anxiety)
Stress Reduction	Rimm & Masters, Wolpe	Substitution of relaxation for anxiety in social situation
Assertive Training	Wolpe, Lazarus,[d] Salter[e]	Direct, spontaneous expression of feelings in social situation
Desensitization	Wolpe	
Direct Training	Gagne[f] Smith and Smith[g]	Pattern of behaviour, skills

[a] B. F. Skinner, *Science and Human Behavior* (New York: Macmillan, Inc., 1953).

[b] David C. Rimm and John C. Masters. *Behavior Therapy: Techniques and Empirical Findings* (New York: Academic Press, Inc., 1974).

[c] J. Wolpe, *Psychotherapy by Reciprocal Inhibition* (Stanford, Calif.: Stanford University Press, 1958); *The Practice of Behavior Therapy* (Oxford: Pergamon Press, Inc., 1969).

[d] J. Wolpe and Arnold A. Lazarus, *Behavior Therapy Techniques: A Guide to the Treatment of Neuroses* (Oxford: Pergamon Press, Inc., 1966).

[e] A. Salter, *Conditioned Reflex Therapy* (New York: Farrar, Strauss, 1949), "The Theory and Practice of Conditioned Reflex Therapy," in *Conditioning Therapies: The Challenge in Psychotherapy*, eds. A. Salter, J. Wolpe, and L. J. Reyna (New York: Holt, Rinehart & Winston, 1964).

[f] Robert Gagne et al., *Psychological Principles in Systems Development* (New York: Holt, Rinehart & Winston, 1962).

[g] Karl U. Smith and Margaret Foltz Smith. *Cybernetic Principles of Learning and Educational Design* (New York: Holt, Rinehart & Winston, 1966).

One of the characteristics of these behavioural models is that they break down the learning task into a series of small behaviours. Although either student or teacher may have control of the situation, in education we have been more familiar with behavioural models in which control is in the teacher's hands. [However, among our seven examples] we are including less familiar uses of behaviour theory, especially models based on the premise of self-control.

Common and unique features

These families of models are by no means antithetical or mutually exclusive, although each represents a distinctive approach to teaching. Whereas debates about educational method have seemed to imply that schools and teachers should choose a single approach, students need growth in all areas. To tend the personal, but not the social, or the informational but not the personal, simply does not make sense in the life of a growing student.

Hence, growth in teaching is the increasing mastery of a variety of models of teaching and the ability to use them effectively. Some philosophies of teacher education maintain that a teacher should master a single model and use it well. We believe that very few teachers are so limited in capacity. Most of us can quite easily develop a basic repertoire of six or eight models of teaching, which will meet the needs generated by our teaching assignment. Certain models are more appropriate for some curriculums than for others; that is, the curriculum helps define our role and the kinds of competencies that we need. For example, a secondary school science teacher of biology who is using Biological Sciences Study Committee materials will want to master the particular kind of inductive approach that fits best with those materials. Or, a teacher of elementary school social studies who is helping children study values will want to master one of the models appropriate to clarifying values and analyzing public issues.

Once a teacher masters the 'basic' repertoire of appropriate models, he or she can then expand it by learning new models and by combining and transforming the basic ones to create new ones. In the midst of a social studies unit, a teacher may use one model (say, Inductive Thinking) to help children master map skills, and combine this model with group-dynamic models that help students attack social issues (for example, Group Investigation). A highly skilled performance in teaching blends the variety of models appropriately and embellishes them. Master teachers create new models of teaching and test them in the course of their work, drawing on the models of others for ideas that are combined in various ways.

Concepts for describing a model

[Each model can be analyzed] in terms of four concepts: syntax, social system, principles of reaction, and support system. These descriptions are the operational heart of each model: they tell us what activities should occur and, when appropriate, in what sequence. . . . [Following the analysis we include] a short section on instructional and nurturant learnings that can be expected from the model.

The four concepts for describing the operations of the model (syntax, social system, principles of reaction and support system) were invented by us as a way of communicating the basic procedures involved in implementing any instructional model.

Syntax

The syntax or phasing of the model describes the model in action. For example, if teachers were to use the model as the basis for their strategy, what kinds of activities would they use? How would they begin? What would happen next? We describe syntax in terms of sequences of activities we call *phases*; each model has a distinct flow of phases.

For example, one model begins with a presentation to the learner of an organizing concept called an 'advance organizer', which the leader presents to the student verbally, in either written or oral form. In the second phase, data is presented to the learner. He or she reads it, watches a film, or is exposed to the data in some other way. This phase is followed by another in which the learner is helped to relate the material to the organizing concept. In a different model, the first phase of a typical activity includes data collection by the students. The second phase involves organization of the data under concepts the student forms himself or herself, and the third, a comparison of the concepts developed with those developed by other people. As shown in Table 5, these two models have a very different structure or set of phases, even though the same type of concept might emerge from both models, and they were in fact designed for somewhat different purposes. The first was designed for the mastery of material, and the second, to teach students inductive thinking processes.

A comparison of the phasing of the two models in Table 5 reveals the practical differences between them. An inductive strategy has different activities and a different sequence than a deductive one.

Table 5   Illustration of phasing in two models

	Phase One	*Phase Two*	*Phase Three*
Model 1	Presentation of concept	Presentation of data	Relating data to concept
Model 2	Presentation of data	Development of categories by students	Identification and naming of concepts

The social system

The social system describes student and teacher roles and relationships and the kind of norms that are encouraged. The leadership roles of the teacher vary greatly from model to model. In some models the teacher is a reflector or a facilitator of group activity, in others a counsellor of individuals, and in others a taskmaster. In some models the teacher is the centre of activity, the source of information, and the organizer and pacer of the situation (high structure). Some models distribute activity equally between teacher and student (moderate structure), whereas others place the student at the centre, encouraging a great deal of social and intellectual independence (low structure).

One way to describe a model of teaching, then, is in terms of the degree of structure in the learning environment. As roles, relationships, norms, and activities become less externally imposed and more within the students' control, the social system becomes less structured. . . . Some models are inherently more structured than others. However, the structure of all models can be varied greatly to adapt to the skill personality of the students. We can tighten or loosen the structure considerably.

Principles of reaction

Principles of reaction tell the teacher how to regard the learner and how to respond to what the learner does. In some models the teacher overtly tries to shape behaviour by rewarding certain student activities and maintaining a neutral stance toward others. In other models such as those designed to develop creativity the teacher tries to maintain a non-evaluative, equal stance so that the learner becomes self-directing. Principles of reaction provide the teacher with rules of thumb by which to tune in to the student and select model-appropriate responses to what the student does.

Support system

We use this concept to describe not the model itself so much as the supporting conditions necessary for its existence. What are the additional requirements of the model beyond the *usual* human skills and capacities and technical facilities? For example, the Human Relations Model may require a trained leader; the Nondirective Model may require an exceedingly patient, supportive personality. Suppose a model postulates that students should teach themselves, with the roles of teachers limited to consultation and facilitation. What support is necessary? Certainly a classroom filled only with textbooks would be limiting and prescriptive. Rather, support in the form of books, films, self-instructional systems, and travel arrangements is necessary, or the model will be empty.

Instructional and nurturant effects

The effects of an environment can be *direct* – designed to come from the content and skills on which the activities are based. Or, effects can be *implicit* in the learning environment. One fascinating question about models is the implicit learnings they engender. For instance, a model that emphasizes academic discipline can also (but need not) emphasize obedience to authority. Or one that encourages personal development can (but need not) beg questions about social responsibility. The examination of latent functions can be as exciting and important as the examination of direct functions.

Hence, the description of the effects of models can validly be categorized as the direct or *instructional* effects and the indirect or *nurturant* effects. The instructional effects are those directly achieved by leading the learner in certain directions. The nurturant effects come from experiencing the environment created by the model. High competition toward a goal may directly spur achievement, for example, but the effects of living in a competitive atmosphere may alienate people from each other. Alienation would be, in this case, *nurtured* by an *instructional* method. In choosing a model for teaching, curriculum building, or as a basis for materials, the teacher must balance instructional efficiency, or directness, and with the predictable nurturant effects, as shown in Figure 1.

If we have two models whose instructional effects are both appropriate for our goal, we may choose one over the other because its nurturant effects further other goals or because they reinforce the direct instructional effects. Three models might be considered as shown in Figure 2. If we assume equal efficiency, we might choose model 1 because its instructional and nurturant effects reinforce one another, and there are no undesirable nurturant side effects. (Model 3 does not reinforce goal A, and model 2 nurtures an undesirable effect.)

It is possible to defend the selection of a model chiefly on the basis of its nurturant effects, even though it might not have high direct efficiency. The

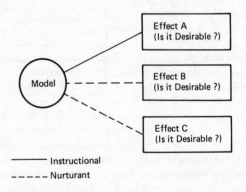

Figure 1   Instructional and nurturant effects

```
Model 1  Instructs _____ A (Desirable)
         Nurtures _ _ _ _ _ _ _ _ A (Desirable)
         Nurtures _ _ _ _ _ _ _ B (Acceptable)

Model 2  Instructs _____ A (Desirable)
         Nurtures _ _ _ _ _ _ _ B (Acceptable)
         Nurtures _ _ _ _ _ _ C (Undesirable)

Model 3  Instructs _____ B (Acceptable)
         Nurtures _ _ _ _ _ _ _ A (Desirable)
         Nurtures _ _ _ _ _ _ _ B (Acceptable)
```

Figure 2

Progressive movement, for example, emphasized teaching academic subjects through democratic process less because it would be an efficient way to teach content (although many believed it would be) than because it would be likely to *nurture* later democratic behaviour and citizen involvement and would *instruct* citizens in democratic skills. Figure 3 illustrates these instructional and nurturant effects.

Educators must choose among models that differ considerably from one another. And the models we choose create a certain kind of reality for our students.

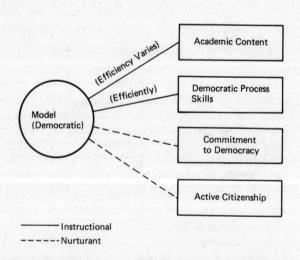

Figure 3   Instructional and nurturant effects: sample model

Developing a repertoire of models

Some view teaching as an exceedingly personal art; to them, the available models of teaching represent the *arts* of master teachers – a collective wisdom on which to build one's personal art.

We feel that the teacher should view these models of teaching as ways of accomplishing a wide variety of purposes. Since no single teaching strategy can accomplish every purpose, the wise teacher will master a sufficient repertoire of strategies to deal with the specific kinds of learning problems he or she faces. For example, the Nondirective Model is especially useful in helping people to become more open and aware of their feelings, to free their inquisitiveness and initiative, and to help them develop the drive and the sensitivity to educate themselves. Similarly, the Laboratory Method Model can greatly improve human relations skills.

The teacher's repertoire of models is particularly important if he or she is responsible for teaching many children in several curriculum areas. But even the subject-matter specialist, whose responsibilities may be confined to teaching a single discipline to fairly mature students, faces teaching tasks for which no one single model can be completely adequate. For instance, the secondary teacher of English can draw on several models. Synectics may be used in the teaching of creative writing, Skinnerian techniques for the teaching of skills, and Behavioural Nondirective methods to help students develop a sense of their own potentialities and a willingness to capitalize on them.

Teams of teachers working together can discover the models most amenable to each member of the team. Some teachers will use the counselling models effectively, while others will use the behaviour modification strategies, and so on. Together, a large team of teachers, able to draw on teacher aides and other support systems, should be able to create a fine spectrum of opportunities for children.

To develop repertoire means to develop flexibility. Part of this flexibility is professional. Every teacher faces a wide range of problems, and if he or she has an equally wide range of teaching models to draw from, more creative and imaginative solutions to those problems can be generated. On the personal side, repertoire requires the ability to grow and expand one's potential, and the capacity to teach oneself more varied and interesting ways of coping with one's own need to develop. The environment for personal growth is greatly enhanced when people can define their present situations and see the alternatives. The growing, developing teacher can embrace more forms of experience, explore more aspects of his or her students, and find more ways of helping them grow.

Note

1 A good example of evidence and opinion that gives pause to those who feel that the issues about how to teach are largely settled in favour of inductive teaching

procedures is the fine collection of essays in SHULMAN, LEE, S. and KEISLAR, E. R. (eds) (1966) *Learning by Discovery: A Critical Appraisal*. Skokie, Ill.: Rand McNally & Company.

Reference

JOYCE, B. and WEIL, M. (1980) *Models of Teaching* (2nd ed.). Englewood Cliffs, New Jersey: Prentice-Hall.

2.11 Technology: the analytic style

I. K. Davies

One of the very first steps in developing an educational or training program is to analyze the nature of the actual task involved. Some tasks, of course, are purely academic or intellectual in nature, others are primarily concerned with physical skills. However, regardless of the nature of the task, it is necessary to determine both the ingredients and the characteristics of the topic or job that the student has to learn. It is only when these precise characteristics are known that the training need can be established, and the learning objectives written. For this reason, great care must be exercised in carrying out the task analysis, for the ensuing document forms the basis of the learning prescription.

In some ways, the term 'task analysis' is an unfortunate one. It suggests that what is primarily involved is the breaking down of the task into its constituent parts. This, however, only describes part of the process, for it is also necessary to consider how these constituent parts are related and organized. Task analysis, therefore, is concerned with both analysis and synthesis. Its ultimate aims are to:

1 Describe the task which the student has to learn.
2 Isolate the required behaviours.
3 Identify the conditions under which the behaviours occur.
4 Determine a criterion of acceptable performance.

Without a proper task analysis, it is not possible to justify what you intend to teach, nor is it possible to decide on an optimal teaching strategy.

Types of task analysis

Three different types of task analysis are readily recognizable, each fulfilling entirely different needs:

1 *Topic analysis.* This involves a detailed analysis of intellectual tasks such as Ohm's law, latitude and longitude, solving simultaneous equations, and considering the character of Brutus in Shakespeare's *Julius Caesar*.
2 *Job analysis.* This involves a detailed analysis of tasks involving physical or psychomotor skills. The technique concentrates on *what* is done when the task is carried out. Job analysis would involve such tasks as renewing the contact points in a car, setting up a lathe, fitting film in a camera.
3 *Skills analysis.* This involves the further analysis of psychomotor tasks,

Source: DAVIES, I. K. (1971) *The Management of Learning*. Maidenhead, Berks.: McGraw-Hill (UK), pp. 36–42.

but this time concentrating on *how* the job is accomplished. Skills analysis will need to be carried out, in addition to job analysis, when either the whole task or part of the task involves complex, intricate and subtle hand-eye coordinations. For instance, a full skills analysis would be necessary for such jobs as glassblowing and panel-beating; whereas renewing the contact points in a car would include a skills analysis, for instance, for that part of the job that involves using a feeler gauge.

There has been a tendency among many teachers and trainers to imagine that task analysis is only applicable to tasks involving psychomotor skills; furthermore, skills analysis and job analysis have often been regarded as competing rather than complementary techniques. Indeed, in the past, certain industrial organizations went so wholeheartedly for skills analysis that they created the impression that all training should be based upon it. This was a time wasting and costly error of judgment. An essential component of the teacher's and trainer's role is to recognize the circumstances in which one strategy of analysis is likely to be more efficient than another.

Sources of information for task analysis

In carrying out a task analysis, whether it involves topic, job, or skills analysis, a number of sources of relevant information must be tapped, so as to ensure that a complete picture has been obtained. Obviously, the most important source of information must always be the 'master'; in other words, the person who can do the job at the required level of mastery. He must always be selected with great care, and steps must be taken to ensure that he is, indeed, proficient at the level which all students will be expected to attain. If the master's level of proficiency is too high, then the task analysis will set

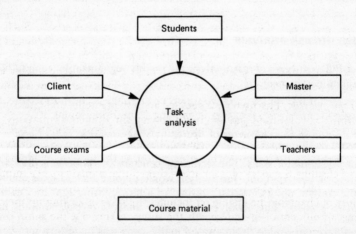

Figure 1   Main sources of information for a task analysis

needlessly high levels of performance, with all the resultant dangers of overtraining. If the master's level of proficiency is set too low, the resulting task analysis will be invalid, with a consequent danger of undertraining.

Once the master's behaviour has been analyzed, his performance must be checked for accuracy and completeness. It is also important to check the analysis under other operating environments and conditions, for these can sometimes affect the way that the task is accomplished. Other sources of information are indicated in Figure 1. Teachers and instructors must be consulted, course materials and examination papers studied, students who are either learning or have just finished learning the task interviewed, and the person who initially sparked off the project questioned. All kinds of procedures can be used in consulting these sources, but the most common ones include observation, interviews, questionnaires, work diaries, film, closed circuit television, job checklists, and activity analysis.

Components of a task analysis

A task analysis is really an audit and inventory. In it, knowledge, skill, and attitudes are identified and isolated, with a view to ultimately synthesizing them into a hierarchical organization relevant to the writing of a learning prescription. In carrying out such an analysis, the analyst or teacher must consider not only the physical components of the subject (use of tools, references, job aids), but also the mental components (procedures, decisions, abstractions).

The task analysis must isolate all those overt acts which characterize either the subject material or job mastery. One way of doing this is to think of a topic or job as a hierarchical organization of levels or components, each of which describes the job in successively greater detail. At the highest level is the topic or job itself. This consists of a number of duties; each duty contains a number of tasks, and each task consists of a number of task elements. Such an organization is schematically illustrated in Figure 2. In topic analysis and job analysis, the task element is the smallest meaningful unit; in skills analysis, the task element is further broken down into 'acts'. An act is very similar to a therblig in time and motion study, and consists of a basic movement that must be repeated if it is interrupted. Four acts or therbligs occur most frequently: reaching for an object, grasping it, moving it, and positioning it.

Let us take an example. In making a job analysis of a psychomotor skill, the job could be that of an engine mechanic. His job is made up of a number of duties, including tuning the carburettor, adjusting the tappets, changing the oil, and cleaning the spark plugs. Each of these duties is made up of a number of separate tasks, all closely related to each other in sequence. For example, the duty of changing the engine oil includes the tasks of jacking up the car, placing an oil container underneath the sump, taking out the sump drain plug, allowing the oil to drain away. Finally, each task includes a number of task elements. Jacking up the car, for instance, involves acquiring the right

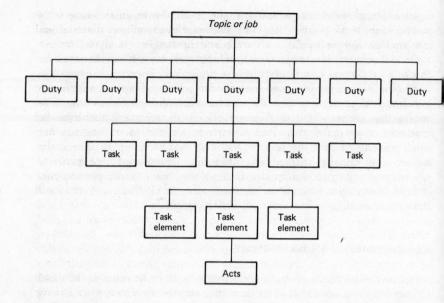

Figure 2   The hierarchy of behavioural levels in a task analysis

kind of jack, positioning it underneath the jacking-up points, and manipulating the jack so that it raises the car to the required level.

Even in more specifically cognitive or intellectual skills, a similar classification can be employed. The job or topic of solving mathematical problems by using logarithm tables could include the duty of multiplying two numbers together. This duty would consist of the following tasks: finding the characteristics and mantissa of the two numbers, adding the logarithms together, antilogging the sum, fixing the decimal point, and connecting the answer to the appropriate number of significant figures. Finally, the task elements involved in finding the mantissa, for example, would consist of locating the first two significant figures of each number in the lefthand column of the logarithm tables, locating the third figure of each number in the appropriate middle columns headed 0–9, and locating the fourth figure in the add column headed 1–9 on the righthand side of the page.

Writing a topic analysis

Although there are a number of different ways of making a topic analysis . . . few of them are structurally detailed enough as to make them practicable for our purpose. One of the most useful methods of topic analysis is based on the well-known matrix technique of program writing (Thomas, Davies, Openshaw, and Bird, 1963). . . .

In order to make a topic analysis, the teacher – who in this case is the master – will need to collect together all the relevant subject material and ensure that it is technically accurate and up-to-date. It would be old-fashioned, for instance, to cite the use of fishplates between lengths of railway line as a precaution against the effects of expansion. Science and technology have now become popular, and scientific facts and applications, which were previously the preserve of the enlightened, are now everyday knowledge. This means that the teacher can no longer rely on the standard textbooks and reference books, but must look elsewhere for the latest findings and applications. Many teachers may well feel that this step is unnecessary because of their level of scholarship or their considerable teaching experience, but no step highlights deficiencies in knowledge more than topic analysis.

Once the subject material has been collected, the next step is to refine and limit the topic that the student is required to learn, and to ensure that it is as self-contained as possible. For instance, the topic of the theory of conservation of energy involves duties such as Ohm's law and Joule's law. Often these topics and duties will be laid down in the syllabus, or prescribed in some other way, but usually in only the vaguest of terms. In any case, syllabuses are only an indication of content, and do not attempt to prescribe the order in which topics should be taught. Many teachers fall into the trap of slavishly following the order given in a syllabus to the detriment of their students' learning. One of the most important duties of the teacher is to reconcile the dictates of the syllabus, on the one hand, with the educational and learning needs of their students on the other.

Identifying task elements or rules

Once the duty has been carefully delimited, it must be broken down into its *smallest* constituent parts. These, as we have seen, are called task elements, but in topic analysis they are more usually referred to as 'rules'. The identification of rules is probably the most skilled part of the whole process of topic analysis, and it demands that the teacher or analyst is – in every sense of the term – a subject matter expert. Although the teacher-analyst will be aided in his task by his experience, there is a considerable risk that the rules that he identifies will be too wide. It is also essential to ensure that the rules are carefully written and sequenced. Although the task of rule writing will be initially somewhat lengthy and laborious, experience and practice soon speed up the process.

In order to identify the rules, the teacher-analyst should ask himself five critical questions:

1 What does he expect the student to *do* to demonstrate that he has learned the topic?
2 What questions does he expect the student to answer?
3 What tasks, procedures, and techniques does he expect him to perform, and at what level does he expect them to be executed?

4   What discriminations does he expect the student to make, and in what terms does he expect these discriminations to be made?
5   What total changes in behaviour does he expect, and in what form does he expect to observe and measure them?

Such a definition of what the student is intended to *do* as a result of the planned learning experience, can best be referred to as the anticipated or *criterion* behaviour.

Writing the rule-set

Writing rules is a way of life, a habit soon acquired by practice. In essence, a rule is a statement of generality, a definition, a fact, or an item of information. For instance, each of the following statements constitutes a rule:

1   Metals expand when heated.
2   A sonnet has fourteen lines.
3   A contract is an agreement enforceable by law.
4   Latitude is angular distance north and south of the Equator.

Each rule should be complete in itself, a complete fact or idea. They form the raw materials or building blocks, which – related and interrelated together – will make up first the duty and then the topic.
Rules should be written in such a way that:

1   They contain only *one* fact or idea.
2   They are written at the same level of generality as all preceding rules.
3   They take the form of simple, declarative (kernel) sentences.
4   They avoid negative forms, qualifications, and conjunctions.
5   They possess only *one* active verb.
6   They are critical and essential to the task.

Generally speaking, they will rarely contain more than a dozen words; indeed, the shorter and simpler the rule, the better it will be.
   It must be borne in mind that the objective is not to write as many rules as possible, but only to write those that are intellectually necessary to the task. Every step must be taken to avoid the common mistake of attempting to teach too much in too short a time. Accordingly, the rules must be carefully sifted; each fact should be considered in relation to the task, and material outside the chosen parameters should be rejected. In this way, rules can be gradually revised and refined until only the absolutely essential ones remain.

Arranging the rules into a logical sequence

As the rules are written, of course, they will be arranged into some type of natural sequence. Steps must now be taken to ensure that this sequence is a completely logical one from the point of view of the subject material. Each rule should lead naturally to the next, so that – in effect – they set up and completely describe the duty. This sequence is likely to be based upon the teacher's own subject expertise, upon his teaching experience, upon intuition, and upon his own learning experience.

The following, traditional rules of sequence will often prove helpful in arranging the rules:

1   Proceed from the known to the unknown.
2   Proceed from the simple to the complex.
3   Proceed from the concrete to the abstract.
4   Proceed from observation to reasoning.
5   Proceed from a whole view to a more detailed view to a whole view.

In accomplishing this, it will often be found useful to so write and arrange the rules that they appear to complement each other. A word, topic, or concept introduced in one rule is built on or expanded upon in the next. In this way, the rules are chained or dovetailed together, and new teaching points are not suddenly, but gradually, introduced into the sequence. . . .

Reference

THOMAS, C. A., DAVIES, I. K., OPENSHAW, D. and BIRD, J. (1963) *Programmed Learning in Perspective*. London: Larson. Chicago, Ill.: Educational Methods.

2.12 Conventional classrooms, 'open' classrooms and the technology of teaching

Ian Westbury

[. . .]

To understand what teachers do we have to look to the context that is the classroom, to the tasks, structures and resources that define that social setting. I . . . want to turn to the task of developing this . . . assumption by showing firstly, that proposals for change in classroom behaviours that do not address the issue of tasks and resources do not show how change in teaching real groups of students can be effected and, secondly (contrary-wise), that changes in teaching technologies *are* possible (at least potentially) when resources to permit that change are made available. The vehicle for both of these discussions will be the literature of 'open' education, the reforming ideology and practices that Americans have come to associate with English infant and junior schools.

Two insistently-maintained sets of principles run through the literature advocating 'open' education; one set draws upon a conception of the relationship of the child to his learning environment, the second makes certain stipulations about the role of teacher vis-à-vis the child. The two sets run something like this:

Students and their learning

1   Children's innate curiosity leads to exploratory behaviour that is self-perpetuating.
2   The child will display natural exploratory behaviour if he is not threatened.
3   Play must not be distinguished from work as a predominant mode of learning among children.
4   When children are interested in exploring the same problem or the same materials they will often choose to collaborate in some way. Similarly, when a child learns something which is important to him he will wish to share it with others.
5   Concept formation proceeds very slowly. Children learn and develop intellectually not only at their own rate but in their own style, and intellectual development takes place through a sequence of concrete experiences followed by abstraction. Verbal abstractions should follow direct experiences with objects and ideas, not precede them or substitute for them.
6   Errors are necessarily part of the learning process; they are to be expected and even desired for they contain information essential for further learning.

Source: *Journal of Curriculum Studies*, 5, 2, 1973, extracted from pp. 109–21.

Teachers and their teaching

1 Teaching must proceed from the interests and capabilities of pupils.
2 The teacher must take an active role in the classroom and seek to understand and direct the pupil's interests in order to attach these to subject-matters that might not ordinarily interest him.
3 Learning must be sustained; the teacher must bring out in children the interests that underlie sustained involvement in learning.
4 The teacher cannot, in the nature of things, find an ideal match between the 'interests' and 'abilities' of pupils and a programme for such a match cannot exist. The teacher's task is to search for meaningfulness in the activities whatever they may be. More important, though, the teacher must create a situation in which the child is willing to project himself into an activity so as to bring his own innate resources and innate sense of orderliness into play.
5 The teacher can only do these things if he provides an environment in which (*a*) children can move from activity to activity as they wish and need to, (*b*) the activities *available* for children are rich in educative potentiality, and (*c*) there is a balance of activities available in the classroom – raw materials, structured materials, reading materials, dramatic play – which truly communicate to the pupils who live in *specific* classrooms.[1]

The creation of an environment that will support student-initiated learning is the most important task of the open teacher. The selection of materials which become, in their turn, the bases for student activities is the most important planning task of the teacher. In the classroom the teacher must guide students through the activities he has made available with vigour and authority.

Three problems lurk in this conception of the open teacher's tasks. As Roland Barth has pointed out, by selecting the activities available to students the teacher controls the scope of the curriculum in the classroom. The kinds of activities the teacher chooses determine in their turn the quality and intensity of the learnings available to students. The kinds of decisions the teacher makes about when and how students should move from one activity to another determine the breadth and depth of the curriculum that students experience.[2] In these problems we have the issues of *coverage, mastery* and *management* even if the environment of the room and the teacher's attitudes allay the issue of *affect*. What coping strategies (to use the term suggested earlier) does the current literature on open education offer to escape the dilemmas that these issues present to teachers in conventional classrooms?

The topic of provisioning . . . is central to an educational philosophy that stresses the importance of choice for children . . .

Sand not only lends itself to all kinds of numerous measurement operations (sifting, pouring, weighing) but provides a rich variety of tactile, aesthetic and conceptual materials as well. Wet sand feels and acts differently than dry sand. Dry sand is good for making pictures and designs; wet sand affords the added possibility of three-dimensional construction . . . Whole towns and road systems can be constructed, and those in turn may become the subject of mapping exercises as children learn to represent their three-dimensional sand town on a two-dimensional plane . . . In short, the potential for developing quantitative operations and concepts; artistic ability; notions of city planning; rudimentary principles of architecture, engineering, drafting, and mapping; and symbolic representation skills – are all inherent in sand and water.[3]

We can adopt two stances as we read material of this kind. We can ask whether or not we believe that prescriptions for method couched in terms such as these are meaningful, given our view of the problems presented by the realities of the classroom, or we can accept the claims of proponents of open education that open classrooms work and then proceed to ask how they might or can work. Let me address both of these problems.

If the view of problems of managing the conventional classroom stands, prescriptions for teaching methods of the kind that I have been citing clearly fail to address the complex realities of the classroom. We are not given any set of concrete strategies that tell us how the involvement of many students in tasks is sustained, how involvement is actually transformed into mastery of a conventional (or even unconventional) kind, or how the teacher manages the series of simultaneous learning settings that are implicit of open classrooms. We are not told how the need for very active planning on the part of teachers can be reduced so that open teaching can become a method suitable for teachers of only average interest in teaching. We are not given any insight into the concrete optimizing strategies by which the trade-offs between manage-ment, mastery and coverage are secured, or interest is made compatible with coverage, or how mastery is built into materials.

Likewise, we are given no real understanding of the concrete theoretical principles that should underlie the provisioning of the open classroom. Coverage and mastery are addressed in terms of productive and 'unproduct-ive' materials, but this distinction seems to cut directly across conceptions of interest and involvement. As Roland Barth writes:

We find open educators inconsistent and even somewhat confused on the question of criteria for selection of materials. On the one hand there is some confidence that any activity on which the child is fully engaged and interested is productive and will result in learning, and on the other hand there is an inclination to make distinctions between productive and 'unproductive' materials.[4]

Two different sets of classroom goals are implied in this ambiguity, but no clear coping strategy for trading between these goals is hinted at so that we could have a feel for what we should be doing were *we* trying to run an open classroom. The examples we are given of method are singularly unhelpful in this search for clarity: it is undeniable, for example, that a sand tray has potential for developing quantitative operations and concepts, artistic ability, etc., but how does the teacher go about extracting real learnings of this kind from a sand tray and how does he do this when he has other groups doing similar open-ended tasks? Without an understanding of how these things are done, without a sense of the classroom strategies that an open teacher should employ in situations of this kind, we have no way of generating a picture of what such a teacher might do in other similar situations.

These objections to the hortatory literature can be met, however, by the claim that, while concrete teaching strategies are not set forth clearly, a picture of the character of the open classroom is adequately sketched in this writing. This claim is true, to some extent at least, but when we seek to penetrate the kind of characterizations that we are offered by such writing, the same kind of inadequate specification emerges.[5]

Thus we can see that the open classroom, with its centres of activity (reading corner, maths corner, sand tray and the like) and its emphasis upon physical movement of students between many different kinds of activity as the interests of individual students change, permits a manipulation of both time and space by the teacher. Students can move between activities and spend as much time as is appropriate with a single class of activities. The insistent emphasis within the literature of open education on the need for intrinsic involvement by students in relatively freely-chosen activities may meet the problem of involvement that conventional self-paced instruction faces. The emphasis on warmth and honesty in encounters between students and teachers and the emphasis on teacher-student inquiry offers the possibility – so often missed amid the managerial problems of the conventional classroom – of liberating a task-focused emotionality that can, in its turn, engender both intrinsic and productive work, i.e. learning.[6]

This kind of analysis of the nature of the open classroom gets us, as I have suggested, some way in our search for understanding of how such a classroom should work. But only some of the way! We can still ask what vague notions like intrinsic involvement or aspirations like warmth or honesty of encounter mean in the world of the classroom and its routines. And what of the demands of mastery and coverage? As Roland Barth has pointed out, activities can be intrinsically rewarding and motivating without being educative:

There are many activities in which children engage, such as learning to play the piano, which are tedious, laborious, and even painful. Others, such as playing ball, are fun, unrestrained and carefree for most children. Both may be characterized by active involvement with materials, but they have considerable differences, as any child knows. One appears, from the adult point of view, to be 'work' and the other 'play'.[7]

Open educators meet this problem by eschewing any attempt to claim that piano playing (i.e. work) is more educative than playing ball (i.e. play); rather they would attempt to distinguish between activities using such terms as 'educationally productive' and 'educationally unproductive' and then seek to show how productive such activities as ball-playing can be. However, if we assume that 'educational productivity' can be defined as a goal for any activity, the pedagogical issue remains of showing how productivity can be secured from activities, i.e. of showing how coverage and mastery can be effected given some specified activity. We can grant that almost any activity (and particularly those chosen *by* children) can be turned to some educative purpose, but we need to ask how the teacher goes about turning activities to educative purposes and how the teacher goes about building *educative* purpose into otherwise educationally neutral activities. . . . We can concede that quantitative operations and concepts, artistic ability, notions of city planning, or principles of architecture and the like are pregnant in any sand tray, but how should a teacher go about extracting these purposes from the sand tray, and particularly how should he go about doing this when he has other groups in his classroom doing similar tasks?

The literature of open education seems to give two different answers to these questions: one of these answers is of little theoretical interest and, on the face of it, would seem to imply the presence of a rock on which open education might founder; the other answer is of great theoretical and practical significance.

The simple solution to this problem of input, and that implied by the sand tray example, is to station a teacher or a teacher-substitute near all productive or potentially-productive activities with the implication that he should intervene to turn an activity to productive ends. A learning activity thus becomes externally-paced although the experience itself, from the viewpoint of the students, might well have intrinsic qualities. The problem with this solution lies in its trivial character: it is merely an extension of the existing classroom practices to smaller activity centres. Given the real problem of management in a decentralized classroom environment, this solution demands either that classrooms be manned more intensively than they are at present or that teachers must expend greater than normal energy on teaching. The implications of either of these possibilities for the institutional viability and cost of open education have not been widely discussed.

These rocks can be avoided, to some extent at least, by recognizing that there are problems in any attempt to run an open classroom and by then facing the theoretical issue of what the problem of the open classroom is. Thus, although activity units can be decentralized in the interests of organizational and pedagogical flexibility, the classroom goals of coverage and mastery of subject matters of one kind or another nevertheless remain; the open classroom has to teach its students and if, for any reason, the teacher cannot do this, then something else has to. This something else must, of course, be materials of some kind.

We can gain some glimpses of what this claim might mean and how this problem might be met – although not in the hortatory literature of open education. Let me attempt to demonstrate this possibility by means of a simple illustration from the nursery school.

David Olson has reported the development of an educational toy that is an effective means of teaching the concept of diagonality to preschoolers but, at the same time, makes no demands on the teacher. His toys were placed in a nursery school with the request that teachers were not to provide any instruction on how to make the patterns but merely to keep the toys, properly assembled, on the shelf; they were to let the children play with them as they would with any other toy in the school. After seven months control and experimental children were tested on their mastery of the concept of the diagonal. 64.1 per cent of the experimental group received maximum scores on the test for diagonality as compared to 39·6 per cent of the control group; even the unsuccessful children in the experimental group went about their attempts to solve the task problems with strategies which were superior to those used by the control children.[8]

Olson's toy seems to offer a way of avoiding the pitfalls that are pregnant in the open classroom notion. Little teacher energy was expended on injecting specific instruction on the diagonal into the classroom setting – the toy itself was responsible for specific instruction and the toy itself exerted its own motivational press on students. The toy was, in other words, self-instructional and thus imposed no special demands on the teacher.

I have emphasized this one, in some way trivial example of materials-induced instruction because I believe that the open classroom can only be made to work if devices of this kind become the primary instruments of routine explicit instruction in these classrooms, thus leaving the teacher free to address the demands of classroom management and non-routine instruction. I am arguing, in other words, that the open classroom can only be regarded as a real and plausible alternative form of schooling if the teacher can be relieved, to a substantial extent, from traditional responsibility for mastery and task attention. As a corollary to this belief I would argue that the effective development and dissemination of the open classroom notion demands that significant attention be given the issues entailed in the development of devices of this kind.[. . .]

[. . .] Materials such as Dienes' *Multibase Arithmetic Blocks* or the *Cuisenaire Rods* are packages of toy-like stimuli developed for teaching elementary mathematics. The literature which surrounds these packages provides the bases for teacher understanding of what they should do with these toys and, indirectly at least, provides the basic discourses which the teacher is to use in his classroom as he operationalizes an 'open' method. This literature is, if my inference is correct, the *real* literature of open education, and the issues which this literature raises are the real issues in open education. As Zoltan Dienes writes in his discussion of the teaching of open mathematics:

Let it be immediately understood that decentralization does not mean chaos: nor does it mean any abrogation of the teacher's responsibility as regards the conduct of the class. The way this responsibility is discharged will, however, be different in a decentralized classroom from the way it is discharged in a centrally controlled one. The children must feel with certainty that the teacher is in charge of things, but at the same time *he has arranged that information can reach children without his intervention. The children must also feel that they can check their own or each other's work in an independent manner, and they will consult the teacher if some problem arises which they are unable to solve by themselves.*[9]

[. . .]

The technology of teaching and the goals of schooling

A conception of knowledge as a content which can be stored in books which can be opened for and by students, controls, of course, the goals of the conventional school. The methods employed in the conventional classroom are designed to perform this task; in the classroom the book is, in one sense, an aid to the teacher but, in another sense, it is the sole object of the teacher's attention – other methods, discussion, and most audio visual aids and the like, are devices which the teacher can use to ease the approach to the book. The real work of conventional schooling is focused on the book or on proxies drawn from books.[10] It is this conception of tasks of education that legitimizes the methods of the conventional classroom. [. . .] They are designed to open, more or less systematically, the boxes of knowledge symbolized by subjects to students. The existing classroom draws upon a technology of books and teacher talk to effect these goals.

The open classroom movement, of course, is an assault on the validity of this conception of knowledge and of methods that have their legitimacy in an image of schooling as information-giving and box opening. Thus, at the heart of Dienes' prescriptions for mathematics is a conception of all mathematical thinking as experiential and intuitive, not formal.
[. . .]

[. . .] Teaching methods must conform to this understanding of the nature of mathematics; the student must be allowed to learn mathematical structures through an inductive examination and manipulation of physical and game-like embodiments of the concepts we are seeking to teach them. In [Dienes'] words,

> In the natural concept formation process which goes on uninterruptedly all the time, artificially structured games are rarely played and, if they are, the structure itself is supposed to provide the amusement, as in a game of chess. Nevertheless, experiences have their own structures and so some experiences will tend to lead towards a concept more quickly than others. The 'play' quality of these early experiences is probably a powerful stimulus towards the attainment of concepts, and a careful selection of these play experiences could accelerate such growth considerably . . . Unfortunately, these natural situations and games do not take us all the way . . . As higher and higher order concepts are aimed at, the number of life situations that could usefully lead up to them diminishes. Eventually we are faced with having to teach concepts for which they have absolutely no background in experience at all . . . Clearly, if we still wish to teach the child to form concepts as a result of experience, then we must provide him with artificial experiences to lead up to these more complex concepts and processes.[11]

Dienes' materials are an attempt to engineer ways in which play- and game-like materials can be used in classrooms as the basis for mathematical experience. They represent a technological form which can be used to support a classroom environment which is appropriate to the attainment of the 'proper' goals of school mathematics.

This conclusion brings us back to the claims of open education, but in a somewhat different context. For Dienes, play-like school experience is a tool which he uses in the classroom to achieve a congruence between the demands of mathematics and the psychological capabilities of children to learn this demanded form of mathematics. These goals of means and ends require him to search for an appropriate organizational structure for the classroom; to effect play the classroom must differ from the conventional room: he needs to group children by interest, level of cognitive maturity, level of learning, and the like, and place them close enough to *experience* for them to manipulate truly the materials he puts before them. He can do all of these things if he moves students through activities over *both* time *and* space, but only if pedagogical control is transferred to materials which are both self-instructing and, as far as possible, self-managing.

This discussion of Dienes' pedagogy can be generalized in some important ways. His invocation of an intuitionist metamathematics represents an awareness of the place of the person as an active agent in both mathematical knowing and learning. This turning of the person into the act of knowing represents one of the crucial understandings of twentieth-century philosophy. For us there is no content that is not inextricably entangled in the act of questioning. As Marjorie Grene writes, we understand that knowing is a form of doing, and 'it is the full, concrete, historical person who is the essential agent of knowledge'.[12] We believe that our discourses are discourses about a world, but this world is a world that is created by the questions we ask, not a world that is given. For us there is no content that is not inextricably entangled in the act of questioning. As a consequence of this awareness, a manifestation of what Father Ong has called our recognition of 'the interior aspects of the person',[13] most of our current reconstructions of knowledge, most of the ways in which we conceptualize what knowledge is, give a higher priority to the question and the act of asking questions than they give to the bodies of answers that we have to past questions. This is the import of, say, Collingwood in history, Polanyi in epistemology, Kuhn in science, Piaget in psychology, and Dewey. For us the encyclopaedia, the ordered body of accumulated knowledge, is not the symbol of knowledge; instead we attempt to symbolize our conceptions of the knowledge most worth having by talking of masteries of the methods by which new questions can be asked of subject-matters or by which discoveries of new subject-matters can be achieved. Moreover, our awareness of the many forms of knowledge has led us to ask why *this* man is asking *this* kind of question; and our psychological awareness has led us to ask why I (and we and they) habitually ask this kind of question. These questions have shifted easily and naturally into the further, specifically psychological question of 'How do I (or we or they) learn to ask questions of this kind?' This whole chain of questions and the considerations about teaching that it implies is, of course, totally disquieting to anyone who thinks about schooling. The prescription for instruction that the chain implies – 'Teach students to think' – is old hat, but, as we know all too well, the schools do not do these things. Schools are as obsessed with the encyclopaedia of content as they ever were.

One source of the failure of the schools to take the point of prescriptions that students must be taught to think is to be found in the classroom itself, in its structures, and ultimately in the technology that needs and makes possible given structures. The technologies of the conventional classroom – the recitation, the lecture, the textbook – were designed to teach the eighteenth-

and nineteenth-century encyclopaedia of established facts and established doctrines. In their time these technologies were responsive to the goals that the schools were designed to enact. However, these technologies are not responsive to the goals that are implicit in our present conceptions of what the schools should do; we cannot execute the programme of teaching implicit in Dewey, Kuhn or Piaget within the structures, and given the materials and methods of these old forms.

It is this conclusion which brings us back to open education. The ideology of open education articulates goals which the conventional school cannot address. The structures of the open classroom, derived from the methods of the preschool or kindergarten (where students cannot conform to the institutional demands of the classroom) are designed to meet needs that the structures of the conventional classroom cannot fulfil. But prescriptions for structure alone do not tell us how the *work* of the classroom, the tasks associated with mastery, coverage, management and affect, can be performed. Dienes has shown us some ways in which aspects of this work might get done, but his technologies are only a beginning.

If we want to execute a new programme in the schools we must develop an array of new ways and new means that are real alternatives to the tried and true method of the conventional classroom. We must see what new purposes imply for the classroom and focus our attention on this latter problem. Infant methods as developed by Montessori and the English Froebel movement offer us one, clearly viable set of models that we can ransack for our new needs. We can equally readily explore how we can turn the principles that lie behind these procedures and artifacts to more complex purposes. But this source of ideas is too limited in scope to cope in any sustained way with the real problem of implementing a new conception of the goals of schooling. We need to turn as well to technologies such as advertising and the computer, and to television, and to such understanding as we have of play, of the nature of learning, of the potentialities of group interaction. Most important of all we must address the question of what new purposes mean when we face the problem of initiating millions of children into the forms of discourse and behaviour that 'education' connotes.[14]

Acknowledgments

I wish to acknowledge the assistance of Jon Abrahamson and Ilene Harris in developing many of the ideas outlined in this paper. For valuable criticism of earlier drafts of the paper, I would like to thank my colleagues Robert Dreeben and Benjamin Wright. Extracts from *The Complexities of an Urban Classroom* are reproduced by arrangement with Holt, Rinehart and Winston Inc., New York.

Notes

1 See BARTH, ROLAND, S. (1969) 'Open education – assumptions about learning.' *Educational Philosophy and Theory*, 1, passim; BUSSIS, ANNE, M. and CHITTENDEN, EDWARD, A. (1970) *Analysis of an Approach to Open Education*, Educational Testing Service, Report No. PR-70-13, August 1970, passim; and RATHBONE, CHARLES (1972) 'Examining the open education classroom.' *School Review*, 80, pp. 521–49.

2 BARTH, 'Open education', 32–4.

3 BUSSIS and CHITTENDEN, *Analysis of an Approach to Open Education*, pp. 37, 39–40.

4 BARTH, 'Open education', pp. 33–4.

5 RATHBONE, 'Examining the open education classroom', does offer a characterization of the open classroom that meets this stricture.

6 For a discussion of the potentialities inherent in the class as a group, see THELEN, HERBERT, A. (1959) 'Work emotionality theory of the group as an organism', in KOCH, SIGMUND (ed.) (1959) *Psychology: A Study of a Science*, Vol. 2. New York: McGraw-Hill.

7 BARTH, 'Open education', p. 32.

8 OLSON, DAVID, R. (1970) *Cognitive Development: The Child's Acquisition of Diagonality*. New York: Academic Press (Chapter 9).

9 DIENES, ZOLTAN, P. (1966) *Mathematics in the Primary School*. London: Macmillan (pp. 208, 209: italics added).

10 For this argument, see ONG, WALTER, J., S.J. (1958) *Ramus, Method and the Decay of Dialogue*. Cambridge, Mass.: Harvard University Press (Chapter 13).

11 DIENES, ZOLTAN, P. (1959) 'The growth of mathematical concepts in children through experience.' *Educational Research*, 2, 16.

12 GRENE, MARJORIE (1966) *The Knower and the Known*. New York: Basic Books (158).

13 ONG, WALTER, J., S.J. (1968) 'Introduction: Knowledge in time', in ONG, WALTER, J., S.J. (ed.) (1968) *Knowledge and the Future of Man*. New York: Holt, Rinehart and Winston.

14 For some fascinating approaches to this task, see FURTH, HANS, G. (1970) *Piaget for Teachers*. Englewood Cliffs, New Jersey: Prentice-Hall; and BROWN, DEAN and EL-GHANNAN, MOHAMMED A. (1971) *Computers for Teaching* (a summary of papers presented to the Second Specialised Course on New Technologies in Education, Regional Centre for the Planning and Administration of Education for the Arab Countries, Beirut, Lebanon). Menlo Park, Calif.: Stanford Research Institute.

2.13 Meaning making

Neil Postman and Charles Weingartner

Adelbert Ames died in 1955, largely unknown to the people who could profit most by his work, namely, teachers.

Beginning in 1938, Ames created a series of demonstrations designed to study the nature of perception. His laboratory included oddly shaped rooms, chairs, windows and other objects which seemed to distort reality when perceived by ordinary people. Perhaps his most impressive demonstration is the trapezoidal window which revolved in a 360° circle. The perceiver, however, observes that the window turns 180°, stops, and then turns back 180°. Some of the people who were shown the demonstrations were not convinced that they had any significance and labelled them 'optical illusions'. But a few thought otherwise, including Albert Einstein, Dewey, Hadley Cantril and Earl Kelley. Dewey believed that Ames had provided empirical evidence for the 'transactional psychology' he and Arthur Bentley had formulated in *Knowing and the Known*. This term was used by them to minimize the mechanistic oversimplification caused by the use of the term 'interaction'. The sense of 'transactional psychology' is that what human beings are and what they make their environment into is a product of a mutually simultaneous, highly complex and continuing 'bargaining' process between what is inside their skins and outside. Dewey believed that Ames had provided substantial understandings of the nature of that bargaining process.

Cantril sensed that Ames's work had great significance for social psychology and developed the point in his book *The 'Why' of Man's Experience*. Kelley saw at once the meanings of the demonstrations for education. In his book *Education for What Is Real* (with an introduction by Dewey), he describes Ames's experiments in detail, and suggests how these studies in perception, if understood and applied, would change the schooling process. In our judgment, it is the best education book written in the past twenty years and probably one of the least known. What is it Ames seemed to prove? The first and most important fact uncovered by his perception studies is that we do not get our perceptions from the 'things' around us. Our perceptions come from us. This does *not* mean that there is nothing outside of our skins. It does mean that whatever is 'out there' can never be known except as it is filtered through a human nervous system. We can never get outside of our own skins. 'Reality' is a perception, located somewhere behind the eyes.

Secondly, it seems clear from the Ames studies that what we perceive is largely a function of our previous experiences, our assumptions and our purposes (i.e. needs). In other words, the perceiver decides what an object is, where it is, and why it is, according to his purpose and the assumptions that he

Source: POSTMAN, N. and WEINGARTNER, C. (1969) *Teaching as a Subversive Activity*. New York: Delacorte Press; London: Pitman.[1]

makes at any given time. You tend to perceive what you want and need to perceive and what your past experience has led you to assume will 'work' for you.

Thirdly, we are unlikely to alter our perceptions until and unless we are frustrated in our attempts to do something based on them. If our actions seem to permit us to fulfil our purposes, we will not change our perceptions no matter how often we are told that they are 'wrong'. In fact, the meaning of 'wrong' in this context is a perception that does not 'work' for the perceiver. This does *not* mean, however, that we automatically change our perceptions if we are frustrated in our attempts to act on them. This does mean that we have available the alternative of changing our perceptions. The ability to learn can be seen as the ability to relinquish inappropriate perceptions and to develop new – and more workable – ones.

Fourth, since our perceptions come from us and our past experience, it is obvious that each individual will perceive what is 'out there' in a unique way. We have no common world, and communication is possible only to the extent that two perceivers have similar purposes, assumptions and experience. The process of becoming an effective social being is contingent upon seeing the other's point of view.

Fifth, perception is, to a much greater extent than previously imagined, a function of the linguistic categories available to the perceiver. As we said, reality is a perception located somewhere behind the eyes. But behind the eyes there is a language process. We know that nature never repeats or standardizes. We do it. And how we do it depends on the categories and classifications of our language system. It is only a slight exaggeration to say we see with our language.

Sixth, the meaning of a perception is how it causes us to *act*. If rain is falling from the sky, some people will head for shelter, others will enjoy walking in it. Their perceptions of what is happening are different as reflected in the fact that they do different things. The fact that both groups will agree to the sentence 'It is raining' does not mean they perceive the event in the same way.

In the light of all this, perhaps you will understand why we prefer the metaphor 'meaning making' to most of the metaphors of the mind that are operative in the schools. It is, to begin with, much less static than the others. It stresses a process view of minding, including the fact that 'minding' is undergoing constant change. 'Meaning making' also forces us to focus on the individuality and the uniqueness of the meaning *maker* (the *minder*). In most of the other metaphors there is an assumption of sameness in all learners. The garden to be cultivated, the darkness to be lighted, the foundation to be built upon, the clay to be moulded – there is always the implication that all learning will occur in the same way. The flowers will be the same colour, the light will reveal the same room, the clay will take the same shape, and so on. Moreover, such metaphors imply boundaries, a limit to learning. How many flowers can a garden hold? How much water can a bucket take? What happens to the learner after his mind has been moulded? How large can a building be, even if constructed on a solid foundation? The 'meaning maker' has no such limitations. There is no end to his educative process. He continues to create new meanings, to make new transactions with his environment.

We come then to the question 'What difference does it all make?' It seems clear to us that, if teachers *acted* as if their students were meaning makers, almost everything about the schooling process would change. For example, most school practices are based on the assumption that the student is fundamentally a *receiver*, that the object (subject matter) from which the stimulus originates is all-important, and that the student has no choice but to see and understand the stimulus as it is. We now know that this assumption is false. To quote Earl Kelley:

Now it comes about that whatever we tell the learner, he will make something that is all his own out of it, and it will be different from what we held so dear and attempted to 'transmit'. He will build it into his own scheme of things, and relate it uniquely to what he already uniquely holds as experience. Thus he builds a world all his own, and what is really important is what he makes of what we tell him, not what we intended.

In other words, you end up with a student-centred curriculum not because it is good for motivation but because you don't, in fact, have any other choice.

There is no such thing as 'subject matter' in the abstract. Subject matter exists in the minds of perceivers. And what each one thinks it is, is what it is. We have been acting in schools as if knowledge lies outside the learner, which is why we have the kinds of curricula, syllabi and texts we have. But knowledge, as Kelley points out, is what we know *after* we have learned. It is an outcome of perception and is as unique and subjective as any other perception.

Note

1 First published in Great Britain by Penguin Books in association with Pitman Publishing, 1971, pp. 92–5.

2.14 Power or persons: two trends in educatio

Carl R. Rogers

The educational system is probably the most influential of all institutions –
outranking the family, the church, the police, and the government – in
shaping the interpersonal politics of the growing person. We will take a look at
the politics of education as it is and has been in this country [USA] and
compare it with the politics of an educational enterprise when it has become
infused with a person-centred approach.

Here is how the politics of the traditional school is experienced:

The teacher is the possessor of knowledge, the student the recipient. There is a great
difference in status between instructor and student.

*The lecture, as the means of pouring knowledge into the recipient, and the examination
as the measure of the extent to which he has received it, are the central elements of this
education.*

The teacher is the possessor of power, the student the one who obeys. The
administrator is also the possessor of power, and both the teacher and the
student are the ones who obey. Control is always exercised downward.

Authoritarian rule is the accepted policy in the classroom. New teachers are often
advised, 'Make sure you get control of your students the very first day.'

Trust is at a minimum. Most notable is the teacher's distrust of the student.
The student cannot be expected to work satisfactorily without the teacher
constantly supervising and checking on him. The student's distrust of the
teacher is more diffuse – a lack of trust in teacher's motives, honesty, fairness,
competence. There may be a real rapport between an entertaining lecturer
and those who are being entertained. There may be admiration for the
instructor, but mutual trust is not a noticeable ingredient.

*The subjects (the students) are best governed by being kept in an intermittent or
constant state of fear.* There is today not much physical punishment, but public
criticism and ridicule, and a constant fear of failure, are even more potent.
This state of fear appears to increase as we go up the educational scheme,
because the student has more to lose. In elementary school the individual may
be an object of scorn, or scolded as stupid or bad. In high school there is added
to this the fear of failure to graduate, with its vocational, economic and
educational disadvantages. In college all these consequences are magnified
and intensified. In graduate school, sponsorship by one professor offers even
greater opportunities for extreme punishment due to some autocratic whim.
Many graduate students have failed to receive their degrees because they have
refused to obey every wish of their major professor. They are like slaves,
subject to the life and death power of an Oriental despot. It is the recognition
of this abjectness which caused Farber (1969) to title his biting criticism of
education *The Student as Nigger*.

Source: ROGERS, C. R. (1977) *On Personal Power*. New York: Delacorte Press. (1979) London:
Constable, pp. 69–88.

Democracy and its values are ignored and scorned in practice. The student does not participate in choosing his goals, his curriculum, his manner of working. They are chosen for him. He has no part in the choice of teaching personnel or in educational policy. Likewise the teachers have no choice in choosing their principal or other administrative officers. Often they, too, have no participation in forming educational policy. The political practices of the school are in striking contrast to what is taught *about* the virtues of democracy and the importance of freedom and responsibility.

There is no place for the whole person in the educational system, only for the intellect. In elementary school the bursting curiosity of the normal child and his excess of physical energy are curbed and, if possible, stifled. In secondary school the one overriding interest of all the students – sex and the relationships between the sexes – is almost totally ignored and certainly not regarded as a major area for learning. In college the situation is the same – it is only the *mind* that is welcomed.

[. . .]

Here are the fundamental conditions that may be observed when person-centred learning develops in a school, college, or graduate school.

Precondition. A leader or a person who is perceived as an authority figure in the situation is sufficiently secure within himself and in his relationship to others that he experiences an essential trust in the capacity of others to think for themselves, to learn for themselves. If this precondition exists, then the following aspects become possible.

The facilitative person shares with the others – students and possibly also parents or community members – the responsibility for the learning process. Curricular planning, the mode of administration and operation, the funding, and the policy making are all the responsibility of the particular group involved. Thus a class may be responsible for its own curriculum, but the total group may be responsible for overall policy.

The facilitator provides learning resources – from within himself and his own experience, from books or materials or community experiences. He encourages the learners to add resources of which they have knowledge, or in which they have experience. He opens doors to resources outside the experience of the group.

The student develops his own program of learning, alone or in cooperation with others. Exploring his own interests, facing the wealth of resources, he makes the choices as to his own learning direction and carries the responsibility for the consequences of those choices.

A facilitative learning climate is provided. In meetings of the class or of the school as a whole, an atmosphere of realness, of caring, and of understanding listening is evident. This climate may spring initially from the person who is the perceived leader. As the learning process continues, it is more and more often provided by the learners for one another. Learning from one another becomes as important as learning from books or films or community experiences, or from the facilitator.

It can be seen that *the focus is primarily on fostering the continuing process of learning.* The content of the learning, while significant, falls into a secondary place. Thus a course is successfully ended not when the student has 'learned all he needs to know', but when he has made significant progress in learning *how to learn* what he wants to know.

The discipline necessary to reach the student's goals is a self-discipline and is recognized and accepted by the learner as being his own responsibility.

The evaluation of the extent and significance of the student's learning is made primarily by the learner himself, though his self-evaluation may be influenced and enriched by caring feed-back from other members of the group and from the facilitator.

In this growth-promoting climate, the learning is deeper, proceeds at a more rapid rate, and is more pervasive in the life and behaviour of the student than learning acquired in the traditional classroom. This comes about because the direction is self-chosen, the learning is self-initiated, and the whole person, with feelings and passions as well as intellect, is invested in the process.

*   *   *

The political implications of person-centred education are clear: the student retains his own power and the control over himself; he shares in the responsible choices and decisions; the facilitator provides the climate for these aims. The growing, seeking person is the politically powerful force. This process of learning represents a revolutionary about-face from the politics of traditional education.

What is it that causes a teacher to reverse the politics of the classroom? The reasons are multiple.

First I cite my own experience. As my point of view in therapy became more and more trusting of the capacity of the individual, I could not help but question my teaching approach. If I saw clients as trustworthy and basically capable of discovering themselves and guiding their lives in an ambience I was able to create, why could I not create the same kind of climate with graduate students and foster a *self*-guided process of learning? So, at the University of Chicago, I began to try. I ran into far more resistance and hostility than I did with my clients. I believe this had the result of making me more defensively rigid, putting *all* the responsibility on the class rather than recognizing myself as a part of the learning group. I made many mistakes, and sometimes doubted the wisdom of the whole approach. Yet with all my initial clumsiness the results were astonishing. Students worked harder, learned more, did more creative thinking than in any of my previous classes. So I persevered, and improved, I believe, in my ability as a facilitator.

Although I began to talk and write about my experience, and some of my students worked in similar ways with classes they were conducting, there was always the nagging doubt that perhaps this procedure worked simply because of something in me, or some peculiar attitudes we had developed in the Counseling Center at Chicago. Consequently it was enormously supportive to find that others had gone through similar struggles, were adopting the principles we had outlined, and were having parallel – indeed almost identical – experiences.

[. . .]

Change is never easy. To pioneer is anxiety-arousing for the teacher and threatening to colleagues. It seems it would be much simpler to go back to being the authority. It is hard being a person to one's students. And then there are, at the elementary and secondary level, the attitudes of sceptical or antagonistic parents to deal with. Many teachers have found that the only way to handle parental doubts is to find ways of including parents in the learning process. Some have invited parents to volunteer in different ways in the classroom. One imaginative secondary school teacher invited parents of her students for 'An Evening of Learning' where they were exposed to, and discussed, the facilitative approach she was using with their children.

A new approach to education demands new ways of being and new methods of handling problems. Individuals are also finding that if they are to carry out a quiet revolution in the schools, they definitely need a support group. This can be small, perhaps only two or three people, but a resource of persons where one does not need to defend one's point of view, and can freely discuss the successes and failures, the problems faced, the difficulties unresolved.

I have spoken mostly of the risks the teacher takes in the teacher-student relationship when the politics of the classroom changes. But a facilitator is also taking the risk of threatening the administration. How is this dealt with?

In many states and communities, instructors are being held more and more accountable. They are expected to write down 'behavioural objectives' for each student or for each course, and later to give evidence that these objectives have been achieved. The anxiety that underlies these demands – sometimes encased in law – is understandable. The public hopes that young people are learning, and this has been the only way they can see of determining whether learning is taking place.

From the viewpoint of any good teacher, conventional or innovative, this becomes a new strait jacket which prevents any deviance from the expected, any ventures into exciting bypaths of learning. Dr David Malcolm, a university professor, tells how he met this request for behavioural objectives.

'My university is on an "accountability" kick right now, and writing "behavioural objectives" for students is the big thing. Both do total violence to all my personal beliefs about learning and what people are for. My protest has been to refuse to write objectives for "my" (what arrogance!) classes. Instead I wrote down some tentative ideas trying to express objectives for my own behaviour. They fell into place pretty well, and I'd like to share them with you' (Malcolm, 1972).

Here they are, in shortened form.

A set of behavioural objectives written by and for Dave Malcolm

(The following is written on the assumption that behavioural objectives begin at home.)

QUESTION: Okay, just what *does* the faculty member (specifically, *me*) do in my idealized 'learning place', i.e., one *not* contaminated by gate-keeping?

ANSWER: Well . . . *first,* I have to give the learners accessibility to me as a person, to my experience, to my expertise . . . *second,* I have to be as ready as I can to suggest experiences (materials to read, things to do, people to touch, processes to observe, ideas to ponder, practices to try, whatever) that they might not otherwise have thought of, thereby increasing the options open to them; *third,* I have to respect each learner's autonomy and freedom, including the freedom to fail; and *finally,* I have to be willing to (perhaps, better, I should say *have the courage to*) give each learner honest feedback, as straight as possible, to the very best of my ability, on as many of the following as I can:

(He describes nine areas, including ability to conceptualize; demonstrated skill in practice; effectiveness in oral and written communication; degree of self-understanding, insight and skill in interpersonal relationships; innovativeness; my best judgment as to his progress or growth. He is *willing* to give feedback in these areas if the student desires.)

Here is a conscientious and inspiring statement of the true 'objectives' of one person-centred facilitator of learning. Malcolm is up against the impossible task of defining his aims for students, being expected to follow the old conventional authoritarian framework. His own politics of education simply does not permit this. So he bravely sets forth, thoughtfully and precisely, the objectives he has for *himself,* not the student. His statement can be a guideline for teachers. Most of all, however, it shows the complete incompatibility of the old politics and the new, and thus fits a definition that has been given of revolution. 'What is a revolution? A redefinition of the facts of life, such that the new definition and the old definition of the same facts cannot coexist' (Ramey, 1975). Clearly, to advance a revolution threatens the power of a conventional administration, and a consequent risk to the facilitator, who is a radical in the true sense of going to the root of the problem. This risk cannot be ignored.

Too little attention has been paid to the problems of the student in meeting the challenge of a person-centered way of education. Initially students feel suspicion, frustration, and anger, and then excitement and creativity replace those feelings. No one has caught these changing reactions better than Dr Samuel Tenenbaum, who was a member of a seminar I offered at Brandeis University in 1958. His account (Tenenbaum, 1961) indicates the impact upon the learner of a sharp change in the power relationship in a class.

I have often pondered the reasons why, in this seminar, the reactions were more strongly negative, and eventually more strongly positive, than in any other class I have led. I believe it is due in part to the fact that they were so eager to learn from the 'master', the 'guru', that they were loath to accept any shift in authority. Perhaps another reason is that they were all graduate students, most of them already employed professionally, or, like Dr Tenenbaum, taking the course as a postdoctoral seminar. Such students are, I believe, even more dependent upon authority than are elementary school children.

I took up most of the first meeting of the seminar (about twenty-five students) by introducing myself and my purpose and asking if others wished to do the same. After some awkward silences, the students told what brought them to the seminar. I told the group about the many resources I had brought with me – reprints, mimeographed material, books, a list of recommended reading (no requirements), tapes of therapeutic interviews, and films. I asked for volunteers to organize and lend out these materials, to run the tapes, and find a movie projector. All of this was easily handled, and the session ended. As Dr Tenenbaum takes up the story:

Thereafter followed four hard, frustrating sessions. During this period, the class didn't seem to get anywhere. Students spoke at random, saying whatever came into their heads. It all seemed chaotic, aimless, a waste of time. A student would bring up some aspect of Rogers' philosophy; and the next student completely disregarding the first, would take the group away in another direction; and a third, completely disregarding the first two, would start fresh on something else altogether. At times there were some faint efforts at a cohesive discussion, but for the most part the classroom proceedings seemed to lack continuity and direction. The instructor received every contribution with attention and regard. He did not find any student's contribution in order or out of order.

The class was not prepared for such a totally unstructured approach. They did not know how to proceed. In their perplexity and frustration, they demanded that the teacher play the role assigned to him by custom and tradition; that he set forth for us in authoritative language what was right and wrong, what was good and bad. Had they not come from far distances to learn from the oracle himself? Were they not fortunate? Were they not about to be initiated in the right rituals and practices by the great man himself, the founder of the movement that bears his name? The notebooks were poised for the climactic moment when the oracle would give forth, but mostly they remained untouched.

Queerly enough, from the outset, even in their anger, the members of the group felt joined together, and outside the classroom, there was an excitement and a ferment, for even in their frustration, they had communicated as never before in any classroom, and probably never before in quite the way they had. . . . In the Rogers class, they had spoken their minds; the words did not come from a book, nor were they the reflection of the instructor's thinking, nor that of any other authority. The ideas, emotions, and feelings came from themselves; and this was the releasing and the exciting process.

In this atmosphere of freedom, something for which they had not bargained and for which they were not prepared, the students spoke up as students seldom do. During this period, the instructor took many blows; and it seemed to me that many times he appeared to be shaken; and although he was the source of our irritation, we had, strange as it may seem, a great affection for him, for it did not seem right to be angry with a man who was so sympathetic, so sensitive to the feelings and ideas of others. We all felt that what was involved was some slight misunderstanding which once understood and remedied would make everything right again. But our instructor, gentle enough on the surface, had a 'whim of steel'. He didn't seem to understand; and if he did, he was obstinate and obdurate; he refused to come around. Thus did this tug-of-war continue. We all looked to Rogers and Rogers looked to us. One student, amid general approbation, observed: 'We are Rogers-centred, not student-centred. We have come to learn from Rogers.'

After more of this, individual students attempted to take leadership and organize the seminar around certain topics or ways of planning, but these attempts at structure were largely disregarded. Gradually the group became insistent that I lecture. I told them that I was just completing a paper, and would be willing to give that as a lecture, but I also informed them that I was quite willing to have it duplicated so that each could read it. They insisted that I give it as a talk, and I agreed. It was a topic I was much involved in, and I believe I delivered it as well as I was able, taking somewhat more than an hour. Tenenbaum reports the results.

After the vivid and acrimonious exchanges to which we had been accustomed, this was certainly a letdown, dull and soporific to the extreme. This experience squelched all further demands for lecturing.

By the fifth session, something definite had happened; there was no mistaking that. Students spoke to one another; they by-passed Rogers. Students asked to be heard and wanted to be heard, and what before was a halting, stammering, self-conscious group became an interacting group, a brand-new cohesive unit, carrying on in a unique way; and from them came discussion and thinking such as no other group but this could repeat or duplicate. The instructor also joined in, but his role, more important than any in the group, somehow became merged with the group; the group was important, the centre, the base of operation, not the instructor.

What caused it? I can only conjecture as to the reason. I believe that what happened was this: For four sessions students refused to believe that the instructor would refuse to play the traditional role. They still believed that he would set the tasks; that he would be the centre of whatever happened and that he would manipulate the group. It took the class four sessions to realize that they were wrong; that he came to them with nothing outside of himself, outside of his own person; that if they really wanted something to happen, it was they who had to provide the content – an uncomfortable, challenging situation indeed. It was they who had to speak up, with all the risks that entailed. As part of the process, they shared, they took exception, they agreed, they disagreed. At any rate, their persons, their deepest selves were involved; and from this situation, this special, unique group, this new creation was born. . . .

After the fourth session, and progressively thereafter, this group, haphazardly thrown together, became close to one another and their true selves appeared. As they interacted, there were moments of insight and revelation and understanding that were almost awesome in nature; they were what, I believe, Rogers would describe as 'moments of therapy', those pregnant moments when you see a human soul revealed before you, in all its breathless wonder; and then a silence, almost like reverence, would overtake the class. And each member of the class became enveloped with a warmth and a loveliness that border on the mystic. I for one, and I am quite sure the others also, never had an experience quite like this. It was learning and therapy; and by therapy I do not mean illness, but what might be characterized by a healthy change in the person, an increase in his flexibility, his openness, his willingness to listen. In the process, we all felt elevated, freer, more accepting of ourselves and others, more open to new ideas, trying hard to understand and accept.

This is not a perfect world, and there was evidence of hostility as members differed. Somehow in this setting every blow was softened, as if the sharp edges had been removed; if undeserved, students would go off to something else; and the blow was somehow lost. In my own case, even those students who originally irritated me, with further acquaintance I began to accept and respect; and the thought occurred to me as I tried to understand what was happening: Once you come close to a person, perceive his thoughts, his emotions, his feelings, he becomes not only understandable but good and desirable. . . .

In the course of this process, I saw hard, inflexible, dogmatic persons, in the brief period of several weeks, change in front of my eyes and become sympathetic, understanding and to a marked degree nonjudgmental. I saw neurotic, compulsive persons ease up and become more accepting of themselves and others. In one instance, a student who particularly impressed me by his change, told me when I mentioned this: 'It is true. I feel less rigid, more open to the world. And I like myself better for it. I don't believe I ever learned so much anywhere.' I saw shy persons become less shy and aggressive persons more sensitive and moderate.

One might say that this appears to be essentially an emotional process. But that, I believe, would be altogether inaccurate in describing it. There was a great deal of intellectual content, but the intellectual content was meaningful and crucial to the person. In fact, one student brought up this very question. 'Should we be concerned,' he asked, 'only with the emotions? Has the intellect no play?' It was my turn to ask, 'Is there any student who has read as much or thought as much for any other course?'

The answer was obvious. We had spent hours and hours reading; the room reserved for us had occupants until ten o'clock at night, and then many left only because the university guards wanted to close the building. Students listened to recordings; they saw motion pictures; but best of all, they talked and talked and talked. . . .

The Rogers method was free and flowing and open and permissive. A student would start an interesting discussion; it would be taken up by a second; but a third student might take us away in another direction, bringing up a personal matter of no interest to the class; and we would all feel frustrated. But this was like life, flowing on like a river, seemingly futile, with never the same water there, flowing on, with no one knowing what would happen the next moment. But in this there was an expectancy, an alertness, an aliveness; it seemed to me as near a smear of life as one could get in a classroom. For the authoritarian person, who puts his faith in neatly piled up facts, this method I believe can be threatening, for here he gets no reassurance, only an openness, a flowing, no closure.

I have nowhere found such a vivid account of the initially chaotic, gradually more fluid way in which the group, as it fearfully takes responsibility for itself, becomes a constructive organism, listening and responding sensitively to its own needs. It is the outwardly confused, inwardly organized, politics of an ever-changing group purpose, as the class moves to meet its intellectual, personal, and emotional needs.

Does a person-centred education bring results? We have a definitive answer from research. For ten years Dr David Aspy has led research studies aimed at finding out whether human, person-centred attitudes in the classroom have any measurable effects and if so what these effects are (Aspy and Roebuck, 1974; Aspy and Roebuck *et al.*, 1974). He collected 3,700 recorded classroom hours from 550 elementary and high school teachers and used rigorous scientific methods to analyze the results. He and his colleague, Dr Flora Roebuck, have found that students of more person-centred teachers contrast sharply with students of teachers who are less person-centred. They showed greater gains in learning conventional subjects. They were more adept at using their higher cognitive processes such as problem solving. They had a more positive self-concept than was found in the other groups. They initiated more behaviour in the classroom. They exhibited fewer discipline problems. They had a lower rate of absence from school. They even showed an increase in I.Q. among their students.

[. . .]

References

ASPY, D. N. and ROEBUCK, F. N. (1974) 'From humane ideas to humane technology and back again many times.' *Education*, 95, No. 2, Winter 1974, pp. 163–71.

ASPY, D. N. and ROEBUCK, F. N. *et al.* (1974) *Interim Reports 1, 2, 3, 4*. Washington, D.C.: National Consortium for Humanizing Education.

FARBER, J. (1969) *The Student as Nigger*. North Hollywood, Calif.: Contact Books.

MALCOLM, D. (1972) in personal correspondence with Carl R. Rogers.

RAMEY, J. W. (1975) 'Intimate Networks.' *The Futurist*, 9, No. 4, August 1975, p. 176.

TENENBAUM, S. (1961) 'Carl R. Rogers and non-directive teaching', in ROGERS, C. R. (1961) *On Becoming a Person*. Boston, Mass.: Houghton Mifflin, pp. 299–310.

2.15 A critique of Logo as a learning environment for mathematics

Tim O'Shea

Two important claims have been made for the computer programming language Logo (see Papert, 1972). The first claim is that despite being as powerful as the 'high-level' programming languages such as Algol, Fortran, or Pascal it is learnable by school children. The second claim is that it provides a revolutionary way to teach mathematics which makes it possible for pupils to learn to '*be mathematicians* rather than do mathematics'. In this article I will describe Logo and its uses in the classroom by means of a series of vignettes. These are based on my observations during a four-year research project carried out with eleven- to thirteen-year-old school-boys (Howe *et al.*, 1980). I will then discuss the strengths and weaknesses of Logo as a learning environment for mathematics.

In the first vignette a class of pupils are having their first encounter with Logo. They are using a box with sixteen buttons to control a small truck with wheels and a pen. The truck is called a floor turtle.

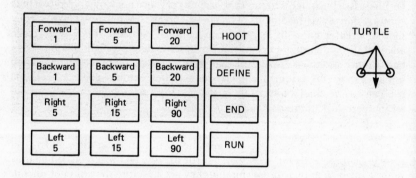

Figure 1

When they press the button 'Forward 5' the turtle moves forward 5 units. When they press the button 'Turn 90' the turtle moves through 90 degrees on the spot. They can teach the turtle to remember and then perform sequences of instructions by using the 'Define' and 'Run' buttons. They try to predict what the turtle will do or understand what it has drawn by playing turtle. When they do this one pupil shouts out the button box instructions and another carries out the turtle movements. The turtle and button box are a toy that school-age pupils enjoy playing with. You press a button and something

Source: Written for this Reader.

happens: the turtle has a pen attached so it leaves a visible trail and it can remember to do things and repeatedly do them. The learnability of Logo depends on the one to one association of turtle actions with stored button box presses. This activity provides a simple metaphor for the process of writing, inputting, storing and running computer programs.

In the next scene we watch two pupils from the class a few weeks later. The button box and turtle have been replaced by a computer keyboard connected to a computer screen.

Now pupils are typing programs in rather than buttoning them in. Instead of seeing a floor turtle move they see a turtle moving on the screen. When they make a mistake in their programming they get a picture they did not intend. This often makes them laugh. For example, they try to draw a house using programs they have made which draw a square and a triangle.

House	Square	Triangle
1 Square	1 Forward 100	1 Forward 100
2 Triangle	2 Right 90	2 Right 120
	3 Forward 100	3 Forward 100
	4 Right 90	4 Right 120
	5 Forward 100	5 Forward 100
	6 Right 90	6 Right 120
	7 Forward 100	
	8 Right 90	

Figure 2

The drawing is a result of running the Logo House program which uses the triangle and square programs. ▰▰▰ gives the starting position and orientation of the turtle.

Trying to understand their mistake the pupils do not 'play turtle' by walking around. But they say to each other things like: 'The square procedure tells the turtle to go forward 10, right 90, forward 10, right 90 . . .' As they say this, they move their shoulders left or right, imagining themselves to be the turtle on the screen. Sometimes they are really pleased by their mistakes. They are trying to draw concentric circles but all the edges of the circles touch. So instead they decide to draw a snail. They are very happy with the

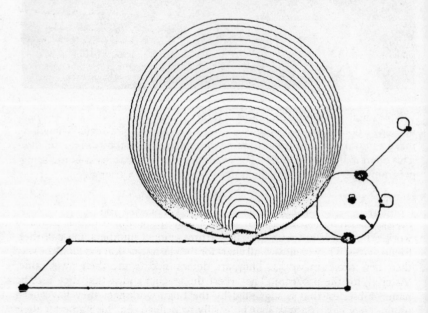

Figure 3   'Snail'

result. In later weeks when they start using Logo the first thing they always do is draw a snail.

Later when they wish to explain that they are going to use one Logo program as part of another they explain to their teacher in terms of 'like the snail program uses the circle program to draw the shell'.

In the third scene two pupils with one year's Logo experience are attempting to write a Logo program that generates Fibonacci series. First they write out the series. Then they search through the Logo programs they have stored in previous weeks but none of these seems useful. Then they ask some other pupils using other Logo computers in the classroom for help. One of their friends offers them a program he has written that takes a single number, doubles it, doubles that, etc., and continues forever. They take this and adapt it so that instead of taking one number it takes two. But the behaviour of the program does not change and it just keeps doubling the first number. After half an hour's experimentation there is great excitement. They

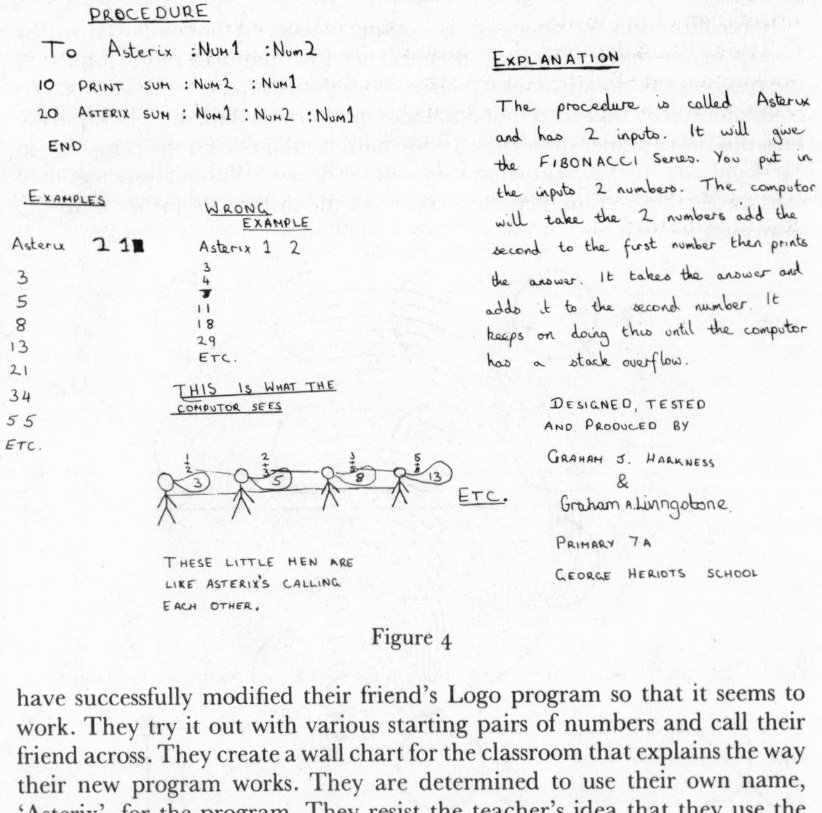

PROCEDURE

```
To  Asterix  :Num1  :Num2
10  PRINT SUM :Num2 :Num1
20  ASTERIX SUM :Num1 :Num2 :Num1
    END
```

EXAMPLES

	WRONG EXAMPLE
Asterix 2 1	Asterix 1 2
3	3
5	4
8	7
13	11
21	18
34	29
5 5	ETC.
ETC.	

THIS IS WHAT THE COMPUTOR SEES

THESE LITTLE MEN ARE
LIKE ASTERIX'S CALLING
EACH OTHER.

EXPLANATION

The procedure is called Asterix and has 2 inputs. It will give the FIBONACCI Series. You put in the inputs 2 numbers. The computor will take the 2 numbers add the second to the first number then prints the answer. It takes the answer and adds it to the second number. It keeps on doing this until the computer has a stack overflow.

DESIGNED, TESTED
AND PRODUCED BY

GRAHAM J. HARKNESS
&
Graham A. Livingstone.

PRIMARY 7A

GEORGE HERIOTS SCHOOL

Figure 4

have successfully modified their friend's Logo program so that it seems to work. They try it out with various starting pairs of numbers and call their friend across. They create a wall chart for the classroom that explains the way their new program works. They are determined to use their own name, 'Asterix', for the program. They resist the teacher's idea that they use the name 'Fibseries' that is suggested by the Logo worksheet they have been using. They clearly think that he is silly to believe that his name for their program would be better than theirs for helping them to remember what their program does.

In the fourth scene we observe a whole class of twelve-year-olds who have spent a year learning Logo. They are working through mathematics worksheets on factorisation that invite them to write a Logo program that computes the common factors for a pair of numbers and gives the example that 3 is the common factor of 15 and 21. Some of the programs they write are very long and include separate checks to test whether 3, 5 and 7 are factors. But when they type them in to the computer and run the programs they get annoyed. The program usually turns out only to 'work' for the particular pair of numbers they were considering when they designed it. So the programs work correctly with 15 and 21 but fail to work out the common factors for 4 and 8. Eventually one pupil looks in the computer's memory for the Logo program the teacher uses. The pupils all copy this and use it. Some of them attempt to understand how the teacher's program works but they eventually give up.

In the fifth scene the same class is working in pairs on the computers with a Logo program that combines positive and negative numbers. As the pupils get the computer to do arithmetic such as −3−4 they see pictures drawn on the computer screen that correspond to the steps in the arithmetic. They quickly turn this into a game where they devise 'hard' arithmetic for the computer to carry out and then predict what they will see drawn. Without noticing, they start predicting the mathematical result of the arithmetic rather than the drawing they will see.

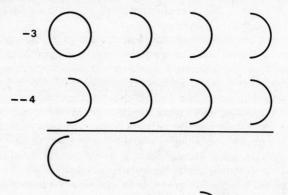

Note: The pupil types in −3−−4 . On the screen) signifies a negative 1 and (signifies a positive 1, ◯ signifying zero. So the result is seen to be positive one. The characters are drawn in sequence left to right by the computer.

Figure 5   Subtraction of negative numbers

Now let me offer some general comments about Logo as a learning environment. I have chosen this clumsy term for Logo because I want to distinguish its use in the classroom from attempts to use computer programs as surrogate teachers or as classroom apparatus. There is no sense in which the Logo programming language can be said to teach or instruct. It does what the pupils tell it to and when, for example, the House program fails to draw a house it does not tell the pupils they have made a mistake because it has no view about their intentions. This allows the learner to attach the values that he wants to the results of running his programs. This means that the learner is able both to enjoy and learn from his mistakes. In some ways Logo is just a well-designed piece of classroom apparatus in that the pupil can easily see the result of his programming experiment. The Logo turtle and the way that the learner can understand its function by using his own body movements are a result of Papert's (see Papert, 1980) earlier work with the Swiss developmental psychologist Piaget. But Logo is also an environment for learning because the learner can use the computer to remember the programs he has created. Then the next week the learner can use his old programs as building blocks to create new ones. The Logo programs become the personal intellectual property of the learner to be stored and re-used or given to friends.

The programming style that Logo is designed to support is to use or adapt old programs as parts of the new program that is being created. So the problem-solving strategy that Logo facilitates is that of breaking problems down into sub-problems. Logo is very well designed. Three- to seven-year-olds use the button box and older children quickly learn to use the keyboard to input more complicated programs.

The interactive quality of Logo does lead to one type of observed behaviour that is worrying. I have sometimes watched individual pupils have the same conversation with the computer week after week. Sometimes the same sequence of pictures is produced and occasionally I have observed learners write programs with names like 'Friend' that print out phrases such as 'I like you' and 'How are you today?' when they are run. My own observations have been over limited time spans of usually less than a year, but clearly it would be disturbing if a proportion of pupils who did not mix well socially with their classmates used computer programming as a surrogate for social interaction. It is much more common to observe learners working cooperatively in pairs on the design and testing of programs. In fact I have never been in an ordinary mathematics classroom which bustled with the activity of happy pupils in the way that classrooms equipped with Logo computer equipment do.

Logo can contribute to a learner's mathematical development via metaphor, visual experience and illuminating personal mathematical processes. I will discuss these three distinct types of contribution in turn. Firstly, programs and the programming activity can serve as metaphors for mathematical concepts and mathematical reasoning, so that the pupils who produced the Asterix program for Fibonacci series can use that program, which they intellectually own, as a metaphor for the mathematical concept of a function with arguments. Likewise the process by which they adapted another program to create Asterix serves as a metaphor for the type of mathematical reasoning that involves generalisation.

Secondly, Logo is especially well designed to give the learner visual experiences related to mathematical ideas. I have used the clumsy term visual experience rather than drawing because I want to emphasise something that is difficult to convey in a written paper. When a Logo program draws a house it does it step by step so that the learner can relate these to the components of the program. Likewise the Logo program for combining negative numbers generates a sequence of pictures rather like a cartoon film. So Logo can be used to give a visual experience that illustrates a mathematical process rather than generates a mathematical product.

The third type of contribution to mathematical development depends on the learner writing a Logo program that solves a problem in the way *he* does. Then when he runs the program he can stand back and watch *himself* as embodied by the program tackle the problem. This is a powerful source of insight as it allows him to pose questions of the type 'I wonder why I never try to solve equations by . . .' This works particularly well in turtle geometry where a mistake results in a 'cartoon film' in which a character appears in a surprising and unexpected place.

These three types of contribution to mathematical development, namely metaphorical, visual and personal reasoning, seem very powerful. But Logo pupils have to date not performed stunningly better at school mathematics than non-Logo learners. One reason for this is that much of the metaphorical content of Logo is inappropriate to *school* mathematics. In general current school work is not based on creative problem-solving but rather on the recall of particular algorithms. So the powerful problem-solving strategies that Logo supports, such as decomposing problems into sub-problems, will not necessarily be helpful. Even more problematic is the fact that many algorithms taught in school, such as long division, depend on physical layout on the paper. A pupil who is forgetting to carry will not obtain an insight related to this by implementing a Logo program that does not lay out numbers in columns and rows and does not cross out digits. But to write a program that will do the layout is very difficult and not relevant to an improved understanding of the algorithms.

Logo, like a number of other programming languages, was developed in the late 'sixties when an epistemological philosophy which advocates the 'procedural representation of knowledge' was current. The result is that it is very easy to use Logo programs as elements of other Logo programs and Logo is a real high-level programming language unlike other teaching languages such as BASIC. But because of the heavy emphasis in the design of Logo on expressing procedures or processes it turns out to be hard to write Logo programs which themselves create and manipulate passive structures like data-bases. So using Logo it is easy to write a program which, say, divides numbers, but it is hard to store number facts such as 21 is 7 times 3. However, we use number facts to make short cuts in our mathematical reasoning. So as constituted Logo makes it easy to express procedural knowledge (mathematical processes) but almost impossible to express declarative knowledge (mathematical facts). The mismatch with some school mathematics, the difficulty of expressing paper and pencil working and the emphasis on procedural knowledge are permanent limitations of Logo.

An area that is open to further development is the visual aspect of Logo. Obviously it is useful for geometry and extensions have been added to Logo that draw appropriate pictures as the pupil manipulates negative numbers, fractions and equations. Non-text presentation of mathematical concepts and processes is not currently well understood, but Logo is clearly a suitable environment which will support the development of interactive visual presentations of mathematical processes for and by the learner.

Overall the evaluations (see Howe *et al.*, 1980) of Logo have demonstrated that it is learnable by young pupils, that they can work autonomously with it and that its acquisition can contribute to the overall learning of school geometry and some specific concepts in school algebra. These studies have also shown that pupils' verbal reasoning skills improve as a result of learning Logo and that they can use Logo experiences and progress as metaphors in non-mathematical problem-solving. But Logo is not useful for acquiring or understanding many of the standard algorithms taught in schools, particularly those used in arithmetic. Some criticism can be levelled at school mathematics curricula which encourage learning without understanding. But some aspects of a learner's mathematical competence, particularly the mathematical facts and heuristics he uses, are really quite difficult.

Other programming languages are being developed (see O'Shea, 1978) that will not be subject to the same limitations that Logo is. My hope is that eventually a programming language for schools will be available that has the learnability of Logo and which is also easy to use to express both procedural and declarative knowledge. Logo is designed to help the learner express mathematical *processes* as computer programs which generate visual experiences. Its strengths and limitations as an environment in which to develop mathematical understanding arise from the ways its designers successfully followed the work of Piaget and the philosophy of expressing knowledge as procedures.

Acknowledgments

The work described here was carried out as part of a research program funded by the SSRC under a grant held by Jim Howe at the University of Edinburgh.

References

HOWE, J., O'SHEA, T. and PLANE, F. (1980) 'Teaching mathematics through Logo programming: an evaluation study in computer assisted learning', in LEWIS, R. and TAGG, W. (eds) *Computer Assisted Learning: Scope, Progress and Limits*. Amsterdam: North-Holland, pp. 85–101.

O'SHEA, T. (1978) 'Artificial intelligence and computer based education.' *Computer Education*, 29, pp. 25–8.

PAPERT, S. (1972) 'Teaching children to be mathematicians v. teaching about mathematics.' *International Journal of Mathematical Education in Science and Technology*, 3, pp. 249–52.

PAPERT, S. (1980) *Mindstorms: Children, Computers, Powerful Ideas*. Brighton: Harvester Press.

Index

Main entries are shown in *italics*.

accountability
 aspects of, *64–8*
 and Education Committees, LEAs,
  64
 teacher, 236
action, communicative vs instrumental, 196ff
Adams, R. S., 119ff
American Association of Medical Colleges, 82
Ames, Adelbert, 230
assessment procedures, 118, 187
association, voluntary vs involuntary,
  39
attainment, 74
attitudes and values, *151*ff
 and evaluation, 170
 of teachers, 221
audio visual techniques, 111
Ausubel, David, 202
authority, *35*ff, 182
 management of, 156
 vs leadership, 38
 vs power, 37
 Weberian notions of, 37ff
 see also teachers and authority

Barth, Roland, 221
behaviour, 45
 pupil, 99
 teacher classroom, 94, 99
 see also context and process variables,
  interaction analysis, teacher–
  pupil interaction
behavioural objectives, *142*ff, *160*ff, 183,
  195, 236ff
Bennett, Neville, *118–41*
Biddle, Bruce J., *92–103*
Bierstedt, R., 38
Bruner, Jerome S., *178–81*, *182*ff, 202

career success, 42

class meetings, 52ff
 organisation, 73
classroom
 contexts, 98
 conventional and 'open', *220–9*
 goals, 222
 management and organisation, 118
 observation, 104
 politics of, 235ff
 research, *104*ff
  'anthropological', 105, *109*ff, *189*ff
classroom teaching
 characteristics of, *92*
 a model for, *92–103*
cluster analysis, 123ff
community
 and classroom, *92*
 involvement, 71
 procedures, 43
 and school, 16, 97
 see also school
computer language, *242*ff
conflict situations
 management of, 156
coverage, 221ff
cultural location, 153
curriculum
 content and planning, 118, 150, *182*ff
 control, 21, 23, 33
 design and development of, *18*ff, 142,
  *178*ff
 development, 104, 163ff
 development as a context for research, *193*ff
 development, school-based, *18–34*
 objectives, 23ff, 163ff, 183
 organisation, 144, 150
 process model, *182*ff
 reform movement, 31, 202
 subject centred, 123

Dancy, John, *41–6*
Davies, I. K., *213–19*

Deal, Terence E., *11–17*
decision-process, 53, 79
Delamont, Sara, *104–17*
democracy and the educational system, 234
democratic organisation, *51*ff
Dienes, Zoltan P., 225ff
discipline
  behavioural, 42, 123
  and control, 233
  critical work as, 175ff
  educational, 83
  procedural, 186
Doyle, W., 192ff
Dunkin, Michael J., *92–103*

East Sussex Accountability Project, *64–8*
Easthope, Gary, *8–10*
education and participation, *35*
Education Committees, 64ff
educational
  action research, *193*
  aims, 188, 195
  goals, 57ff, 199ff
  models, *see* teaching styles/strategies
  objectives, *160*ff
  perspective on teaching and learning, *196*
  philosophy, 18, 221
  programmes, evaluation of, 79ff
  research, 79ff, 104ff
  structure, 57ff
  system as an influential institution, 233ff
Educational Testing Service, 181
educative purpose, 224
Eight Year Study, 21
Elliott, John, *189–98*
environment, 76
  learning, *242–50*
ethos
  definition of, 41
  of universities, 43
  values, aims, attitudes, procedures, 42ff
ethnographic research, 109ff
evaluation
  adversary, 85

and curriculum development, 166
  goal-free, 85
  issues of, 81
  methods of, 79ff
Evaluation Strategies, 185
examinations, 42, 180
  as an objective, 187
examining board, 21, 24

Fenstermacher, G. D., 189

Glasser, William, 203
government agencies, 21
grammar school, 9, 45
group dynamics, 186

Habermas, J., 196
Hadow Report, 118
Hamilton, David, *104–17*
headteacher
  as an authority figure, 38
  influence of, 10
  self-assessment questionnaire, 77
head of department as manager, 47ff
Her Majesty's Inspectorate (HMI)
  Secondary Survey, 41ff
Hetman, Francois, 84
historical causation, 182
Humanities Curriculum Project, *183*ff, 194
Hunt, David, 203

ideologies, 19, 220
  culture and counterculture, 11
  educational, *11*ff
  and management, *51–63*
Inner London Education Authority Inspectorate, *69–78*
in-service programmes, 33
inspectors, 24
interaction analysis, *105*ff
Intergroup Education Project, 156
International Evaluation of Achievement, 22
interpersonal relations, 156

James Committee, 32

John, Denys, *47–50*
Joyce, Bruce, *199–212*

knowledge, *142*ff
  conception of, 225, 227
  distortion of, 182
  as a framework for education, 185ff
  measurement of, 169
  structures of, 185
  see also learning
Kohlberg, Lawrence, 202
Kreiner, Kristian, *51–63*

Langford, G., 43
Lawton, Denis, *35–40*
leadership, 47ff
  collective, 51
  roles, 157
learning, 5ff, 145, 220ff
  computer-based, *242–50*
  and early childhood, 5
  and evaluation, 173
  experiences, 163ff
  and participation, 35
  and school, 5ff, 13
  systems, 22
  tasks, 192ff
  vs education, 5, 35
  see also behavioural objectives,
    knowledge
Leavis, F. R., *175–7*
liberal curriculum, 8
Local Education Authority (LEA), 64ff
  advisers, 126
logical reasoning, 149
Logo, as a learning environment,
  243–50
Lorayne, Harry, 202
Lucas, Jerry, 202

Malcolm, David, 236ff
Man: a course of study, *183*ff, 194
management, 72, 221
  analysis, *85*
  and ideologies, *51–63*
  procedures, 43
  see also classroom management and
    organisation

mastery, 221ff
memory, 179, 192
middle management, 47ff
Ministry of Education, 21
models, educational
  of teaching, 200ff
Moore, Terry, *35–40*
Mortimore, Peter, 42
motivational techniques, 118
multiple causation, 148

National Council for the Accreditation
  of Teacher Education, 82
National Union of Teachers, 126
Nolan, Robert R., *11–17*

Oakeshott, Michael, *5–10*
objectives, form of, *160–74*
  model vs process model, 187
Olson, David, 224
open assembly, 51ff
open-ended curriculum, 31
O'Shea, Tim, *242–50*

parent–teacher association (PTA), 98
parents, 16, 52, 71, 236
  and accountability, 65
  beliefs and attitudes, 58
participant observation, 109
participation, 35ff, 61
pedagogical aims, 184, 194
perception, 230ff
Perls, Fritz, 203
permissiveness
  see teacher control and sanctions
person-centred vs power education,
  233–41
Piaget, Jean, 202, 247
Plowden Report, 83, 118, 130
Postman, Neil, *230–2*
power, 182
  vs authority, 37
  vs leadership, 38
  vs person-centred education, *233–41*
primary school, self-assessment of, 69ff
process-product study, *189*ff, 194
programme, educational training, *213*ff
programme of work, 72

progressive teachers, 119
public school, 8, 52
    administration of, 8
    and social structure, 8ff
    and team games, 9
pupil participation, 37
    achievement, abilities and intelligence, 97
    formative experiences, 96
    properties, 97

Roe, Ann, 101
Rogers, Carl R., 102, 203, *233–41*
Rutter, Michael, 41

sampling as a research method, *121*
school, *5*ff
    -based accounting, 68
    -based curriculum development, *20*ff
    board, 51
    and classroom, *92*
    and community, 97
    computers and, *242*ff
    and ethos, *41*ff
    goals of, *225*
    as a hierarchical community, *8–10*,
        *41*ff
    as a human social institution, 19
    and ideologies, *11*ff
    as involuntary associations, 39
    and languages, 6
    objectives of, 160
    as organisations, *13*ff
    as an organised anarchy, 53
    politics of the traditional, *233*
    and support structures, 28
    and teachers, 6
Schools Council, 21, 29
Schutz, William, 203
Schwab, Joseph J., 202
Scriven, Michael, 79ff
Sigel, Irving, 202
Simon, A. and Boyer, G. E., 105ff
Simon, B., *119*ff
Skilbeck, Malcolm, *18–34*
skills
    acquisition of, *155*
    communication of, 184
    see also task analysis

social action, 37
social policy analysis, *85*
social sensitivity, *153*
socialisation, 153
staff
    meetings, 75
    resources, 74
state school, 9ff
Stenhouse, Lawrence, *182–8*
Suchman, Richard, 202
Sullivan, Edmund, 202

Taba, Hilda, *142–59*, 202
task analysis, *213*ff
teacher
    accountability, 236
    associations, 21
    causality, 190ff
    classroom behaviour, 94, 99
    control and sanctions, 118, 122, 233
    education, 28, *31*, 189, 193
    effectiveness, 105
    formative experiences, 94ff
    freedom and autonomy, 18
    as learner or expert, 184ff, 189ff
    properties, 95ff
    –pupil interaction, 100
    resource centres, 28
    training, 193
    training experiences, 95ff
teachers, 13
    and authority, 36, 195, 233
    board of, 51, 60
    and curriculum development, 18ff
    and decision making, 33, 36
    and management, *47*ff
    and participation, 35, 61, 194
    progressive vs traditional, 119
    self-assessment questionnaire, 78
    and selection process, training, 32
teaching styles/strategies, *118–41*, 150,
        199–212, 223
    approach, 118, *199–212*
    discussion based, 186
    methods, 144, 226
    performance, 189ff
    technology of, *220–9*
    for understanding, 195ff
    of values, 153

Tenenbaum, Samuel, 237
thinking, reflexive/critical, 146, 161
traditional teachers, 119
topic analysis, *216*
Tyler, Ralph W., *160–74*, 183
Tyler rationale, 23, 26

university, ethos of, 43

validation and research into teaching
    styles, 125
  scientific validity, 144
  validity and evaluation, 170

value judgements, 148
values and attitudes, *151*ff
variables
  context, 96
  process, 99
  product, 100

Walberg, H. J. and Thomas S. C., 119ff
Weber, Max, 37
Weil, Marsha, *199–212*
Weingartner, Charles, *230–2*
Westbury, Ian, *220–9*
Wilson, Bryan, 43
work procedures, 44

Acknowledgments

The editors and publisher wish to thank the following for permission to reprint copyright material in this book:

Professor Michael Oakeshott for an excerpt (here called 'The idea of school') from his paper 'Education: the engagement and its frustration' originally printed in *Proceedings of the Philosophy of Education Society*, 5, 1, January 1971, and The Philosophy of Education Society; Routledge and Kegan Paul Ltd for an excerpt (here called 'The school as a hierarchical community') from *Community, Hierarchy and Open Education* by Gary Easthope, and for an excerpt from chapter 5, 'Authority and participation', by Terry Moore and Denis Lawton, from *Theory and Practice of Curriculum Studies* by Denis Lawton *et al*.; University of Chicago Press and Dr T E Deal for an excerpt from an article, 'Alternative schools: a conceptual map' by T E Deal and R R Nolan, originally printed in *School Review*, November 1978, copyright © 1978 by the University of Chicago, reprinted by permission of the publisher; Professor Malcolm Skilbeck for material from his paper 'School-based curriculum development and teacher education'; Professor John C Dancy for his article 'The notion of the ethos of a school' from *Perspective I* (University of Exeter School of Education); Heinemann Educational Books for an excerpt (here called 'Leadership in middle management') from *Leadership in Schools* by Denys John, and for an excerpt (here called 'A process model') from *An Introduction to Curriculum Research and Development* by Lawrence Stenhouse; Professor R A Becher, Dr M Eraut, Mrs Julia Knight, Mr A Canning and Mr J Barton for an excerpt (here called 'Aspects of accountability') from the report of the East Sussex Accountability Project (University of Sussex); Inner London Education Authority Learning Materials Service for an excerpt from *Keeping the School under Review: a method of self-assessment for schools devised by the ILEA Inspectorate*; OECD, Paris, for an excerpt (here called 'The methods of evaluating') from *Evaluating Educational Programmes: the need and the response* by Robert E Stake; Holt, Rinehart and Winston, Inc., CBS College Publishing, New York, for an excerpt (here called 'A model for classroom teaching') from *The Study of Teaching* by Michael J Dunkin and Bruce J Biddle, copyright © 1974 by Holt, Rinehart and Winston, Inc., reprinted by permission of the publisher; Manchester University Press for the article 'Classroom research: a cautionary tale' by David Hamilton and Sara Delamont from *Research in Education*, 11, May 1974; Open Books Publishing Ltd for an excerpt (here called 'A typology of teaching styles') from *Teaching Styles and Pupil Progress* by Neville Bennett; Harcourt Brace Jovanovich, Inc., New York, for an excerpt (here called 'The types of behavioural objectives') from *Curriculum Development: Theory and Practice* by Hilda Taba, copyright © 1962 by Harcourt Brace Jovanovich, reprinted by permission of the publisher; University of Chicago Press and Dr R W Tyler for an excerpt (here called 'The form of objectives') from *Basic Principles of Curriculum and Instruction* by Ralph W Tyler, copyright 1949 by the University of Chicago, reprinted by permission of the publisher; The Literary Estate of F. R. Leavis and Chatto and Windus Ltd for an excerpt from *Education and the University: a sketch for an 'English School'* by F R Leavis; Harvard University Press, Cambridge, Mass., for an excerpt (here called 'The importance of structure') from *The Process of Education* by Jerome S Bruner, copyright © 1960 by the President and Fellows of Harvard College, reprinted by permission; Kogan Page Ltd for an excerpt (here called 'Implications of classroom research for professional development' by John Elliott from *World Yearbook of Education 1980, Professional Development of Teaching*, edited by Eric Hoyle *et al.*; Prentice-Hall, Inc., Englewood Cliffs, N.J., for an excerpt (here called 'Against dogmatism: alternative models of teaching') from *Models of Teaching* by Bruce Joyce and Marsha Weil, second edition copyright © 1980, pp. 1–2, 7–19, reprinted by permission of the publisher; McGraw-Hill Book Company (UK) Ltd for an excerpt (here called 'Technology: the analytic style') from *The Management of Learning* by I K Davies, copyright © 1971 by McGraw-Hill Book Company (UK) Ltd, reprinted by permission of the publisher; Taylor and Francis Ltd and Professor Ian Westbury for an excerpt from his article 'Conventional classrooms, "open" classrooms and the technology of teaching' from *Journal of Curriculum Studies*, 5, 2, 1973; Pitman Books Ltd for an excerpt (here called 'Meaning making') from *Teaching as a Subversive Activity* by Neil Postman and Charles Weingartner (published in the USA by Delacorte Press); Constable and Co. Ltd for an excerpt (here called 'Power or persons: two trends in education') from *On Personal Power* by Carl R Rogers (published in the USA by Delacorte Press); Dr Timothy O'Shea for his paper 'A critique of Logo as a learning environment for mathematics'.

Every effort has been made to trace copyright holders of material reproduced in this Reader. Any rights not acknowledged here will be acknowledged in subsequent printings if notice is given to the publisher.